BASHING SARAH PALIN

THOMAS R. MEINDERS

iUniverse, Inc.
Bloomington

Bashing Sarah Palin

iUniverse books may be ordered through booksellers or by contacting:

iUniverse
1663 Liberty Drive
Bloomington, IN 47403
www.iuniverse.com
1-800-Authors (1-800-288-4677)

Because of the dynamic nature of the Internet, any Web addresses or links contained in this book may have changed since publication and may no longer be valid. The views expressed in this work are solely those of the author and do not necessarily reflect the views of the publisher, and the publisher hereby disclaims any responsibility for them.

Any people depicted in stock imagery provided by Thinkstock are models, and such images are being used for illustrative purposes only.

Certain stock imagery © Thinkstock.

ISBN: 978-1-4502-9863-6 (sc)
ISBN: 978-1-4502-9864-3 (dj)
ISBN: 978-1-4502-9865-0 (ebook)

Printed in the United States of America

iUniverse rev. date: 02/23/2011

INTRODUCTION

The Democrats must really be scared of the power of Sarah Palin. The main stream media and television has been bashing the former Governor of Alaska from the time she was selected to be the running mate of Senator John McCain in 2008.

Compared to our last 4 presidents, a President Palin would be a breath of fresh air, a true conservative, American citizen and stateswoman like our founding fathers intended and if you listen to her, you will find her right on the mark. Plus, she's got the guts to go up against the crooked people who are trying to bring this nation to its knees. What more could we ask for?

I would like to try and collect some of the hate campaign ads that have been broadcast in print or on television. The Democrats have stooped to a level so low it is embarrassing.

The main stream media is very biased and pro Democratic and the President they are backing is the biggest fake that has ever been elected President. In my opinion Obama does not have any qualifications what so ever to be the President of the United States.

Instead of printing the facts about Governor Palin's history of accomplishments they are concerned about what she has done from the time she was in Kindergarten. We are going to make a collection of the biased reports so that the Democrats will not have anything to left to bash Sarah Palin with.

The Democrats are going to be in the deep Caribou dung when they have to campaign on their record. In addition, we are going to present detailed information about the record and comments of President Obama.

Many are saying that eliminating earmarks will not save the taxpayer a single dime. I don't believe the reports from the Democrats concerning this and we will address the earmark problem later. Perhaps that is true, but it certainly eliminates the bribery of Congressmen to vote for bills the citizens do not want, and it sheds light on requests for taxpayer money to be given to states for needless projects that do nothing to bring about economic health. In fact, I wonder if a request for millions of dollars to study ants or save field mice is not actually going into the state coffers to shore up their pay/pension/ benefits of public employees. Government employees, from the President on down, must be put on the same pay/pension/benefits programs that the non-unionized private sector must adhere to. When the President talks about "shared sacrifices," why are so many being given exemptions from the burdens he is placing on the rest of us? Congress has been given too much power and has turned themselves into royalty and that has to stop. Term limits are necessary to cut some of the abuse.

Sarah Palin is the most captivating, charming and influential Republican in America — and therefore a viable contender for the Republican presidential nomination in 2012.

Didn't Palin think that the Republican kingmakers who were now supposedly scheming to kneecap her were mainly just concerned about how voters viewed her? "If that were the case, then they need to be courageous enough to put their names behind their criticisms," she said, referring to anonymous quotations attacking her. "As I replied to Politico, these fellows want to be trusted to tend to our nation's economic woes? They want to be trusted to take on the likes of Ahmadinejad, but they won't take on a hockey mom from Wasilla? Until they do that, I dismiss them."

Sarah Palin is in touch with the average Americans. That is because of what she is. The people that surround Palin are common sense Americans who just want the government on their side and not riding on their backs or telling them what is best for them. Palin tweets to reach out to the common American.

This book is written in simple language to help educate some of the voters about what is going on now and what can be done to make our country a much better place. We need to return to "America the Beautiful"

TABLE OF CONTENTS

CHAPTER ONE:

Sarah Palin's Credentials

Sarah Palin's was the Governor of Alaska for two years and Mayor of Wasilla Alaska for ten years. She also served as President of Alaska Conference of Mayors and was also a City Council member (1992-1996). Palin was the youngest governor of Alaska and the first female. During her time as governor she displayed a tough and dedicated desire to improve the quality of life in Alaska and did it with integrity.

I believe that Sarah Palin will return the role of President of the United States of America back to the people of this great nation. She has the courage to fight the corruption that has been rampant in the Congress. Palin will listen to the will of the people and strive to pass the legislation that is what Americans want. We need a strong willed individual as President that will fight for what our founding fathers decided when they wrote the Constitution. America needs to vote for Sarah Palin because she stands for our principles. Unlike the current President, do not vote for her because she is white and a female. Voting for a President of the United States because of color is totally racist and there is no place in this country for racism.

AGIA License bill signed August 27, 2008. Energy Package signed August 25, 2008. Administrative Order 242 signed August 20, 2008.

AGIA License bill signed August 27, 2008

House Bill 3001 for awarding a contract to Trans Canada Alaska for developing and building a pipeline stretching for 1,715 miles from the Prudhoe Bay treatment plant to Alberta Canada.

Natives of Alaska have dreamed of a pipeline for more than 30 years. Sarah Palin in less than two years got the bill passed and the framework is now laid for them to move forward with the project.

This legislation brings Alaska closer than we've ever been to building a gas pipeline and finally accessing our gas that has been languishing for so many decades on the North Slope.

More than 36,000 miles of pipeline is now operated by Trans Canada Corporation in North America. They have built many pipelines also and are appreciative of the Governor's support.

Energy Package signed August 25, 2008.

House Bill 4001 and Senate bill 4002 were signed into law by Governor Palin on August 25, 2008. SB 4002 pays $1,200 to each resident who qualifies. The money for these payments comes from the state's natural resource revenue. This bill also suspends the state's tax on gasoline.

"Alaskans who signed up for direct deposit will see these funds on September 12, along with their dividend," said Governor Palin. "In rural Alaska, particularly, many people are facing a choice between feeding their families and heating their homes, and they could use this payment from the state's energy-generated surplus to cover some of those bills."

She also signed a proclamation declaring September to be energy efficiency month in Alaska. She encourages residents to use energy more efficiently during this month.

Administrative Order 242 signed August 20, 2008.

This order puts together a co-op of the Department of Natural Resources and the Department of Revenue to work with organizations who wish to commercialize Alaska's North Slope natural gas.

"This solidifies our commitment to facilitating an LNG project that is a product of market interest," Governor Palin said. "By committing both project capital and natural gas resources to a pipeline that would transport North Slope natural gas to tidewater, an LNG project can remain an integral element of the state's effort to deliver Alaska's gas to market"

The Order encourages the departments to support any who are pursuing development of natural gas projects which are liquefiable and economic.

Sarah Palin sold the private jet of the State of Alaska which saved the state $62,492 in quarterly payments. The jet was purchased by the previous governor. The jet was sold to a businessman from Valdez that paid $2.1 million for the jet.

When Sarah Palin took office as Governor of Alaska one of the initial things that Palin did was fire the chef. She said she is able to make meals for her children and the chef is no longer necessary.

It seems to me that one thing she is against, is wasteful spending of taxpayers dollars. I think she has integrity, if nothing else to bring to the position of President of the United States. Her campaign for Governor centered on eliminating corrupt politics.

Internet rumors have been going around claiming Palin cut funding for Special Needs Education by 62%. The rumor has been found to be false and the funding in fact tripled for these special needs children education.

More Internet Rumors

Palin supposedly demanded that certain books be banned by the library at Wasilla. This is a false rumor. Many of the books that were mentioned in the rumor weren't even published yet. The librarian said that Palin asked a what if question. The original rumor also stated that the librarian was fired, but she in fact worked at the same library through most of Palin's first term.

She was charged with being a member of the Alaskan Independence Party which has pushed for succession from the United States. Fact is that she was never a member of that party.

She never endorsed Pat Buchanan. She merely wore a Buchanan pin during his visit to Wasilla.

She has not pushed for teaching creationism in Alaska's schools. She has said that students should be allowed to debate both sides of the evolution question, but she also said creationism doesn't have to be part of the curriculum.

Bridge to Nowhere

Originally the report was that Sarah Palin was against the bridge to nowhere. After doing some digging here are the facts about the bridge. Sarah Palin originally was for the bridge and even made a statement to that affect which has been recorded.

Palin, Sept. 2006: The money that's been appropriated for the project, it should remain available for a link, an access process as we continue to evaluate the scope and just how best to just get this done. This link is a commitment to help Ketchikan expand its access, to help this community prosper.

When the proposal came before the Senate, the bill was passed with a vote of 91 for and 4 against it, with 5 senators not voting. John McCain was one of the 4 who voted against it. Barack Obama and Joe Biden both voted for the bill...

The Bridge to Nowhere became a symbol of Pork Barrel spending and earmarks, which is something that every representative of Congress should be against.

The accomplishments of Sarah Palin rank her as one of the most effective Governors of the State of Alaska. It is pathetic that the Democratic Party does not recognize any of these accomplishments. Instead they would rather bash Sarah Palin at every chance they get. It is cheap politics as usual for the Democrats.

Barack Obama's Accomplishments

Barack Obama learned early in his political career to be shrewd and practical. Learning how to play hardball with the big wigs is a must for anyone who goes into politics. He endured racial slurs from many of the opposing party and hazing by other African American colleagues and learned how to recognize an opportunity when presented and a willingness to work with opposing party members.

Having learned his lessons well Obama is now the 44th President of the United States.

The record of achievements accomplished by President Obama's during his tenure as Illinois State Senator. Some of his key votes are listed below.

Voted to end $300 million worth of tax breaks for businesses. (2004)

Voted for having Illinois endorse embryonic stem cell research. (2004)

Voted against restrictions on public funding of abortion. (2000)

Successfully co-sponsored a prescription drug discount buying club program for seniors and the disabled. (2003)

Unsuccessfully co-sponsored ban on discrimination based on sexual orientation. The measure became law after Obama was elected to the U.S. Senate. (2003)

Successfully co-sponsored major ethics reform called the Gift Ban Act. (1998)

There was the speech by Barack Obama where he indicated that he had visited all 57 states during his campaign. I do not know which country he was referring to but at the last count the United States only had 50 states. I have no idea but does Kenya have 57 states?

Obama played a key role in getting death penalty laws changed in Illinois. The state had previously been deeply divided because of problems with their death penalty laws before 2003.

One key point in the new death penalty law was how interrogations are handled. Interrogations of murder suspects, according to the new law, are to be recorded. Previously 13 death row inmates were released because they were found innocent or were convicted using improper procedures.

"We brought police officers and civil rights advocates together to reform a death penalty system that had sent 13 innocent men to death row," he declared in a recent presidential debate.

How about the Nobel Peace Prize? Obama has received the Nobel Peace Prize. The decision has stunned many around the world. The Prize was awarded not for action, but promises more than anything. Obama hasn't had any major success in foreign policy as of yet.

Then there are the bills that were passed into law by the President that were not in the best interest of the voting citizens of the United States.

Based upon the study of the qualifications of Sarah Palin and Barack Obama our vote for the most qualified to be President of the United States based on a scale of 1 to 10 "By the People, For the People"

Sarah Palin   7

Barack Obama`   4

Additionally, Sarah Palin has two years as Commander in Chief of the Alaska National Guard. Barack Obama didn't even have one day of military service when he became President.

What is troubling is that during all of Obama's speeches he does not mention about winning the war in Iraq and Afghanistan. The only thing that Obama mentions is bringing our troops home regardless of how the world is going to look at us for not finishing these wars. I am very uncomfortable with just saying the troops will leave on a certain day regardless of the status of the conflict. I am proud to be an American and believe we should win what we start and not quit at any time. I believe that Obama has in reality put our troops in harms way with his policies.

CHAPTER TWO:

Drill Baby Drill

During Sarah Palin's speech at The Oil Palace, she hit all of the right wing keywords: czars, energy, lame stream media, bowing and of course, "*Drill Baby Drill*". The half-term governor of Alaska's voice gets higher with each word and faster after each sentence in her speech.

After the Gulf oil disaster many of the House Republicans ran away from Sarah Plain's famous 2008 campaign slogan "Drill, Baby Drill". In a Face book posting Palin herself declared that the United States "must" "drill, baby, drill," but "the public will not trust" oil companies to do so "unless government appropriately regulates oil developments and holds oil executives accountable."

Palin invoked the mantra again at a speech in Tyler, Texas saying, I chant, "Drill Baby Drill" because it will help make the United States energy independent. The NBC affiliate KETK in Tyler, Texas aired an extended excerpt of Palin's speech including her claim that if America doesn't "Drill Baby Drill" the United States soon we're going to be bowing to the foreign countries that drill for us.

We've learned more about government's proper role and not violating the separation of powers. It appears that Obama is kind of flirting with these powers. We are a rule of laws, not a rule of presidential fiats that it appears

President Obama would rather have. Anyone who wants to chastise a person for believing in "Drill Baby Drill" should keep this in mind. Palin said those three little words when she was running for the number two job in the United States and if she had won her duty in the White House would have been to help our country towards becoming more energy independent. Palin understands that we need to be energy independent to make a major improvement in the federal deficit. We are sending too much of the United States money to foreign countries.

Palin is trying to have it both ways when she correctly says "we have to make sure that BP will pay up what they owe" to victims of the oil spill, but then asserts that President Obama is "kind of flirting with also, some government overreach." Earlier President Obama got BP to agree to set up a $20 billion escrow fund that will provide substantial assurance that the claims people and businesses have will be honored. Palin claims that she too wants a guarantee that BP compensates victims. Palin recently bashed the escrow fund as an unconstitutional power grab.

The following comments were from citizens that are scared of the power of Sarah Palin. The content tends to indicate that the majority are Democrats. What is puzzling is that the Democratic Party has a vast majority of the members that are unable to think for themselves and will follow the leader no matter what he says.

Who is making things up Sarah? She should also be reminded that she is the lame stream media. We've also had Czars since the 70s. Czars are not a new concept.

Sarah Palin is so embarrassing. I don't know why Republicans are proud to have her in their party. When she tries to become the Republican nominee she will be told she should leave by the RNC and she is going to become angry at the Republican Party for not letting her run for the presidency.

Sarah Palin is finally keeping her mouth shut; which is a good thing because she is putting her foot in it time and again. I'd rather hear fingernails on a chalk board than listen to her or Rep Moo Bachmann. The only proven things these morons can do are to lie like rugs.

How's that drill baby drill thing working for you Sarah Palin, air headed Vanna White wanna be, half finished governor, shot gun wedding gone bad, queen of dingbats? When is America going to wake up and figure out this half brains, quitter governor, who talks in fear mongering platitudes smacking of sophomoric valley girl jabs, tweaked in urban legend logic, is a complete idiot?

You can bash Vanna White, when she pretends to be an expert on oil exploration. Only to once again be proven wrong. Intelligent citizens would agree that we need oil. We also realize that alternative energy sources need to be tapped. Drilling to the center of the earth isn't the answer. I hope we can agree on that. This spill should have awoken you and everyone else with a brain. I Hope that's the case.

When we produce the oil and natural gas from the resources of the United States we will provide for the countries vast consumption but we will decrease our national deficit each year. How simple can it be? We need people with common sense in Washington and not people with Doctors Degrees. History has shown that some of the most highly educated individuals do not have one iota of common sense and are not able to listen to what the American public wants. The truth about producing our natural resources is following.

Not everyone is against the production of our natural resources. Some are just clinging to the past. Oil has been produced for about 80 years. Other sources of energy are in fact expensive when you compare it to oil. And that's why no one really wants to do it right now. But eventually we will have to do it because we will run out of oil. I honestly think solar is the way to go. However, it's a very limited resource. It's only good for a few things whereas oil can be used for over 6000 different products throughout the world.

Oil is the energy source in our lifetime. Stop and think about that for a moment. It is the source of energy in our lifetime. We need oil, we must have it. It is the source of so many products. Did you know plastic requires oil? Oil is here to stay. At least in our lifetime it is. I understand that in the future other energy sources will take over but for now oil is king.

The Gulf oil spill is a good example of the misinformed leading the misinformed. I hope everyone who thinks this way can afford to pay $10.00 per gallon for gas. You have been lied to by the militant environmentalist movement. The spill, while regrettable, certainly could have been minimized if our leaders would have taken the proper steps to solve the situation early. The truth is they wanted it to be this bad so that they could further their agenda to bring America to its knees through the green movement. The Obama administration gave British Petroleum 274 passes on failed safety inspections in the last year alone. So who is really at fault? You won't hear about these facts being reported by the main stream media. The main stream media is blinding you and they haven't had to work very hard to accomplish the fact. They lie straight to your face yet you are too lazy to go get the facts yourself.

Information gathered from the biological, seismic and geological studies was used to complete a Legislative Environmental Impact Statement (LEIS) that described the potential impacts of oil and gas development. This LEIS study included the Secretary's final report and recommendation, and was submitted to Congress in 1987. The report concluded that oil development and production in the 1002 Area would have major effects on the Porcupine Caribou herd and muskoxen. Major effects were defined as "widespread, long-term change in habitat availability or quality which would likely modify natural abundance or distribution of species." Moderate effects were expected for wolves, wolverine, polar bears, snow geese, seabirds and shorebirds, arctic grayling and coastal fish. Major restrictions on subsistence activities by Kaktovik residents would also be expected. In the report, the Secretary of Interior recommended that Congress authorize an oil and gas leasing program that would avoid unnecessary adverse effects on the environment.

Congress failed to act on the recommendation, first in 1989 following the Exxon Valdez oil spill, and again in 1991 when a provision to open the Arctic Refuge to development was dropped from the National Energy Policy Act. In 1995, Congress passed budget legislation that included a provision to allow drilling in the Refuge. Citing a desire to protect biological and wilderness values, President Clinton vetoed the bill.

The estimated oil reserves in the Artic Refuge's 1002 Area are in excess of 30 billion barrels that could be recoverable. With oil prices over $80.00

per barrel and going higher it would be in the best interest of the United States to commence drilling in this area. These reserves would reduce the national debt and provide the United States with independence from foreign oil producers. Every barrel of oil that the United States can produce eliminates one that has to be imported.

Newer technologies that are applied today in Alaska's expanding North Slope oil fields include directional drilling that allows for multiple well heads on smaller drill pads; the re-injection of drilling wastes into the ground, which replaces surface reserve pits; better delineation of oil reserves using 3-dimensional seismic surveys, which has reduced the number of dry holes; and use of temporary ice pads and ice roads for conducting exploratory drilling and construction in the winter. As the oil fields expand east and west, additional oil reserves are consequently being tapped from smaller satellite fields that rely on the existing infrastructure at Prudhoe Bay and Kuparuk.

Here are the Obama administrations answers to our energy problems. These are directly from the President's proposed budget for the year ending September 30, 2011.

Because we know the nation that leads in clean energy will be the nation that leads the world, the Budget creates the incentives to build a new clean energy economy—from new loan guarantees that will encourage a range of renewable energy efforts and new nuclear power plants to spurring the development of clean energy on Federal lands. More broadly, the Budget makes critical investments that will ensure that we continue to lead the world in new fields and industries: doubling research and development funding in key physical sciences agencies; expanding broadband networks across our country; and working to promote American exports abroad.

Funding Highlights:

• Supports high-risk, high-payoff transformational research and development projects with $300 million for the recently established Advanced Research Projects Agency–Energy (ARPA-E).

• Supports and encourages the early commercial deployment of innovative energy technologies with an additional $36 billion in guaranteed loan volume authority for advanced nuclear power plants and an additional $500 million in credit subsidy to support $3 to $5 billion in loan guarantees for innovative energy efficiency and renewable energy projects.

• Provides a 4.6 percent, or $226 million, increase in funding at the Office of Science for basic research and world-leading laboratories to support transformational scientific discoveries and accelerate solutions to our Nation's most pressing challenges.

• Invests $2.3 billion in applied energy research and development to position the United States as the world leader in energy technology that will address climate change, develop new industries, and create new jobs.

• Accelerates the transition to a low-carbon economy through support of development and deployment of clean energy technologies such as solar, biomass, geothermal, wind, nuclear, and low-carbon emission coal power.

• Reduces security risks through major increases in funding for the detection, elimination, and securing of nuclear material and radiological sources worldwide and the maintenance of a safe, secure, and effective nuclear weapons stockpile.

• Continues the Nation's efforts to reduce environmental risks and safely manage nuclear materials.

Nowhere in the President's proposed budget is there any mention of reducing the independence on foreign oil. There is also nothing mentioned about developing our own natural resources. The President's proposals are more on the lines of spend, spend and then spend some more to develop green energy sources that should be funded by corporate enterprises. The oil industry will fund the development of our natural resources in the state of Alaska and the Rocky Mountain Region of the United States. That would be proper management of our resources and reduce the national deficit at the same time. Let private businesses fund their own green energy ideas and not the taxpayers.

Encourages the Early Commercial Use of New, Innovative Energy Technologies that Will Reduce Greenhouse Gas Emissions.

The Budget substantially expands support for DOE loan guarantees for innovative energy technologies, by adding $36 billion in new loan authority (for a total of $54.5 billion) for nuclear power facilities and an additional $500 million in credit subsidy to support $3 to $5 billion in loan guarantees for innovative energy efficiency and renewable energy projects. The loan guarantee program also will continue to support a range of commercial renewable energy programs and other facilities that help reduce pollutants and greenhouse gases while simultaneously creating clean energy jobs and contributing to long-term economic growth and international competitiveness.

Invests in Smart, Energy Efficient and Reliable Electricity Delivery Infrastructure.

The Budget continues to support the modernization of the Nation's electric grid, by investing in research, development and demonstration of smart-grid technologies that will spur the transition to a smarter, more efficient, secure and reliable electric system. The end result will promote energy and cost-saving choices for consumers, reduce emissions, and foster the growth of renewable energy sources like wind and solar. In addition, the Budget supports the Power Marketing Administration to reliably operate, maintain, and rehabilitate the Federal hydropower and transmission systems.

Advances the Development of Carbon Capture and Storage Technologies.

The Budget supports a balanced research and development (R&D) portfolio of carbon capture and storage technologies. The $545 million for climate change technology funding provided for Fossil Energy R&D in the 2011 Budget will help reduce greenhouse gas emissions by focusing resources to develop carbon capture technologies with broad applications to advanced power systems, existing power plants, and industrial sources.

Invests in Clean Energy Technologies to Reduce Dependence on Oil and Accelerate the Transition to a Low-Carbon Economy.

The Budget provides support for accelerating research, development, demonstration of nuclear technologies, and the commercialization of new nuclear power facilities and various clean energy technologies. Nearly $2.4 billion is provided for energy efficiency and renewable energy programs, an increase of $113 million over the 2010 appropriation, including $302 million for solar energy, $220 million for bio-fuels and bio-mass R&D, $325 million for advanced vehicle technologies, and $231 million for energy efficient building technologies. These investments will help reduce dependence on oil and create long-term, sustainable economic growth in the low-carbon industries of the future, helping to foster long-term job creation. The Budget also eliminates funding for programs that provide inefficient fossil fuel subsidies that impede investment in clean energy sources and undermine efforts to deal with the threat of climate change.

Reduces Proliferation Risks and Promotes the Safety, Security, and Reliability of the Nuclear Weapons Stockpile Without Nuclear Testing.

The Budget provides $2.7 billion, an increase of $550 million over the 2010 appropriation, to prevent the proliferation of nuclear weapons. This increase supports the strategy to move toward a world without nuclear weapons that the President announced in his April 2009, speech in Prague. This investment fully funds efforts to: secure nuclear material; develop technology to detect and deter nuclear testing and smuggling; and support international nonproliferation treaties, regulatory controls, and safeguards. Development work on the reliable replacement warhead has ceased. The 2011 Budget funds $8.1 billion, $750 million over the 2010 Budget,

to improve the nuclear stockpile's safety, security, and effectiveness with more extensive life extension programs, upgrades to the infrastructure supporting the life extension programs, and new initiatives in naval reactors work. Funding for the stockpile and naval reactors work increases by about 10 percent over 2010 funding.

Protects the Public from Harmful Exposure to Radioactive Waste and Nuclear Materials.

The Environmental Management program continues to clean up the legacy of waste and contamination at sites used to produce nuclear weapons and conduct energy research. The Administration has determined that Yucca Mountain, Nevada, is not a workable option for a nuclear waste repository and will discontinue its program to construct a repository at the mountain in 2010. The Department will carry out its responsibilities under the Nuclear Waste Policy Act within the Office of Nuclear Energy as it develops a new nuclear waste management strategy.

The President does not support developing the natural resources of the United States the budget also eliminates funding for fossil fuel development. The President needs to understand that all the wind farm development he is pushing uses products such as the propellers that are not produced in the United States. How does that create production jobs for the Americans?

Could there be more to the cap and trade then is disclosed. Just who is going to benefit the most from the cap and trade? The history of that bill needs to be investigated before the Congress passes the bill.

When everything is compared and the results about who has a better understanding of the needs and welfare of the United States? Sarah Palin has a much better understanding of the problems than the President. Not to mention that the majority of the American citizens are wondering why we are not developing our own natural resources?

Which would be the best? Have the government fund these clean energy projects that will take many years to develop or have the oil companies pay for the development of our natural resources without any cost to the government? Seems like a no-brainer to me.

In our vote for the most qualified to be President of the United States based on a scale of 1 to 10 "By the People, For the People"

Sarah Palin   **9**

Barack Obama`   **3**

The environmentalists are concerned about saving the calving grounds for the Caribou. With the size of the ANWR there should be plenty of room for the calves to be grown. That is if we shoot enough of the wolves to let them grow up.

President Obama is preaching about using clean energy for our automobiles. During the Presidents visit to Lisbon where the Portuguese hosts of Friday's NATO summit hoped to use the event to promote clean energy and electric cars, but all eyes were on the President of the United States Barack Obama's diesel-guzzling "Beast" instead.

As is usual when he travels, Obama's eight ton armored behemoth of a limousine was flown out to Lisbon before the United States leader's arrival, and it ferried him from the airport tarmac to his first meetings of the weekend.

Doubtless he didn't intend the Beast's roar to drown out his hosts' green message, but a United States presidential motorcade and its attendant escort of Secret Service SUVs do attract attention, even at the most elite gatherings.

According to President Obama the clean energy type of vehicle is only for the common folk and not for him. Doesn't the foreign country that Obama is visiting have any form of transportation that is adequate for our President? Why does he have to send a fleet of vehicles all over the world when he travels? Seems like a huge ego problem and a waste of the United States money.

CHAPTER THREE:

The Federal Reserve System

Palin lashes out at Feds stimulus plan

Sarah Palin trained her sights on the Federal Reserve's controversial multibillion dollar move to prime the United States economy, calling on the central bank "cease and desist."

Finally there is a politician that understands a little bit about the Federal Reserve System. Sarah Palin has gone record that the Federal Reserve's move to buy up $600 billion of United States debt would push up prices for ordinary Americans. The Federal Reserve's top economic panel last week said it would take the unusual and risky step to keep a fragile recovery moving and ease the high unemployment.

The Federal Reserve has gone on a frenzy of printing money out of thin air like monopoly money and should not be playing with inflation. The United States does not need any temporary or artificial economic growth that will cause permanent inflation that will erode the value of our incomes and savings.

The value of the United States dollar is going to be much lower as more dollars are pumped into the world market. This is like an extra tax on the earnings of the American citizens. Oil has recently risen to over $87 per barrel which is a six month high. The comments of Sarah Palin echoed the criticisms from conservative economists and some of the United States allies. Our allies are worried that the move could destabilize the global economy.

Barack Obama broadly defended the Federal Reserve moves during his visit to India. "The Fed's mandate, my mandate, is to grow our economy. That is not just good for the United States, that is good for the world as a whole," Obama said during a press conference with Indian Prime Minister Manmohan Singh.

Federal Reserve Chairman Ben Bernanke said that he did not expect rising commodity prices to be passed on to consumers and noted inflation levels were well below the Federal Reserve's target rate. Palin countered that "The Federal Reserve's pump priming addiction has got our small businesses running scared, and our allies worried."

"The German finance minister called the Federal Reserve's proposals 'clueless.' When Germany, a country that knows a thing or two about the dangers of inflation, warns us to think again, maybe it's time for chairman Bernanke to cease and desist," she said.

You do not need to be an economic expert to know what works and what does not. It is quite clear in the last few months there have been sharp increases in the prices of food, gas and so on. Bernanke will not argue the dollar is being weakened by these "Stimulus packages". A weak dollar of course causes the prices of everything to go higher here in the United States. The instability is causing precious metals to sky rocket in last few weeks

I am going to try and figure out why the Federal Reserve is holding the interest rates they are charging the banks to borrow money at close to zero. I have never understood why the Federal Reserve thinks that providing the massive amount of funds to the likes of Bank of America, Chase Manhattan, Wells Fargo and many other banks is going to help the economy. The theory of the program is to provide more capital that the banks can lend to the businesses and middle class Americans. That is really the stupidest program that has ever been designed. All this does is let the banks have huge amounts of capital that they don't have to pay interest on so they can turn around and loan it to the American citizens at any where from 5% to 18% that they charge the consumer. The only one that wins in this situation is the banks. No wonder their financial statements are looking better. If I could borrow $1 billion and earn an average of 10% on the money my financial statements would look much better too. The Federal Reserve is just pumping profits into the banks instead of helping the citizens of the United States. What will eventually happen is that the United States is going to fall into a deeper recession than we are already in.

The American citizens and small businesses are not going to borrow money they do not have any way of repaying. It is too bad that the federal government can not operate on the same principles. The businesses are not going to borrow money unless there are ways they can earn profits from the loan that exceed the costs to borrow. Businesses are not going to hire more employees until those employees can produce enough products or services to pay for the cost to the employer. Borrowing money is not the answer since it eventually has to be repaid. That does not improve the economy. Then we have the banks creating excessive lending requirements so that the majority of the applicants do not qualify. This will keep the funds available for the banks use instead of stimulating the economy.

The Federal Reserve is pumping all this money into the large banks so that they can pump the money into the economy but instead of loaning the money they are investing in the stock market and other high risk commodity futures. With all the buying pressure they are putting on the market it will continue to improve in the short term. The day is going to arrive fairly soon when all these bank investments are going to need to be sold and they are hoping that the small investors will be suckered back into the raising market so they can liquidate their holdings. Again the little guy gets screwed and the big banks reap their huge profits at the expense of the citizens.

The Federal Reserve is not willing to accept the fact that their programs is doomed to fail. It is like most of the programs that the current administration is promoting. The common sense is that by keeping the interest rates at these low levels is that they are killing the 58 million senior citizens that rely on receiving interest on their savings accounts and because of the Federal Reserve policy have been reduced to a 1% return. This cuts into the amount of income the seniors have to spend and further stifles the economic growth of the country.

What we have to overcome in the future elections is the educational capacity of the average voter that supports the Democratic Party. I will present some comments from different articles bashing Sarah Palin. The amount of intelligence that is displayed by these comments reinforces my opinion that the voters that have supported Barack Obama are severely lacking in any common sense or education about what has happened in America. After the comments I will provide some basic history which will reinforce Sarah Palin's views with regard to the Federal Reserve and the Chairman.

Mrs. Palin does not even know where Russia is relative to Alaska, but she is an expert in macroeconomics and monetary policy?

By the way, she accuses both President Obama and Mr. Bernanke day after day for not doing enough to ease unemployment, but when they try something bold to accelerate growth in this country your argument is that the Germans do not like it??? We cannot have it both ways. There is no magic solution to this problem. Sitting and doing nothing will not resolve our problems. Oh, I forgot, her expert economist solution to all the problems of this country is to cut taxes. Sorry Mrs. Palin, Bush tried that and look at the results.

Sarah Palin is saying to Bernanke what Obama should have said to him a long time ago. Those who think Bernanke is totally disconnected from the president should note that the president appoints the Federal Chairman. Obama was lavish in his praise for Bernanke, when he reappointed this architect of the housing bubble, the root cause of the ongoing great recession.

Germany's Finance Minister Wolfgang Schauble: "It doesn't add up when the Americans accuse the Chinese of currency manipulation and then, with the help of their central bank's printing presses, artificially lower the value of the dollar."

Once we start the process of devaluing the dollar, month by month over the next year, who is going to stop it? Can it be stopped? Obama's sending the country to the edge of the river called "Hyperinflation"... he may be sending us all over the falls. But that's what the progressive left does -- creates disaster, then capitalizes on it.

Every politician, when sworn into office should have, tattooed on the back of their hands, "It's not your money!"

Perhaps when they are about to launch a new spending program, or live large, or entitle themselves in any way, they would be reminded as to the fact that they are in office to invest in the country, not in their own indulgences. Printing more money is inflationary, and it is only backed by trust. Printing more money is payment in promises.

A BRIEF HISTORY OF THE FEDERAL RESERVE

The conspiracy to form the Federal Reserve System was carried out during the night of November 22, 1910. A delegation of the nation's leading financiers left the train station in Hoboken, New Jersey on a very secret mission. It would be years before anyone found out what the mission was. Even then they would not understand that the history of the United States underwent a drastic change after that night in Hoboken.

The delegation traveled in a sealed railway car for Jekyll Island. The group was led by Senator Nelson Aldrich, head of the National Monetary Commission. President Theodore Roosevelt had signed into law the bill creating the National Monetary Commission in 1908, after the tragic Panic of 1907 had resulted in a public outcry that the nation's monetary system be stabilized. Aldrich had led the members of the Commission on a two-year tour of Europe, spending some three hundred thousand dollars of public money. He had not yet made a report on the results of this trip, nor had he offered any plan for banking reform.

Accompanying Senator Aldrich at the Hoboken station were his private secretary, Shelton; A. Piatt Andrew, Assistant Secretary of the Treasury, and Special Assistant of the National Monetary Commission; Frank Vanderlip, president of the National City Bank of New York, Henry P. Davison, senior partner of J.P. Morgan Company, and generally regarded as Morgan's personal emissary; and Charles D. Norton, president of the Morgan-dominated First National Bank of New York. Joining the group just before the train left the station were Benjamin Strong, also known as a lieutenant of J.P. Morgan; and Paul Warburg, a recent immigrant from Germany who had joined the banking house of Kuhn, Loeb

These facts can be verified from information on the Internet. Thank God for today's modern technology.

"The Federal Reserve System was established by an act of Congress in 1913 and is not a 'private corporation'." On the next page, Mr. Winn continues, "The stock of the Federal Reserve Banks is held entirely by commercial banks that are members of the Federal Reserve System." He offers no explanation as to why the government has never owned a single share of stock in any Federal Reserve Bank, or why the Federal Reserve System is not a "private corporation" when all of its stock is owned by "private corporations".

The main problem, as Paul Warburg informed his colleagues, was to avoid the name "Central Bank". For that reason, he had decided upon the designation of "Federal Reserve System". This would deceive the people into thinking it was not a central bank. However, the Jekyll Island plan would be a central bank plan, fulfilling the main functions of a central bank; it would be owned by private individuals who would profit from ownership of shares. As a bank of issue, it would control the nation's money and credit.

Thus the proposed Federal Reserve Bank was to be "controlled by Congress" and answerable to the government, but the majority of the directors were to be chosen, "directly or indirectly" by the banks of the association. In the final refinement of Warburg's plan, the Federal Reserve Board of Governors would be appointed by the President of the United States, but the real work of the Board would be controlled by a Federal Advisory Council, meeting with the Governors. The Council would be chosen by the directors of the twelve Federal Reserve Banks, and would remain unknown to the public.

Warburg responded that the administrators of the proposed central banks should be subject to executive approval by the President. This patent removal of the system from Congressional control meant that the Federal Reserve proposal was unconstitutional from its inception, because the Federal Reserve System was to be a bank of issue. Article 1, Sec. 8, Par. 5 of the Constitution expressly charges Congress with "the power to coin money and regulate the value thereof.". Warburg's plan would deprive Congress of its sovereignty, and the systems of checks and balances of power set up by Thomas Jefferson in the Constitution would now be destroyed. Administrators of the proposed system would control the nation's money and credit, and would themselves be approved by the executive department of the government. The judicial department (the Supreme Court, etc.) was already virtually controlled by the executive department through presidential appointment to the bench.

Another member of the "First Name Club" was less reticent. Frank Vanderlip later published a few brief references to the conference. In the Saturday Evening Post, February 9, 1935, Vanderlip wrote: "Despite my views about the value to society of greater publicity for the affairs of corporations, there was an occasion near the close of 1910, when I was as secretive, indeed, as furtive, as any conspirator. . . . Since it would have been fatal to Senator Aldrich's plan to have it known that he was calling on anybody from Wall Street to help him in preparing his bill, precautions were taken that would have delighted the heart of James Stillman (a colorful and secretive banker who was President of the National City Bank during the Spanish-American War, and who was thought to have been involved in getting us into that war) . . . I do not feel it is any exaggeration to speak of our secret expedition to Jekyll Island as the occasion of the actual conception of what eventually became the Federal Reserve System."

Edward Vreeland, co-author of the bill, wrote in the August 25, 1910 Independent (which was owned by Aldrich), "Under the proposed monetary plan of Senator Aldrich, monopolies will disappear, because they will not be able to make more than four percent interest and monopolies cannot continue at such a low rate. Also, this will mark the disappearance of the Government from the banking business."

Vreeland's fantastic claims were typical of the propaganda flood unleashed to pass the Aldrich Plan. Monopolies would disappear, the Government would disappear from the banking business. Pie in the sky.

Nation Magazine, January 19, 1911, noted, "The name of Central Bank is carefully avoided, but the 'Federal Reserve Association', the name given to the proposed central organization, is endowed with the usual powers and responsibilities of a European Central Bank."

CHAIRMAN CARTER GLASS: "Why didn't the Western bankers make themselves heard when the American Bankers Association gave its unqualified and, we are assured, unanimous approval of the scheme proposed by the National Monetary Commission?"

ANDREW FRAME: "I'm glad you called my attention to that. When that monetary bill was given to the country, it was but a few days previous to the meeting of the American Bankers Association in New Orleans in 1911. There was not one banker in a hundred who had read that bill. We had twelve addresses in favor of it. General Hamby of Austin, Texas, wrote a letter to President Watts asking for a hearing against the bill. He did not get a very courteous answer. I refused to vote on it, and a great many other bankers did likewise."

MR. BULKLEY: "Do you mean that no member of the Association could be heard in opposition to the bill?"

ANDREW FRAME: "They throttled all argument."

MR. KINDRED: "But the report was given out that it was practically unanimous."

ANDREW FRAME: "The bill had already been prepared by Senator Aldrich and presented to the executive council of the American Bankers Association in May, 1911. As a member of that council, I received a copy the day before they acted upon it. When the bill came in at New Orleans, the bankers of the United States had not read it."

MR. KINDRED: "Did the presiding officer simply rule out those who wanted to discuss it negatively?"

ANDREW FRAME: "They would not allow anyone on the program who was not in favor of the bill."

CHAIRMAN GLASS: "What significance has the fact that at the next annual meeting of the American Bankers Association held at Detroit in 1912, the Association did not reiterate its endorsement of the plan of the National Monetary Commission, known as the Aldrich scheme?"

ANDREW FRAME: "It did not reiterate the endorsement for the simple fact that the backers of the Aldrich Plan knew that the Association would not endorse it. We were ready for them, but they did not bring it up."

We object to the Aldrich Bill on the following points: Its entire lack of adequate government or public control of the banking mechanism it sets up. It's tendency to throw voting control into the hands of the large banks of the system. The extreme danger of inflation of currency is inherent in the system.

The insincerity of the bond-funding plan provided for by the measure, there being a barefaced pretense that this system was to cost the government nothing. The dangerous monopolistic aspects of the bill.

"Our financial system is a false one and a huge burden on the people . . . This Act establishes the most gigantic trust on earth."--Congressman Charles Augustus Lindbergh, Sr.

Senator LaFollette publicly charged that a money trust of fifty men controlled the United States. George F. Baker, partner of J.P. Morgan, on being queried by reporters as to the truth of the charge, replied that it was absolutely in error. He said that he knew from personal knowledge that not more than eight men ran this country.

The Presidential campaign of 1912 records one of the more interesting political upsets in American history. The incumbent, William Howard Taft, was a popular president, and the Republicans, in a period of general prosperity, were firmly in control of the government through

27

a Republican majority in both houses. The Democratic challenger, Woodrow Wilson, Governor of New Jersey, had no national recognition, and was a stiff, austere man who excited little public support. Both parties included a monetary reform bill in their platforms: The Republicans were committed to the Aldrich Plan, which had been denounced as a Wall Street plan, and the Democrats had the Federal Reserve Act. Neither party bothered to inform the public that the bills were almost identical except for the names. In retrospect, it seems obvious that the money creators decided to dump Taft and go with Wilson. How do we know this? Taft seemed certain of re-election and Wilson would return to obscurity. Suddenly, Theodore Roosevelt "threw his hat into the ring." He announced that he was running as a third party candidate, the "Bull Moose". His candidacy would have been ludicrous had it not been for the fact that he was exceptionally well-financed. Moreover, he was given unlimited press coverage, more than Taft and Wilson combined. As a Republican ex-president, it was obvious that Roosevelt would cut deeply into Taft's vote. This proved the case, and Wilson won the election. To this day, no one can say what Theodore Roosevelt's program was, or why he would sabotage his own party. Since the bankers were financing all three candidates, they would win regardless of the outcome. Later Congressional testimony showed that in the firm of Kuhn Loeb Company, Felix Warburg was supporting Taft, Paul Warburg and Jacob Schiff was supporting Wilson, and Otto Kahn was supporting Roosevelt. The result was that a Democratic Congress and a Democratic President were elected in 1912 to get the central bank legislation passed. It seems probable that the identification of the Aldrich Plan as a Wall Street operation predicted that it would have a difficult passage through Congress, as the Democrats would solidly oppose it, whereas a successful Democratic candidate, supported by a Democratic Congress, would be able to pass the central bank plan. Taft was thrown overboard because the bankers doubted he could deliver on the Aldrich Plan and Roosevelt was the instrument of his demise. *The final electoral vote in 1912 was Wilson - 409; Roosevelt - 167; and Taft - 15.

Glass claimed that the proposed Federal Advisory Council would force the Federal Reserve Board of Governors to act in the best interest of the people.

Under the Federal Reserve Act, note circulation would always expand indefinitely, causing great inflation. However, the later history of the Federal Reserve System showed that it not only caused inflation, but that the issue of notes could also be restricted, causing deflation, as occurred from 1929 to 1939.

The Federal Reserve Act puts it in twelve regional central banks, all owned exclusively by the identical private interests that would have owned and operated the Aldrich Bank. President Garfield shortly before his assassination declared that whoever controls the supply of currency would control the business and activities of the people. Thomas Jefferson warned us a hundred years ago that a private central bank issuing the public currency was a greater menace to the liberties of the people than a standing army."

<u>The real question is who actually owns the Federal Reserve System today?</u>

As astonishing as it may sound the practice of passing legislation without reading it has been going on for over 110 years. The Healthcare bill was passed using these same tactics of voting without reading the bill. You would think that after 110 years that this country would have learned something.

In our vote for the most qualified to be President of the United States based on their knowledge of the Federal Reserve. The vote on a scale of 1 to 10 "By the People, For the People"

Sarah Palin   9

Barack Obama`   2

CHAPTER FOUR

The Decision to Resign as Governor

The Democrats are bashing Sarah Palin's decision to resign as Governor of Alaska stating that she is a quitter. I take exception to the claims that leaving the office was quitting. The idea of being a lame duck Governor did not appeal to Palin. Sarah Palin knew that she would not be running for a second term as governor and did not want to be in the position as a lame duck. Instead of being a lame duck it is better to have the new governor step in and lead the state. By doing so the transition was smooth and the state was able to function the way it should. Sarah Palin on the other hand was able to devote all of her energies to helping others within the Tea Party and Republican Party to get a majority elected in the House and make strides into the control of the Senate by the Democrats.

Sarah Palin kept her future plans shrouded in mystery and it was unclear if the controversial hockey mom would quietly return to private life or begin laying the foundation for a presidential bid.

What scares the Democratic Party is the fact that Sarah Palin is a dynamic and tough opponent and will cause the Democrats to be concerned about winning the Presidency in 2012. The Democrats had better perform better during the last two years of Obama's administration or they are going to really face hostile voters in 2012. They are on course to keep doing what they have done for the last two years. By retaining Reid and Pelosi as the leaders of their party it looks like some more of the same from the Democrats.

When Alaska's Governor Sarah Palin abruptly announced that she is resigning from office, a shocking move that rattled the Republican Party but left open the possibility she would seek a run for the White House in 2012.

Many lame duck politicians just accept that lame duck status and they hit that road. They draw a paycheck. They kind of milk it. Sarah Palin was not going to put Alaskans through that. She should be commended and not chastised since it was the best decision for Alaska.

Sarah Palin's vision of what is best for Alaska also translates into what is best for America.

Jerry McBeath, a veteran political science professor at the University of Alaska Fairbanks, called the pending resignation a "smart move," both for Palin and the state.

Palin felt that the pressures of the job combined with her family obligations and the demands and desires to help other Republican candidates led her to decide not to run again. Once that decision was made, she realized, why not do it now and let the lieutenant governor take over and get a head start on his election.

"I cannot stand here as your governor and allow the millions of dollars and all that time go to waste just so I can hold the title of governor," Palin said, referring to the alleged impact of multiple ethics complaints against her, most of which have been dismissed.

Palin remaining as governor is not good for Alaska, given the "political blood sport" by her critics, Stapleton said. Stepping down is a "fighter's move," Stapleton said, essentially Palin stepping around political barriers in her way and pursuing her vision.

Sarah polled the most important people in her life, her kids, where the count was unanimous, she said. "Well, in response to asking, "hey you want me to make a positive difference and fight for all our children's future from outside the governor's office?" It was four yeses and one 'Hell, yeah!" and the 'Hell, yeah' sealed it.

CHAPTER FIVE

Lisa Murkowski

The citizens of Alaska elected Lisa Murkowski because Sarah Palin did not run. Sarah Palin could have run for Senator of Alaska in the same manner that Barack Obama ran in Illinois. After a year in office she could have declared that she was running for President and then Alaska could have appointed the candidate they wanted. We all know that every time Sarah Palin has ran against a Murkowski that she has won handily. It would not have been any different in this case. The Governor of Alaska would not try to sell the vacant Senate seat that Palin would have left like the ex-governor of Illinois.

Senator Lisa Murkowski (I-AK) whose relationship with fellow Alaska politician Sarah Palin has been rocky for years said that Palin lacks the "intellectual curiosity" to be president. Lisa should be sending Sarah a thank you card for not running against her for the Senate seat.

According to Lisa Murkowski Sarah Palin lacks the Intellectual curiosity to be the President of the United States. That comment is coming from a person whose relationship with Sarah Palin dates back to the time when Frank Murkowski was defeated by her for the Governorship of Alaska in 2006. Frank Murkowski appointed his daughter to the United States Senate over objections from the Republican Party.

When the voters selected Joe Miller as the Republican Party candidate to run for the Senate Lisa Murkowski pouted and refused to back the party's selection. She has won the Senate seat as a write in candidate by bashing Joe Miller from day one. Not once in her campaign did Lisa Murkowski comment on what her policies would be when she returned to the Senate. Probably just more of the same old earmarks that Ted Stevens believed in. How about supporting the legislation that every American will benefit from?

"You know, she was my governor for two years, for just about two years there, and I don't think that she enjoyed governing," Murkowski said. "I don't think she liked to get down into the policy." Murkowski said she would prefer a candidate who "goes to bed at night and wakes up in the morning thinking about how we're going to deal with important issues." Wouldn't it be nice is Murkowski practiced what she is preaching?

For the record, Lisa Murkowski was one of the seven Republicans that voted against banning earmarks.

The following comments are what some American citizens think of Murkowski and her comments.

Ah, so Sarah Palin lacks "intellectual curiosity". Well, good for her. Then just maybe she would be much better for this country than the moronic intellectuals in Washington who got us into the mess we're in today. I wonder just how many of our Founding Fathers would be considered intellectuals by that same bunch of today's Washington intellectuals. We need more people like Sarah Palin who live by the standards of honesty, decency, integrity, and personal responsibility. We certainly don't need more whining losers like Murkowski.

There is obviously some animosity here for not getting her endorsement and for Palin beating her father. It doesn't take a genius to figure out that if Palin would have endorsed her then she would be singing nothing but praises. This is just a little cat fight from a Senator who almost lost her seat because she was not as conservative as her constituents wanted her to be. Maybe she will learn her lesson from this or who knows maybe she will caucus with the Democrats. I put nothing past this angry old lady.

Obviously the voters in Alaska decided that Palin had more governing ability than Murkowski's father did when they voted him out of office and voted Sarah Palin in. Ms. Murkowski actually demonstrates her own lack of suitability for high office when she takes her cat fight to Katie Couric and pleads her case to an all to gleeful liberal media that loves nothing more than seeing Republicans scratch each other's eyeballs out. Ms. Murkowski seems more like a spoiled brat throwing a tantrum than a person worthy of the office as a Senator of the United States.

I cannot believe that this Senator would have the gall to make a comment about anyone seeing how her father was the one to appoint her Senator in the first place. How are we allowed to appoint family in our government? In my opinion any one who would give family jobs just is a form of corruption. Thanks!

Palin is a narrow minded dimwit who has few if any of the talents needed to be President of the United States. That she has gotten as far as she has is nothing short of a miracle. If she were to get the nod from the Republican Party for 2012 it would guarantee a 2nd term for Obama.

Not a word about all the past corruption In the Murkowski family that got brought to light by Palin but a whole lot of garbage trying to trash Palin again. Calling names and throwing false accusations is all the dirt they have on Sarah Palin but no hard facts. Between Obama and Palin when it comes to experience, Palin wins by a mile. Ever notice how the AOL police come out to assure more negative comments get posted when anything is written about Palin. Anyone that scares the Left as much as she does has got to be good.

Now that some of the hate mail is out of the way. We will list some of the accomplishments of Sarah Palin and why the Democrats are so scared of her. The main stream media will keep on bashing Palin due to the fact that it reaches the illiterate section of the voting public that is traditionally voting Democratic.

Those of you that consider Republicans, Tea party supporters to be racist please tell me which you would consider to be more racist. 1) To vote for a man simply because he is Black. 2) To not vote for a man because he is Black. I ask this question because 97% of Black people voted for Obama.

It seems to me it's just as racist to vote for someone because he/she is Black as it is not to vote for the person because he/she is white. I'll take Sarah Palin over Obama any day. At least she won't create policies that stomp all over the United States Constitution or slams programs down the citizen's throats that they do not approve of. The President does not listen to what America wants.

"Real folks" is a very common term in the real world but most folks from the metro areas don't have a clue about real folks. Everyone should spend some time in the Midwest, or the plains states, or the south and then they'll understand what real folks are all about. As for Ms. Palin, so many people criticize her but don't have a clue about growing up in an area like Alaska, and quite honestly she's not dumb. The funny thing is that the people that continue to criticize her seem to be very concerned about her and that truly brings a smile to me. So much nastiness but these same people seem to think Obama, Reid, Pelosi and Holder are really something to aspire to. I sure hope the America wakes up soon.

There is, for example, a pending public records request from Linda Kellen Biegel, an Anchorage blogger who is seeking e-mails showing an effort by the Palin administration to smear her critics including those filing ethics complaints against the governor. Biegel, whose own ethics complaint was dismissed, also is seeking an investigation into the financial profits to the Palin family from racing sponsors of Palin's husband, Todd, in the 2,000-mile Iron Dog snowmobile race.

"No truth whatsoever. Period," she wrote in an e-mail to The Associated Press. "This is Just more nonsense from the same people who choose to waste state resources."

In the presidential race, Palin became the butt of talk-show jokes and Democratic criticism after news broke that the Republican Party had spent $150,000 or more on a designer wardrobe, accessories and hair and makeup services for her. The high-end spending spree contrasted with the down-to-earth image she sought to craft for herself and became an unwelcome issue for the McCain campaign.

She didn't leave the limelight once McCain lost the presidency. She recently led a public spat with "Late Show" host David Letterman over a joke he made about one of her daughters being "knocked up" by New York Yankees baseball player Alex Rodriguez during the governor's recent visit to New York. Palin's 18-year-old daughter, Bristol, is an unwed, teenage mother. Letterman later apologized for the joke.

Palin also complained that her 14-month-old son, Trig, who was diagnosed with Down's syndrome, had been "mocked and ridiculed by some mean-spirited adults recently." She didn't elaborate.

It is despicable that the Democratic followers are capable of stooping so low as to attack the family of any candidate for political office. When will the Democratic candidates and their supporters begin to tell the American people what they are really going to try and accomplish for the benefit of all of the American citizens? Instead of rhetoric how about explaining the method that their policies are actually going to be enforced and what the real results are going to be?

CHAPTER SIX

Democrats Running Scared

Obama's Accomplishments in the News

President Barack Obama's former chief of staff Rahm Emanuel formally announced his bid for mayor of Chicago. He stepped down from what is considered to be the second most important position in the White House on October 1, 2010, to prepare to run for mayor of Chicago, a job he has long coveted. That is good news. There goes one more Chicago politics supporter.

As President Barack Obama's plane headed eastward from New Delhi, he left India on a high. The India-United States partnership had been lifted out of the apparent slowdown of the past two years.

Republicans, who opposed much of President Barack Obama's agenda throughout the administration's first year, took control of the U.S. House of Representatives November 2, 2010 and appear to consider their success a referendum upon the president's policies.

President Barack Obama leaves Asia digesting complex new realities in a region where rising powers like China wield new influence and challenge American global dominance.

It's almost enough to evoke sympathy: the entire journalistic world poring over President Barack Obama's post-election comments and applying a humility meter to his words, his facial expressions and his mood. Does he get it? Is he sufficiently abashed by the voters' rebuke? But just when you think the guy has suffered enough, he short-circuits your pity.

Desperate Advertisements Target Palin

You know you're doing something right when the opposition targets you in one of its final campaign ads, despite the fact that you aren't even a candidate. That's the position of ex-Alaska Governor Sarah Palin. She's the subject of a get-out-the vote Internet ad produced by the Democratic National Committee.

The ad features a picture of Palin with the title "Don't Let Sarah Palin Win." Her nomination for vice president in 2008 produced a huge inflow of donations for the Republican National Committee. And Palin haters contributed to the Democrats.

The Democratic National Committee wants to take advantage of liberals' continued apathy toward the potential Republican presidential candidate for 2012. The new spot is the DNC's "best performing" ad that doesn't feature President Barack Obama.

John McCain and his spokesperson are bashing Sarah Palin.

It was bad enough that many rank and file conservatives began criticizing the spunky winker from Alaska, but now things have simply gotten out of control. Senator John McCain made the following comments in a speech in New Mexico:

I didn't just show up out of nowhere, after all — America knows me. You know my strengths and my faults. You know my story and my convictions. And though familiarity in politics can be both helpful and not so helpful to a candidate, it does at least fill out the picture and answer the essential questions.

You need to know who you're putting in the White House — where the candidate came from and what he or she believes. And you need to know now, before it is time to choose.

Damn! I know McCain is desperate, but this is a Hail Mary that should have never been thrown.

Carly Fiorina made the comment that Sarah Palin couldn't run a computer company. Senator John McCain surrogate and former Hewlett Packard Chief Executive Officer said on a radio interview that Sarah Palin wouldn't have the experience to run her old company. That is really quite a statement since Fiorina is not capable of running the same company either. Thank the people of California for their common sense we will not have to put up with Carly in government either.

Fiorina commented that Hewlett Packard had a global workforce as large as the size of the number of registered voters in Alaska. If she had not been out sourcing so many jobs overseas the work force could have been supporting American jobs instead of a global work force. Then Fiorina suggested that running Hewlett Packard did not generally focus on the issues of the United States such as war, commerce or the welfare of the citizens.

This is the same Carly Fiorina that was drummed out of Hewlett Packard by the Company's board in 2005. Fiorina could tell you exactly what you need to know about how to fail at running Hewlett Packard.

Still Bashing Sarah Palin for Being Decent, Normal American

Sarah Palin's new job as an analyst at Fox News has inspired yet another round of bilious projection from the establishment left. Guess what she was called on dumb-as-a-rock Joy Behar's show? Dumb, of course. Equally amusing, the slavish worshipers of Dear Reader accused Saracuda of over-reliance on a teleprompter.

Do you remember like a couple weeks ago Jon Stewart did a bit where he talked about how the Fox host had to dumb themselves down for the audience? Sarah doesn't have that problem.

The question was asked if Sarah Palin was going to be a hit on the Fox show. I do. If you remember, when she graduated from the six colleges that she attended, she became a sports caster or a news reader as they say. So this is perfect for her. As long as the teleprompter doesn't break, she's going to be great.

It gets worse. Soon they were going after Trig again: That baby, they passed that baby around more than a joint at a Grateful Dead concert. Is she going to bring that baby on the set of Fox? You've just about triggered America's gag reflex.

CHAPTER SEVEN:

Can Sarah Palin Beat the Numbers?

The number of Americans viewing Sarah Palin favorable is at 40% which was her lowest score recorded. Palin, the Republican Party's vice presidential candidate in 2008 is among Republican names being floated as a possible presidential pick in two years time. The poll found she might have a good chance of capturing the nomination with 80 percent of Republicans having a positive opinion of her.

About the same as the Presidents numbers and a lot better then Pelosi and Reid's. Why does the press keep picking on her? Does she have the Democrats running scared?

Palin told the Times that her biggest job would be to prove her record to voters.

"That's the most frustrating thing for me -- the warped and perverted description of my record and what I've accomplished over the last two decades," Palin said. "It's been much more perplexing to me than where the lame stream media has wanted to go about my personal life. And other candidates haven't faced these criticisms the way I have." I can not remember any candidate that has ever been bashed as much as Sarah Palin and I have watched elections for over 50 years. The Democrats are scared and the main stream media is going to do everything possible to keep the lame duck as president in 2012.

Palin might have a harder time in a general election. Polls indicate that 81 percent of Democrats and 53 percent of independents viewed her unfavorably. That means that the majority of the Hispanics and Blacks are hoping for more hand outs and will vote Democratic. We need to get the voters educated and overcome this handicap.

Since the Democrats took control of Congress on January 3, 2007 the Deficit has increased by five trillion dollars. Palin has a higher favorability rating then the present Speaker of the House who is third in line for the Presidency. Being Governor and/or Mayor means you have more Executive experience than the other three that were running as President and Vice President. Being in the Senate or a Community Organizer is not Executive experience. Finally we have the Governors of Arizona and Kansas that quit before their term was up to become one of President Obama's lemmings in Washington.

I was thrilled when McCain announced her as a running mate. I had already checked her experience early in the campaign when her name was mentioned. She has what this country needs in a candidate. It is the same thing that you see in Tea Party Candidates. A belief in our country believing in limited government, following the Constitution and a balanced budget. She has the spunk, tenacity and truthfulness you rarely see in a candidate. We need this in a politician and will be looking for this in anyone who runs for office.

I view myself as an Independent politically, but I'm a Sarah Palin fan. It's not because I always agree with her politically, but because she is a refreshing respite from the otherwise droll spin of Washington politics. She's an outsider, a puzzle piece that doesn't fit, and she injects life, and at times, humor, into the mix. And while she is often polarizing within her own party, just her presence makes the hair stand up on the necks of most Democrats.

Governors and ex-governors do not necessarily make good presidents. To be a good President you should have international experience. Palin does not, nor does she take an interest in foreign affairs.

Other governors that have quit their governorship early are moving up and are still governing. Palin quit being a talking head on Fox, promoting a book she didn't write, and make money. Of course she's more popular than someone who actually has to make decisions. She has nothing at stake in the fight. What shocks me is that 40% of Americans support her. The question I have is: why are those 40% of Americans so afraid of intelligence?

Sarah Palin can beat all the odds by telling America what she is going to be doing for the American citizen instead of filling the media with rhetoric about policies that have absolutely no way of helping the average American citizen. When Palin starts to explain how her policies are going to be implemented and how they will be accomplished America is going to rejoice and support her for President.

CHAPTER EIGHT:

Earmark Policies

The Democratic Earmark Policy

I do not know what the views of Sarah Palin are with regards to earmark policies. But if Palin really wants to run for President it will be important to support the Republican Party on earmark legislation. Although Senate Republicans have vowed to halt the practice, Senate Majority Leader Harry Reid defended it as the obligation of every member of Congress.

"I believe, personally, we have a constitutional obligation, a responsibility, to do congressionally direct the spending. I do not feel comfortable turning that over to the people downtown," Reid said, referring to federal agencies that would assume the responsibility of designating federal funds in the absence of congressional direction. "So I am not going to back off of bringing stuff back to Nevada."

The Congress needs to pass legislation that bans all earmark attachments to any piece of legislation that is proposed in both houses. Every bill that is presented should be able to stand on the merits of the legislation. If it can't be passed without bribing the members with pork the bill probably was not for the benefit of the people of the United States.

On November 30, 2010, The United States Senate voted 56 to 39 to continue to allow congressional earmarking, the practice that lets individual lawmakers designate federal funds for specific projects, usually in their home states. The representatives just can not get it straight about what the voting citizens of the United States want. The citizens want truth in legislation and that will only come when each and every piece of legislation is passed on the merits of the bill. The earmarks just lead to corruption in the Congress.

Although Senate Republicans recently adopted a nonbinding resolution to prevent Republican senators from requesting or supporting earmarks, the bill proposed Tuesday -- by two Democrats and two Republicans -- would have formally changed Senate rules to make it impossible for the chamber to move any bill with an earmark attached.

Despite the GOP caucus' official stand against the practice earlier this month, eight Republicans joined a majority of Democrats to keep earmarking alive, including Alaska Sen. Lisa Murkowski, who defended the practice on the campaign trail this year, arguing that the millions of earmarked dollars that her state gets help with everything from air mail delivery for remote islands to basic infrastructure projects. Also voting yes were Republicans Susan Collins (Maine), Jim Inhofe (Okla.), Richard Shelby (Ala.), Richard Lugar (Ind.), Robert Bennett (Utah), George Voinovich (Ohio), and Thad Cochran (Miss.), the top Republican on the Senate Appropriations Committee.

Democrats were no more united than the GOP on the issue. Although Senate Majority Leader Harry Reid defended congressional earmarks earlier this month as the constitutional obligation of every member of Congress, six Democrats bucked Reid and voted to put an end to practice, at least temporarily.

Russ Feingold (Wis.), Evan Bayh (Ind.), Michael Bennet (Colo.), and Mark Warner (Va.) joined Claire McCaskill (Mo.) and Mark Udall (Colo.) in voting against earmarks. McCaskill and Udall introduced the measure with GOP Senators Tom Coburn (Okla.) and John McCain (Ariz.), two longtime critics of pork-barrel spending.

The issue has roiled both Democrats and Republicans this year as they balanced the chance to send federal funds back to their states and districts with the increasing anger of American voters, who have complained more and more that federal spending is out of control.

But critics say that even if Congress did ban earmarking, the larger question remains as to whether it would reduce overall federal spending or simply take the decision-making process about federal dollars from Congress and move it to federal agencies. It would decrease the budget deficit due to the fact that a large portion of the earmarks would not pass as stand alone bills that only benefit an individual state. The Republicans in the House of Representatives need to bring this to a vote again after the Democrats are removed from their office.

The vast majority of the American taxpayers voted to eliminate all earmarks. The Republicans had better get off the stump and propose legislation that bans all earmarks in January 2011. Then if the President veto's the bill it will be another strike against his re-election goals for 2012.

Sen. Richard Durbin (Ill.), the second-ranking Democrat in the Senate and a member of the Appropriations Committee, argued before Tuesday's vote that senators are already making voluntary efforts to increase transparency in earmarking and that the effort is "virtually unprecedented."

He added that the real abuses in earmarking happened under Republican leadership in the House of Representatives, and that past abuses of the system should not affect his or anyone else's chance to send funding home to their states.

"I believe that I have an important responsibility to the state of Illinois and the people I represent to direct federal dollars into projects that are critically important to the direction of our state and its future," he said.

The Citizens against Government Waste puts out an annual "Congressional Pig Book" that listed 9,129 projects at a cost of $16.5 billion in 2010.

I would like to see a total breakdown of the $800 billion stimulus bill to include each and every project that was in the bill. How many pork projects were attached to the bill to get it passed. The government needs to provide a complete accounting for each project that was funded by the bill. That includes engineering cost, labor cost, material cost and all other expenses. When the accounting is received it could reveal just how many jobs were created for non union members that were not employed by the contractors who received the project money. How many jobs did this massive spending bill create for the unemployed?

The Obama administration needs to make a full disclosure about the healthcare legislation. The citizens of the United States have the God given right to know what pork projects were attached to this bill. We already know that the requirement to have businesses prepare Form 1099's on every business that they sell or buy over $600 from. What other garbage attachments are on the healthcare bill? All of the pork attachments need to be repealed immediately.

Harry Reid the leader of the Senate started his campaigning in Nevada by bragging about his ability to bring hundreds of millions of dollars in federal pork back to the state of Nevada.

The Congress has created a federal government that's too big and too expensive. Every political candidate should swear off the earmarks. Congress needs to know that many of the systems or manifestations of the pork spending, which is the political lubricant that keeps this big machine going and keeps it growing. We need to decrease the size of government and not provide methods of making the government larger. Eliminate all pork spending.

Earmarks that were attached to the legislative bills in 2010 amounted to about $16.5 billion. The government has attached bring home the bacon attachments that the taxpayer's did not know anything about. If these attachments were so good they could have been stand alone bills and the whole Congress could have voted on them. That would be the transparent way of passing legislation.

The Democrats would have been in trouble if it were not for the pork earmarks. Without them the healthcare bill would not have been passed. It is the result of the bribes made to the Democrats that voted to pass the legislation. Every American should be contacting their representatives and demanding an accounting of what bacon went to each state. It is bad enough that there is not any transparency but to add to the insult there is not any accountability.

The following is an example of how the bringing home the bacon works. That's good. Whatever anyone thinks about Harry Reid or the Tea Party bragging about how much pork you've brought to a state is not a good thing.

A residence of Connecticut where they have the Coast Guard Academy and the Electric Boat Company that makes submarines for the Navy. Every year, their two senators would brag about how much money they had procured for the Electric Boat Company to build submarines but the catch was THAT THE NAVY DIDN'T WANT THEM. So in essence, they spent billions building submarines that the United States Navy didn't want or need. That is not very good for all the taxpayers. I'm all for having a few extra jobs but not at the expense of the national economy. Polls rail against discretionary spending but defense spending is the largest portion of discretionary spending in the federal budget. It is just a jobs program and corporate welfare for defense contractors. Another reason the federal government should eliminate all the pork programs. This would not have passed as a stand alone piece of legislation.

Could it be that the pork problem is going to be heard? The anti-earmark candidates promise to shake up a Capitol culture in which earmarking is seen by most lawmakers as a birthright. In the House, Minority Leader John Boehner, R-Ohio, who has never sought an earmark, earlier this year orchestrated a Republican rules change in which the party swore off earmarks. Now they need to pass legislation that makes it illegal to have earmarks.

But renegades like Senators. Jim DeMint, (R-SC), and Tom Coburn, (R-OK) are pushing the party to give up earmarks. DeMint was counting on anti-earmark reinforcements from the election to help him force a vote on changing Republican conference rules to require Republicans to abandon the practice. An overwhelming majority of new Republican candidates have taken the no-pork pledge.

President Obama and all Incumbents your worst nightmare is going to happen. It is the American people waking up. Don't be afraid be very, very afraid, and we know you are, because we can tell by the desperation in the Democratic campaigns and all the fear that you are trying to place in the American voters minds. It is as palpable as the grass roots movement that is picking up speed and sweeping the nation. "We the People" may not be able to dislodge you all from your positions on Pork Hill, but a substantial number of you are about to be evicted and the remaining ones had better pass legislation that is for the people and not for the benefit of some representative's home district. We are your employers and you are the employees. You are supposed to be serving the people and not your political interests. You should be afraid of us and not us afraid of you. These things you have forgotten, in the course of turning deaf ears to your countries needs and wants while you pursue only that which will benefit you and your state. We are tired of the lies, the stealing and the deception. We will reclaim our country and you can't stop us.

Earmarks amount to buying or selling a vote, an action that would put the common voter in prison. In congress it is an acceptable practice done on a daily basis. This practice of give me this and I'll vote yes on this bill that I'm actually against has got to stop.

All of these vote buying earmarks are a huge part of the problem. Ban all earmarks. If you can't get broad support for a piece of legislation without resorting to bribery, it is probably not a good piece of legislation to begin with. The people have had enough of the back door deals and bribery.

CHAPTER NINE

Ending Entitlement Programs

This morning I went to sign my Dogs up for welfare. At first the lady said, "Dogs are not eligible to draw welfare". So I explained to her that my Dogs are mixed in color, race, creed, and origin, unemployed, lazy, can't speak

English and have no clue about who their Daddy's are. They expect me to feed them, provide them with housing and medical care. So she looked in her policy book to see what it takes to qualify. My Dogs get their first checks Friday. Dang this is a great country. By the way, my dogs are here illegally from Mexico.

That was dedicated to President Obama and his policies on entitlement, immigration and amnesty for illegals.

On the news there was a comment by the Speaker of the House Pelosi that giving food stamps would provide more "Bang for the Buck". I have been trying to figure out how Pelosi thinks that giving $1.00 in food stamps will create $1.79 for the economy? I am stumped as to where Pelosi comes up with the idea that giving another entitlement will help the economy. What kind of economics did she study? The fact is that there are 41.8 million citizens drawing food stamps at a cost of $60 billion. If that is helping the economy then Pelosi must think that the people are really stupid. What I would like to know is how many of those 41.8 million are illegals in the United States. It looks like Pelosi, Reid and Obama are grasping for anything they think the less educated will buy to get some more votes.

I think we need to reform entitlement programs. The welfare and unemployment programs need to be addressed to weed out the people that are taking advantage of the system.

This is my philosophy if you are not mentally or physically disabled, and you receive welfare, you should be required to do some sort of labor for the state in which you live. You should be required to submit to job placement programs. You should be required to do something productive even if it's basic community service type stuff. I don't think we should give anyone a free ride, especially if they are physically and mentally capable of working. There are plenty of areas in the community that could use labor in exchange for the unemployment benefits. Clean the parks, streets, highways or any other area that needs picking up. When the people that are receiving the benefits have to do something productive to receive them watch the number of unemployed be reduced. A lot of the recipients think that it is better to do nothing than to find a job paying lower wages than they believe they are worth. Pride is a wonderful thing.

Entitlement programs are supposed to be a stepping stone for people down on their luck. It is not supposed to become a way of life for the lazy who would rather not work.

Give a man a fish and he will be expecting you to feed him forever. Teach him to fish, and he'll know how to feed himself. Entitlement programs teach people nothing, and help them leech off of others. The programs should be limited except for those who are completely disabled, and drug screening as there is for any government employment should be mandatory.

Government entitlement programs create dependency. How else do you explain it when women have more kids to get more welfare? Naturally people are going to vote for candidates that promise more benefits at the cost of those evil rich people. So naturally candidates that promise the most get the most votes. Heaven forbid we elect government officials who actually make it easier to earn our own living.

The way things are dealt with should be changed. Granted, there are some that are severely disabled that will not ever be able to hold a job that pays well enough to survive on, and they should be assessed to determine this and stay with the help they are given, this should be a small number of people.

Private help groups such as those for battered women have a great system worked out. They take the families into a shelter where they receive counseling and training. There are strict rules they must live by if they want help. Very strict rules, they must keep their living quarters clean, they must be in by a certain time. They must train for a job. When they get a job, they are not immediately cut off from help they continue to get to live where they are living in the group home. However, they must turn over 1/2 of their income to the shelter, and account for every penny they spend of the other half. This teaches them things like budgeting. When they have reached the point where they can become self-sufficient, they are given an apartment for themselves, rent prorated to be a certain percentage of their income. Here, they still get food stamps and are united with a sponsor that will help them pay child care expenses, on a sliding scale so they can work and still survive. When their income reaches a sustainable level, they are given back the 1/2 of their paycheck they turned over when they started working, they can spend it on a car and for a down payment on an apartment of their own. They still get help with child care at this point, but are coming off of the system at a pace they can deal with. The help declines as they start earning enough to support themselves and their children. The success rate for this system is fantastic. I really believe that most people want to work, in spite of what we hear, they just can't go from nowhere to somewhere overnight. With working and building your self esteem and taking pride in what you have accomplished will lead to becoming a productive and proud citizen.

CHAPTER TEN

Repealing the NAFTA

The North American Free Trade Agreement (NAFTA) should be abolished between the United States and Mexico. The simple facts are that Mexico has declared war against the United States with their invasion of 20 million illegals that have entered into the United States. Although it has not been a military invasion it is definitely taking our resources and the quality of life from the citizens of the United States.

The United States needs to stop doing business with the Mexican's until such a time as the borders are secure and the illegals that are residing in the country are returned.

We the people of the United States need to practice self discipline and cancel all travel plans that include stops in any part of Mexico. Mexico needs to lose out on all of the American tourist money. We have an abundance of beautiful places in the United States that everyone could use to enjoy on their vacations. Why not go to Hawaii or Alaska instead? We need to return to our roots and enjoy America the Beautiful. For those of you who want to see what it is like in Mexico travel to Southern California.

The United States has lost over one million jobs since NAFTA began in January 1994. The value added tax is one of the most negative economic games that are played on the consumer. Don't kid yourself every country has a value added tax to their imports except America. These value added taxes are one of the primary reasons that American companies ship their jobs out of the United States. They can use cheap labor to produce overly cheap products in a foreign country and ship the manufactured products back to America free of a value added tax. There go our American manufacturing jobs to another country and up goes our unemployment rate.

The United States needs to incorporate a value added tax on all merchandise that comes into the country and protect our manufacturing base and put every company on an equal basis. When everything becomes equal the manufacturing will return to the United States and our economy will start to revive.

The federal government is borrowing trillions of dollars to keep our economy running. Something is seriously wrong our economic priorities are up side down. The economy can not be restarted from the government. It has to be started from the local communities by creating new jobs and saving our housing.

What is the North American Free Trade Agreement?

In January 1994, the United States, Mexico and Canada entered into the North American Free Trade Agreement (NAFTA), creating the largest free trade area and richest market in the world. The NAFTA is the most comprehensive regional trade agreement ever negotiated by the United States and is scheduled to be fully implemented by the year 2008. In 1996, United States two-way trade in goods under the NAFTA with Canada and Mexico stood at $420 billion--a 44% increase since the NAFTA was signed.

What are some of the key goals of the NAFTA?

NAFTA was established to reduce barriers to trade and increase cooperation to improve working conditions in North America. This was great for Mexico because they had lousy working conditions and a way of life that was unacceptable. The program was to have an expanded and safe market for goods and services that are produced in North America. The program was to expand and broaden world trade.

Well the program sure has worked. Look at all the junk that is made in Mexico. It is about time that the United States starts to make its own pottery. We have enough hand carved wooden statues. One thing for certain it sure has developed a world trade of the worst kind. So many drugs and illegals are being exported by Mexico that it is killing the United States and turning some areas into a third world status. America does not need this treaty with Mexico anymore.

We are not against promoting the policies of the NAFTA with Canada since it is not shipping millions of their unwanted citizens into the United States every year. Thank you Canada!

Does the United States really need to provide jobs in Mexico? Why does a company like General Motors need to build a new plant in Mexico? We have outrageous unemployment figures in the United States and a company that the government wants to build a factory in Mexico and transfer the jobs that American's need down to Mexico. This is absurd. What is more disgusting is that the United States government is still stuck holding a 62.1% of the company and they are shipping jobs out of the country. How can anyone in our government justify such a move?

The government needs to step up and stop General Motors from building the plant in Mexico. We have 62.1 percent of the voting power at General Motors use this power and stop the stupidity.

What are the benefits of the NAFTA for U.S. consumers?

These are some of the things that the NAFTA was supposed to provide. More free trade resulting in greater choices in goods and services, lower prices and improved quality products, stronger health and safety standards, improved economic stability in the United States marketplace and a marketplace that is increasingly driven more by supply and demand than by barriers to commerce.

I am finding it very difficult to notice any improvement in the quality of living in the United States due to the NAFTA. There have not been better health or safety standards in the United States. The economic stability in the United States has definitely not improved. In fact the health and safety standards have been made several times worse due to the 20 million illegals. Finally, we really do not need any more baskets, vases or hand carved toys. Not to mention that we need to stop the illegal drug trade that is thriving across out Southern borders.

How does the NAFTA affect the environment?

One of the very important targets of the NAFTA was that the United States and Mexico were to have launched a Border XXI program that would have established a five-year objective for achieving a clean border environment and a blueprint for meeting these objectives.

Wow!! That was a beautiful plan but it has failed miserably. The border is in the worst shape now than in the history of the United States. It will not be cleaned up until the government decides to take the necessary action to complete the border fence and then stop the massive flow of illegals from Mexico into the United States.

The government needs to pass legislation that will eliminate the North American Free Trade Agreement with Mexico. It had some good points when it was passed into law but the negatives surrounding it today are more than enough to abolish the program.

We should replace it with a policy that anyone that enters the United States will be caught and deported immediately. We do not need to be supporting 10% of the Mexican population as we are now. The United States has a big enough job in taking care of the legal citizens of the country.

Thanks to the NAFTA and the policies of out sourcing jobs from America we can expect to receive another stimulus payment in the future. This is a very exciting program but does have a few drawbacks. Let me explain in the following questions and answers.

Q. What is an 'Economic Stimulus' payment?

A. It is money that the federal government will send to taxpayers.

Q.. Where will the government get this money?

A. From taxpayers.

Q. So the government is giving me back my own money?

A. Only a smidgen of it.

Q. What is the purpose of this payment?

A. The plan is for you to use the money to purchase a High-definition TV set, thus stimulating the economy.

Q. But isn't that stimulating the economy of China?

A. Shut up.

Below is some helpful advice on how to best help the United States economy by spending your stimulus check wisely:

* If you spend the stimulus money at Wal-Mart, the money will go to China or Sri Lanka.

* If you spend it on gasoline, your money will go to the Arabs.

* If you purchase a computer, it will go to India, Taiwan or China.

* If you purchase fruit and vegetables, it will go to Mexico, Honduras and Guatemala.

* If you buy an efficient car, it will go to Japan or Korea.

* If you purchase useless stuff, it will go to Taiwan.

* If you pay your credit cards off, or buy stock, it will go to management bonuses and they will hide it offshore.

Instead, keep the money in America by:

1) Spending it at yard sales, or

2) Going to ball games, or

3) Spending it on prostitutes, or

4) Beer. Or

5) Tattoos

These are the only American businesses still operating in the United States.

Conclusion:

Go to a ball game with a tattooed prostitute that you met at a yard sale and drink beer all day.

No need to thank me, I'm just glad I could be of help.

I do not know what either Palin or Obama are planning to do about the NAFTA. Who ever decides to abandon the program will win lots of votes from the other candidate.

CHAPTER ELEVEN

Border Policies

If I was Sarah Palin and running for the office of President of the United States I would make securing our southern border a tremendous work project that would put several hundred thousand people back to work.

There are approximately 1,300 miles of the border fence that still needs to be constructed. In addition to the fence the America's Highway needs to be finished. The America's Highway would run parallel to the border fence and can be completed at the same time as the fence. This will provide access to the fence for the workers and the shipment of the materials necessary to complete the construction of both projects.

The projects can be built in segments with bids from highway construction companies competing for each 20 mile stretch of America's Highway. Other construction companies can compete for 20 mile sections of the border fence. All of these 20 mile sections could be working at the same time and this would allow for a minimum of time to complete the project.

Every section of the border fence would be constructed to the same specifications so that the end project would look exactly the same.

Look at what America has done in the past to solve the unemployment problems. How about Hoover Dam being constructed? Americans can build anything they put their minds and hearts into. Look at the photo of the bridge connecting Arizona and Nevada that was just completed.

If we can build this bridge we can construct a highway through the desert to protect our border. This is the highest support arch bridge in the Western Hemisphere with the exception of the bridge at the Royal Gorge in Colorado which is not a highway bridge.

America's Highway would provide information about every one of the 44 presidents of the United States and all future presidents. There would be history plaques located every 40 miles in rest areas with the accomplishments of each president. This could turn into one of the most exciting trips people could make to learn about the history of all of our presidents. Just look at what Mt. Rushmore did for the state of South Dakota.

The rest areas could be built at an elevation that would provide viewing of the Mexican side of the border for those that would like to see the river and Mexico. The American Flag would be flown and these areas would provide services to the border patrol while they do their jobs along the fence.

The United States has currently constructed about 600 miles of the border fence on the southern border of California. The construction led to a decrease of about 50 percent on the number of illegals that entered through that area. The completion of the remaining 1,369 miles of the border fence and America's Highway would complete the project. All of the border projects would be under the supervision of the Army Corps of Engineers. This would provide for 68 different highway construction projects that can be completed at about the same time. This would provide 68 different fence construction projects that can be completed at about the same time. This would create 34 construction projects for the rest areas.

These projects will also create thousands of jobs in many different support areas. The construction of the materials required for the projects. Transportation jobs to get the materials to the construction projects. Then there would be food services and housing requirements that will provide additional jobs.

This would be expensive to construct but the alternatives are more expensive. It is estimated that the illegals in the United States cost the local, state and federal governments in excess of $50 billion per year. Those costs will more than offset the cost of a permanent border fence and America's Highway to patrol the fence.

America's Highway will be able for all citizens to utilize when they want to travel from East to West or West to East. Currently all of the 42 border crossings have to be reached by traveling from North to South. The border fence will not restrict travel between Mexico and the United States since the 42 border crossings will still be in operation. It will just make it easier to get from one to the other.

Obama's Advice: Put terrorist attacks in perspective.

The Pentagon long ago made a cliché of the phrase, "Failure is not an option." Barack Obama's anti-terrorism crew believes failure is not only optional but inevitable – and Americans need to get over it. Michael Leiter, head of the National Counterterrorism Center, told a conference on intelligence reform, "We're not going to have a perfect batting average, and it's important that Americans understand that." Not to worry, though; the opening line of the story states Leiter believes we can bounce back from another 9/11 or two. The key is to take the terrorist blasts with a happy face. "It's important that we approach this with national resilience that in fact shows that this country is not going to be defeated by "terrorists," Leiter told the increasingly nervous crowd. Instead, we must tell those nasty Muslim fanatics they will not be "cutting into the fabric of our society." What we have to do, Leiter concluded, is "put the threat in perspective."

Were this one loose-lipped, harebrained security official, it would be concerning enough. Unfortunately, this seems to be official policy. We the people need to make sure that we contact enough representatives in the Congress and get the policy of the President corrected. We are not going to accept anything less from our government.

Most of the foreign countries of the world have displayed a total lack of respect for America. This is primarily due to the actions of the President of the United States and some of his policies including the one above.

President Filipe Calderon of Mexico has directly blamed the United States for the drug violence in Mexico. "The origin of our violence problem begins with the fact that Mexico is located next to the country that has the highest levels of drug consumption in the world," Calderon wrote. "It is as if our neighbor were the biggest drug addict in the world."

What I don't understand is why does the President of the United States keep letting Calderon keep trashing our country? Instruct the Department of Drug Enforcement to stop the flow. We have the highest trained military forces in the world and our President refuses to defend our nation against these blatant attacks on our citizens.

The drug cartels have grown rich and they are getting overly bold in how they are killing their own citizens and anyone else that tries to interfere with their activities. Since the Mexican government is not going to eliminate these cartels it is going to be up to the United States. Why are we waiting to accomplish what is going to be best for the United States. We have to be realistic when the cartels are demolished and the drugs stop flowing into the country we will have to stop using these drugs. If the supply is there then the demand will also be there. This is a huge business for the cartel and the Mexican government does not want to stop the flow of American money back into Mexico. The drug business is netting the Mexican people any where from $10 billion to $25 billion per year.

Instead of using the power of the United States to stop this horrible situation right now the Obama administration had dedicated $1.3 billion in aid to train police, reform the courts, supply drug sniffing dogs, armored cars, night vision goggles and Black Hawk military helicopters. Talk about a severe waste of the taxpayer's money. Just use our Air Force and take out the drug cartels hang outs. It would only take a few days and the whole operation would be over.

The problem is that Mexico really does not want the problem solved. They are enjoying the cash from our country. When will our President get some courage and protect our nation?

The solutions are right before our President's eyes and he will not look at them. When the borders become secure then most of these problems will automatically disappear.

The President of Mexico and the President of the United States must have gone to the same school of blame. If both of these presidents want to end the traffic of drugs they need to use some common sense. Let the United States Air Force do a few days surveillance as to where the drug lords are located. Give the citizens in the area a few hours to leave the vicinity of the drug lord's strongholds and then have the Air Force use some of our strategic missiles and blow them to kingdom come. It would take about one day.

The problem we have is that the government of Mexico likes the drug money coming into Mexico and is willing to let the drug lords continue operating to make sure the money comes into their country. President Obama will not do anything for fear of offending Calderon and taking a chance on possibly losing votes from the Hispanic citizens in America. Does anyone else remember that the Democrats stood and applauded Calderon in the Senate while he degraded the Americans? I am proud that the Republicans did not stand.

The Secretary of State of the United States stated that "we are working very hard to assist the Mexicans in improving their law enforcement and their intelligence, their capacity to detain and prosecute those who they arrest. I give President Calderon very high marks for his courage and his commitment. This is a really tough challenge. And these drug cartels are now showing more and more indices of insurgency — you know, all of a sudden car bombs show up, which weren't there before."

When are Obama and Clinton going to stop placating the Mexican government and start looking out for the people of our country? It is so disgusting it can't be put into the proper words. It does not matter where the drugs come from they are crossing into our country through Mexico.

Once again the President of Mexico is trying to dictate to the American people what we should do. What America needs is to have a President that will tell Calderon that he does not have any rights or say in what is done in America. The Mexicans can live in their third world country and stop the flow of illegals into the United States. If it is great to live in Mexico how come over 10% of their population is living in the United States illegally?

President Calderon is concerned that California will pass the proposition 19 which would allow the possession of an ounce of marijuana and pave the way for retail sale. It was a highly debated issue in the United States when we abolished prohibition and allowed the sale of alcohol. The same will happen when and if the sale of marijuana is legalized. The people are going to use marijuana regardless of whether it is legal or not. Create a regulatory process and tax the product the same way the government did with alcohol. It will be a huge tax windfall for the state of California.

Calderon is sticking his nose into our countries business for the sole purpose of protecting Mexico's traffic of marijuana into the United States. He wants to condemn our country while Mexico produces and sells marijuana into the United States. Sounds like he or the Mexican government is on the take from the drug cartels and that provides huge amounts of money to them.

Here is the real reason that Calderon wants to make sure that proposition 19 does not pass. Marijuana cultivation in Mexico increased to 8,900 hectares in 2007 and yielded a potential production of 15,800 metric tons.

The Mexican government wants their share of the drug cartels money from all of this marijuana that is sold in the United States.

Calderon said he was certain that legalizing marijuana will lead to an increase in drug consumption. "It's very sad to see how drug consumption is, little by little, tearing apart American society and, if we don't watch ourselves, it will tear apart ours," Wow, he must be smoking more than anyone realizes or else is using his other drugs.

It would be very hard to tear apart the majority of Mexico. How can it get any worse?

This will go down as one of the major understatements of all time. Calderon said Tijuana continues to suffer from crime but that its problems are no different than other cities in the world — a view echoed by the city's politicians and business elite. While the gruesome displays of violence have diminished, killings continue. Tijuana had 597 murders from January through September, up 33 percent from the same period in 2009 but still at a pace below the record 843 deaths in 2008. Why would anyone want to visit Tijuana?

I do not advocate the use of marijuana but does anyone remember politicians also saying that concealed carry permits would make everyone start carrying guns and having shootouts in the streets. The law was passed and crime dropped almost immediately. The people that got the permits were mostly people who carried anyway, gun sales did not rise and more training was available. This is a similar situation with pot. Anyone who will smoke it already does. The biggest problem is that pot is a naturally occurring plant that the drug companies can't control and make millions from in their labs. It's all about the bottom line. It is amazing that we live in a society where a person can be arrested for pot and pass a dozen stores that sell deadly booze on the way to jail.

What Clinton did not address, is probably the most important aspect of the problem. What can the United States do to protect itself? And the answer to that is simple: Control the border.

When will the government place travel restrictions on Americans that want to visit Mexico and see how their economy starts to crumble. There are reportedly 15 million American tourists that visit Mexico every year. Put a halt to this until the drug problems and border is secure. There are many places in the United States that are wonderful vacation spots that are being overlooked. We could use the billions that are spent vacationing in Mexico. Go to Alaska or Hawaii and enjoy your vacation and help the United States.

During October 2010 there were several incidents that happened that should have indicated to the citizens of the United States that the President should have taken action on when they happened. We heard the President of Iran tell the world that the leaders of the United States should be buried. Then we had an American tourist murdered on Falcon Lake which is about 25 miles long and 3 miles wide on the border between Mexico and Texas and nothing was done. Both of these acts are a disgrace to the American people.

The situation on Falcon Lake has been brewing for the several years. The Mexican drug cartels have taken over control of the Mexican side of the lake. The security of the United States has been in jeopardy for years and the state of Texas and the federal government has done nothing to protect our citizens or the border.

Would anyone care to guess why the government is silent on illegal immigration? Why the government is afraid to tackle this issue? Why Obama is suing Arizona? It's quite simple, politicians are so afraid of upsetting the Hispanic voters with such nonsense like securing our borders. Politicians are more concerned with loosing the Hispanic voters then actually doing what is right for the United States and I don't see it changing any time soon. America needs to wake up and secure all of the borders.

Obama's lawsuit against Arizona and all the Democrats standing up and applauding Mexico's president when he denounced Arizona's law takes the cake. It's nothing less than treason.

The United States will be able to return to the beautiful land that if once was after the country starts dealing with the illegal immigration and drug trafficking that is plaguing the Mexican borders. The amount of drugs that are entering the Unites States is absolutely insane. These drugs are what is fueling the drug gangs and turning the southern California area into despicable living conditions.

The Federal Bureau of Investigation and the Department of Homeland Security reported that 75% of those on the most wanted list in Los Angeles, Phoenix and Albuquerque are illegal aliens. 24.9% of all inmates in California detention centers are Mexican nationals. 40.1% of all inmates in Arizona detention centers are Mexican nationals. 48.2% of all inmates in New Mexico detention centers are Mexican nationals. 29% (630,000) convicted illegal alien felons fill our State and Federal prisons at a cost of $1.6 billion annually. 53% plus of all investigated burglaries reported in California, New Mexico, Nevada, Arizona and Texas are perpetrated by illegal aliens. 50% plus of all gang members in Los Angeles are illegal aliens. 71% plus of all apprehended cars stolen in 2005 in Texas, New Mexico, Arizona, Nevada and California were stolen by Illegal aliens or "transport coyotes". 47% of cited/stopped drivers in California have no license, no insurance and no registration for the vehicle. Of that 47%, 92% are illegal aliens. 63% of cited/stopped drivers in Arizona have no license, no insurance and no registration for the vehicle. Of that 63%, 97% are illegal aliens. 66% of cited/stopped drivers in New Mexico have no license, no insurance and no registration for the vehicle. Of that 66%, 98% are illegal aliens.

Those statistics were from the same people that are advocating amnesty to the illegals. These are real statistics and not some fringe group statistics. With all the negative reports being printed/broadcast in the "liberal/progressive" news media (New York Times, CBS, NBC ABC, MSNBC, CNN, etc) here are the statistics they don't deem news worthy and fail to report. This is really sad for America.

Until the American people force our representatives in Congress to address these problems we are not going to achieve our dream of becoming America the Beautiful again.

I don't know how many of you have ever visited some of the cities along U. S. Highway 1 that winds through California. It is a scary sight to behold. The cities along the coast are a good example of what the Mexicans want to turn the United States into. The businesses are all catering to the Spanish and very few of the signs are in English. They do not make any attempt to resemble what a normal American city looks like. The only way we will ever recover in those areas is to make sure that every illegal that is in this country is deported. California alone has more than 10.8 million illegals living there. The government of California can not understand why they have a $19 billion deficit this year alone. It will not get any better until the system stops giving the illegals free entitlements.

The Homeland Security Department that is headed by Janet Napolitano has an internal memo that is designed to give amnesty to the majority of the illegals in the United States. The memo reportedly will allow this measure to bypass Congressional approval. We can not let this type of policy be enforced in the United States. The majority of the people do not want amnesty of any kind. Why don't the Democrats listen to what the people want?

As reported by Newsmax on September 18, 2010, there is another Arizona sheriff that believes the Obama administration is undermining the rule of law on the border by blocking the border enforcement needed to prevent illegals and narco-terrorists from flooding into the United States from Mexico.

Pinal County Sheriff Paul Babeu stated that the administration has actively thwarted law enforcement efforts to help secure the border. Now why does that not surprise anyone? The Mexican drug cartels now control some parts of the Arizona border. Currently there are militant groups who are escorting drug carriers or human illegals with AK-47's. They are much more organized than the American public is aware of. They have look out points on the miles of Arizona border and know when the border patrols are going to be in the area and when they will have free access to enter into the United States.

The Obama administration has sued the state of Arizona for enforcing the current laws and wants to leap frog over border security and just go right to amnesty. We can not let such a disgrace to the American people happen. The border fence needs to be completed now. We could build the fence and reduce unemployment by hiring thousands to complete this project immediately. Put the Army Corps of Engineering in charge to supervise the labor force and get the job done. It could be a project similar to the

Hoover Dam. Thousands of workers were hired from all over the United States to complete that project.

Some things that the United States could do that will help solve the illegal problems. By solving the illegal problems the country will then be able to start cleaning up the third world mess that the illegals have left. They are as follows:

Close every border and access point into the United States of America. Should the Mexican, Canadian, Cuban or any other government be offended by our border policy that is fine? We can live with that much better than we can live with the illegal migrants into the United States.

Locate every illegal person that is in the United States of America and take them back to the closet border where they came from. The simple fact is that they are criminals and illegal and are not deserving of any type of protection by our laws.

This is to include all the anchor babies born in the United States of America during the time that the illegal parents are living in our country.

Current polls show that approximately 75% to 80% of the legal voting American Citizens are in favor of securing our borders. About the same percentages are in favor of adopting laws similar to the Arizona SB-1070.

The government of the United States of America should provide public notice via the mainstream newspapers, the television media and radio in Spanish and English so that everyone that reads or hears will be able to understand. Every illegal in the United States of America has 30 days to get their belongings together and go back over the border that they came from. The illegals that go back voluntarily will not have any record and will be allowed to apply through legal channels to return to the United States.

Every illegal that does not return voluntarily will be hunted down and taken to the border that they crossed into the United States from. A complete record of these illegals will be maintained and they will never be allowed to apply for citizenship in the United States. The record will include a photo, DNA sample and control number. If they are caught in the United States again they will go to jail for ten years at hard labor.

These types of policy will not only deter any more illegals it will solve the problem of the ones here.

It has been reported that in California 26% of the population are illegals. If you have ever lived in California or visited there you can verify that there that many.

Does anyone really want all of these illegals in the United States and then give them amnesty so they can vote?

The North Korean attitude towards the United States shows total disrespect for our country. The following information was released by the news and is disgusting. Hopefully, they are going to be intelligent enough to realize that they would by annihilated in any attempt to attach the United States or our territories.

The Worker's Party parade was said to be North Korea's largest ever, an impressive display of unity and military might for a country known for its elaborately staged performances.

Thousands of troops from every branch of North Korea's 1.2 million-member military, as well as naval academies and military nursing schools goose-stepped around the plaza to the accompaniment of a military brass band while citizens waved plastic bouquets.

Trucks loaded with katyusha rocket launchers rolled past, but they were dwarfed by a series of missiles, each larger than the last and emblazoned with: "Defeat the U.S. military. U.S. soldiers are the Korean People's Army's enemy."

"If the U.S. imperialists and their followers infringe on our sovereignty and dignity even slightly, we will blow up the stronghold of their aggression with a merciless and righteous retaliatory strike by mobilizing all physical means, including self-defensive nuclear deterrent force, and achieve the historic task of unification," Ri Yong Ho, chief of the General Staff of the North

Some citizens of Grand Junction, Colorado are so irate at the President's policies that they have paid for a billboard depicting President Obama unfavorably. I have a photo of the billboard outside of Grand Junction Colorado on my home page at www.thomasmeinders.com. The Democrats pulled enough political strings that the billboard was only operational for a few days. Part of the problem could be that the President and the Justice Department are not standing up for Arizona. How could the government let foreign countries enter complaints against the state of Arizona in their lawsuit?

The American people are tired of the President and the policies that he has shoved down our throats. When is he going to get some courage and stand up for the United States and our countries rights? First of all it is disgusting that the President and the Justice Department has sued the state of Arizona. Now there are foreign countries that are being allowed to try and sway our court system in the 9th District Court. Then we have another judge trying to change the "Don't Ask and Don't Tell" of the military. How can one individual think they can possible overrule the military?

MY AMERICAN DREAM

Newsletter   December 1, 2010

Volume 2010-48   **www.my-american-dream.org**

What is Happening on the Border?

What is happening on the Texas and Mexican border is just the start of our problem in America. Unless someone gets some courage to stop this we will continue to be invaded by the Mexican illegals. We really do not want these people in our country because they are causing higher unemployment among the Americans. They are also burdening our welfare system and President Obama wants to pass legislation to make them legal. America has to stop this now.

The following email came from a friend that lives on the Texas border.

Good Morning, I Googled Fox News and didn't see anything about this immigration bill. I know they are talking about the «Dream Act» to give citizenship to illegals who are going to college (at our expense) or who serve in the military for two years. I hope & pray that doesn't pass. There are over 600 of those students going to college here in this area according to the paper. This overhaul of our food supply has me worried. That will mean higher prices and food shortages probably...more food stamps. It is scary!!! The mess in Mexico gets worse & worse with Mexicans fleeing their country for the U.S., and we don't hear about it on the news, but it is happening. Drug cartels are taking over whole towns and telling people to get out or die. So, where will they go when they flee???? The situation is grim and I feel that George Soros and the White House are behind the mess in Mexico to get more Mexicans here to vote for Obama, open borders and all the other horrible things that seem to be happening. I hope it won't, but it could. I don't ever remember this country and the world being in such a mess!!!! Maybe we are heading into those «last days!» All we can do is pray!! I'm glad we own land 500 miles north of here....we may need to flee this area if things here get really bad. The city of Donna has been wanting a bridge to connect our area with a town called «Rio Bravo» which is South of Donna in Mexico. Well, after years of wrangling, their idiot, stupid bridge is scheduled to open in January if all goes according to plans. Our side is done, but Mexico hasn't finished their side. I hope they never do. It will make it easier for all those thieves, to roam around here, more kids to plug up our school system, higher taxes, more drugs, wear on our roads, etc.!!! It doesn't look good for us here.

America's Third War: Uncovering Border Tunnels

There is a very simple approach to the tunnel problem. When one is located there is a thing called dynamite that could reduce the tunnel to rubble and put it out of business. Why does our government make everything so difficult? The following was reported on November 30, 2010.

Scores of trucks pass through Otay Mesa, California, each day, loading and dropping off cargo at various warehouses located just yards from the United States and Mexico border.

One warehouse bearing the name "Medi Int Enterprises" an alleged storage facility for toilet paper seemed to be running business as usual, equipped with a front desk and receptionist. Yet, on Nov. 3, 2010, Immigration and

Custom Enforcement agents found they were storing much more than bathroom supplies.

ICE agents intercepted a truck leaving the warehouse and discovered 20,000 pounds of marijuana. An additional 32,000 pounds were found in 10-kilo bricks throughout the warehouse, making it the second largest seizure of marijuana in United States history. But, the biggest find was what lurked below. Agents found 1,800 feet of tunnel running underneath the warehouse to Mexico. Designed with tracks and pulleys, the smuggling tunnel is the most recent to be discovered in a growing number popping up along Border States.

Since Sept. 2001, 113 tunnels have been discovered -- a 63 percent increase in just the last two years. ICE agent Tim Durst said they are becoming an increasing threat with the "growing presence of law enforcement above ground."

With tougher enforcement and new barriers along the U.S.-Mexico border, smugglers have become more creative in their methods, finding alternative routes by sea and land and now underground.

Seventy-one smuggling tunnels have been uncovered in Nogales, Arizona, with San Diego, California, a close second, counting 34 in both Otay Mesa and San Ysidro. The tunnels are "golden goose eggs" and if they're completed and become operational, they are of great value to smugglers, Durst said.

The majority of the tunnels ICE agents have found are unfinished, which makes this find that much more concerning to law enforcement. Durst says the tunnel in Otay Mesa took approximately a year to build, but had been operational for less than a month.

While the tunnels can be sophisticated drug smuggling routes, the engineering behind the creation of the tunnels is not. Would-be smugglers use jackhammers, concrete saws and shovels that can be purchased in retail hardware stores.

Law enforcement isn't empty-handed in their efforts to thwart smugglers from taking over the underground. Durst is part of a tunnel task force, monitoring areas like Otay Mesa and looking for signs of things out of the ordinary.

New technology has aided ICE agents in their battle against smugglers. Ground-penetrating radar detects anomalies in the ground and can find trap doors or exits to potential tunnels. A motorized robot -- controlled like a video game from above ground --serves as a safety precaution. It has a camera on top and navigates through tunnels, allowing law enforcement to scope out the scene before entering.

Joint efforts by ICE and other government organizations including the Department of Defense, universities, and Border Patrol are working to create newer and more effective technology to combat the growing problem of smuggling tunnels.

President Obama's approach

President Obama's approach to protecting our borders is to sue the state of Arizona for enforcing the laws that are currently in effect. It would be really nice if the President would think about the invasion of the United States that is ongoing and start to realize that it needs to be stopped. We can not continue to allow a million illegals to enter the United States every year. Of course there might be another reason that the President does not want to stop the flow. Could it be that the President is thinking along the lines of amnesty for the 20 million illegals in the United States?

Stalled Virtual Border Fence

The Department of Homeland Security Janet Napolitano has already frozen work on the controversial virtual fence that was supposed to secure roughly 1,969 miles along the United States border between the United States and Mexico. Reports are out that the Department of Homeland Security is going to cancel the entire program sometime in November.

That is probably the only intelligent thing that Janet Napolitano has proposed during her entire time in that office. Now the Department of

Homeland Security needs to understand that the Mexicans have invaded the United States and station our military on the southern border.

The questions that most of the American citizens are asking is why in the world the Department of Homeland Security would hire Boeing to be responsible for securing our borders in the first place. Boeing has enough trouble getting their aircraft produced on schedule. Just how lame brained was this selection anyway? Put the United States Corps of Engineers on the job and build a real fence.

The Department of Homeland Security is proposing to increase the number of drones flying along the border. Just look at how effective they have been in Afghanistan after about 10 years of use. Another option would be to increase the number of border patrol agents or rely on the National Guard. The government is hedging on increasing the number of agents due to the 1969 miles of unprotected border. The Department of Homeland Security states that manpower solutions are not cost effective. That is after they have wasted over $1 billion on the program that they intend to scrap. Can anyone figure out these cost effective actions are benefiting our country? Complete the construction of the fence and the America's Highway along the fence which are one time costs. Then the border can be patrolled more efficiently and effectively.

Then if you can believe just how stupid the Department of Homeland Security is they are considering a different type of program that is similar to the one just scrapped. Again with a civilian contractor that is not in the construction business. Starting over with new bids gives the illegals another 24 months of free entry into the United States. How many of the 2 million or more illegals will be terrorists?

The virtual fence should be written off as a very stupid move and move forward with what will be completed in the shortest period of time. The United States is incurring costs because of the illegals at approximately $50 billion per year. How can anyone in government think the cost of the fence is too expensive? Look at the alternative. It is like comparing the problem of getting old compared to dying young.

That brings us to the point. President Bush started the construction of a physical border fence. The Democratic Congress stalled the completion and blamed it on reported legal challenges. It is doubtful that the President would sign any legislation commencing construction of a border fence. The attitude of Janet Napolitano is that is you build a 50 foot fence they will use a 51 foot ladder. What she doesn't understand is that we would have several minutes to use high powered rifles and shoot the illegals while they are climbing the ladder. We would not have to shoot very many and they will take their ladder back to Mexico. That is just another lame excuse by the Department of Homeland Security and Janet Napolitano with the support of President Obama. The Democrats do not want to stop the illegals from entering the United States. There is a hidden agenda to grant amnesty to the 20 plus million illegals that are in the country.

Based on the opinions of President Obama and Janet Napolitano and the rest of the administration we can't stop them so lets just move the border northward about 20 miles per year until they have what they want. Why doesn't someone in the current administration understand that we have military personnel that have the training to defend our borders? We can go all over the world and interfere with other governments and defend their borders. What is the matter with this situation?

People just don't realize how easy it is to cross the border into the United States from Mexico. If you lived in these areas you would realize how sinfully easy it is to make these movements. It is not just an illegal alien issue anymore, national security should be the main goal, so what will it take for people of other countries like Yemen based al-Qaida, terrorist from Iran and others. The United States government is responsible for the nation's borders, instead they're suing the state of Arizona, and other states that are doing what the government is suppose to be doing. It doesn't matter where you live in the United States you should be angry that they're spending taxpayer dollars to go after states that are fighting a border war they should be doing. The only way the citizens are ever going to solve the problem is to send emails and letters every day to the representatives of your local district. Let them know the will of the people and that we will not stand for anything else.

An article from Monterrey, Mexico and reported by Reuters indicated that the Mexican Marines had killed one of the drug lords that was terrorizing the area. The report indicated that this was a victory for President Calderon.

The Mexican report indicated that 3 marines and 4 gunmen were killed. It also claimed that a civilian reporter was killed.

This article fails to mention some import information. According to the Valley Morning Star, which is in Harlingen, Texas, not far from Matamoras, stated that there were 47 people killed in this little gun battle? It is suspicious to me that this Reuters report makes is sound like only 8 were killed. Forty seven people being killed in Matamoras is about the same as 47 being killed in Washington, D.C., a city about the same population. Don't you think if 47 were killed in Washington, D.C. that it wouldn't be plastered all over the news? Come on folks, we have a war raging right next door to us and a mainstream news media is failing to report the real news because of their love for President Obama and his administration who finds it more convenient to look the other way.

Every American needs to question ourselves about why President Obama, Senator Reid and the other Democrats refuse to send troops to the borders? Could it be that Reid won Nevada because of the votes in Las Vegas and Reno was funded by money from the drug cartels and unions through the casino industry to support and attract the Hispanic votes?

The border situation has been an ongoing problem for years. The only President in recent history that cracked down on illegal immigration was President Eisenhower. Everyone else has ignored it or has been too enamored with Hispanic votes or cheap labor to close the border. Calderon would have you believe that most of the drug cartels weapons came form United States. Try buying a full automatic weapon, grenade, or grenade launcher, and it is evident that these are military grade weapons from other places. Our federal government has proven to be totally useless and will continue to dance around the issue until a real massacre or ambush occurs in the United States. Then they will want to disarm the law-abiding citizens so we are defenseless. Note how robust the European economies are, and how successful they are in dealing with the illegal Muslim immigrants there. Nothing will change until Americans quit doping themselves for fun and recreation, and we quit voting the same party hacks in that kowtow to the same cheap vote and union labor interests. The best part is that the United States is still one of the best places on earth to live. I wonder how long this will last if we continue to allow millions of illegals to enter our wonderful country every year?

The latest polls that were available indicated that over 60 percent of Americans want our borders secure. If indeed Sarah Palin were to adopt the above policies our vote for the most qualified to be President of the United States based on their knowledge of the Border. The vote on a scale of 1 to 10 "By the People, For the People"

Sarah Palin   10

Barack Obama`   0

CHAPTER TWELVE

Term Limits

If I was Sarah Palin and running for the office of President of the United States I would be pressing for legislation that would place term limits on both houses of Congress. The Senators would be limited to two terms or 12 years and the Representatives of the House would be limited to 4 terms or 8 years the same as the President of the United States.

There are too many representatives in both houses that have been in control for too many years. We need to remove these individuals because they are presenting programs that are not in the best interest of all of the citizens of the United States. A couple of examples would be Charlie Rangel and Maxine Waters who are both Democrats.

The punishment for Charlie Rangel's crimes ought to be as harsh as they come. Here is a man who sat as the point man for all taxation with which you and I must comply! However, the Chairman thought himself to be above such laws. Never mind the spectacle that he made at not being allowed to present his case with legal representation. Both the Democrat majority leadership (they still are the majority till January) and Charlie Rangel himself knew that if they didn't get this over with quickly, a new majority would be apt to throw the book at him and meet out a harsher sentence then the "slap on the wrist" he will probably get. What he deserves is the very maximum punishment, because he thought himself above the laws he expects us to obey. Every tax cheat who now sits in jail ought to be released if he does not receive this. Rangel was censured when he should have been thrown into a prison cell.

Oh my God, censure! What is that? A piece of paper saying naughty boy, you were bad, don't do those things. If you do this again we will take away your privilege to ride the little train to work everyday. We'll turn off the mike when ever you are up front and speak. Maybe give Rangel KP! How about making him clean the chalk boards, and the erasers too! This guy has been in office 40 years and he does not know what is legal. Where was he when he first came to Washington? Did he play hokey from school? This is all just eye wash to placate the people, we'll show Rangel, and we're upset. Alright for you Charlie Rangel! Shame on you naughty man now you can go back to work.

Then the Ethics Committee has decided to delay the hearings on Waters. Waters happens to be another corrupt black representative that has been in power forever. These life time representatives need to be replaced with fresh ideas and younger people. Sorry John McCain but that also includes you.

I was wondering why the government needs a Black caucus in Washington. Shouldn't the representatives that are elected into these positions of power be able to work on legislation that is for the benefit of every American whether they are black or white? I do not see the need to form a group of individuals that are going to vote as a block no matter what happens. What happened to the voting for the legislations on the merits of the bill? Who are the racists now?

CHAPTER THIRTEEN

The Corporate Tax Structure

The United States will not solve the deficit problem until it takes major steps to correct the way the big corporations are taxed. There are some things that we can do that will change the tax structure of big business.

We need to make sure that the big corporations on Wall Street that are giving out these tremendous amount of stock to their executives are not deducting these from their profits to avoid the taxes. If the corporations are deducting the amount from their incomes, then the individuals that are receiving these benefits must be made to pay the taxes on the stock they are receiving. Someone must be required to pay income taxes on these deductions. They are not only excessive they are cheating the American taxpayers out of the just taxes. The people that are receiving the stock are going to complain that it is unfair since they have not received any cash compensation. The can sell the stock. The other main problem with giving shares is that if they are generally held for a 12 month period so that they will be taxed at the lower capital gain rates. The corporations are not only taking advantage of the taxpayers they are paying bonuses which are outlandish.

What we as taxpaying citizens need to be aware of are that the big businesses have tremendous lobbying forces and it is going to require an all out effort by everyone to overcome that disadvantage. Contact your representatives and make sure that they will work for these changes.

According to the information that is enclosed in the 2011 budget report the corporations of the United States are paying about 16% of the amount of taxes that are collected. The amount of income taxes that corporations are projected to pay during the fiscal year ending September 30, 2011 will only be $410.7 billion. The government needs to pass new legislation that increases the corporate income tax rate from 35% to 40%. This will increase the federal income tax receipts by approximately $58.7 billion per year.

This seems like a small concession from corporate America instead of placing a burden that is exceptionally large on the people that can least afford to be paying the taxes.

We are going to get into some changes in the tax structure and accounting methods of the major corporations that will help level the playing field for all Americans.

The corporations that have operations that are in foreign countries must be audited every year to make sure that all the income that is earned is reported and the taxes paid. The policy of having a subsidiary in a foreign country with a different year ending date to transfer taxes from one place to another to avoid the payment of the income taxes has to be eliminated.

Corporations that are manufacturing products in foreign countries and then shipping them back to the United States to be marketed must be required to start paying taxes on the cost of their labor reduction. We can not allow for the major manufacturing wages to be paid to foreigners and not to the workforce of the United States. One way to make sure that the American workers start getting their jobs back would be to tax the payrolls of the workers in the foreign countries. The tax would be computed on the difference in the amount of the hourly pay paid to the employees of the foreign work force compared to the American work force. If foreign wages are $10.00 per hour and the American wages are $20.00 per hour then the excise tax on the foreign wages would be 100% of the payrolls. The result would be a lot more jobs would be created in the United States as well as the tax base increasing. This would provide an improvement in the unemployment and an increase in the revenue to the federal government.

We read the earning reports of the major companies and they show millions or even billions of dollars in profits. It is time that a disclosure is made concerning the actual amount of income tax that is paid by these corporations. If we could get truthful information from them I am sure that the income tax paid would be several times what it is now. It should be a requirement that in the annual reports they provide how much income tax was paid by the corporation and how they computed it from their earnings. It is going to take a massive effort from the public to get the politicians to address this problem. It must be done; we do not need to keep operating with a deficit. Of course a government that believed in a balanced budget would also help.

How many of the richest Americans have paid any taxes on the stocks that they have received as bonuses from the large corporations? How many of those corporations deducted the bonuses in stock from their income statements and actually paid taxes on them?

Let's take this one step further. As we stated above that the corporations were writing off these bonuses as expensed during the tax year. We will use Citigroup as an example. They reportedly granted payments of stock in lieu of cash because the government had a maximum cash limit on how much they could be paid of $500,000. Now if they gave stock to their senior executives in the amount of $20 million to make the numbers simple. The corporate tax rate of 35% would have saved Citigroup at total of $7 million in taxes that were not paid to the government because the corporation expensed the bonuses in the current tax year. Then the executives who received the stock would not have to pay any taxes on the $20 million until they sold the shares which would currently be taxed at 15% if they held the stock over one year. That means that they would only pay taxes of $3 million. This would over a period of time that the government would lose $4 million on this transaction. However if the executive who received the bonuses in stock were taxed in the year he received it the current year taxes would be in the $6 million range. It does not seem like a very good system for the taxpayers of the United States. Now the solution would be to make the recipient of the shares in their company to pay income taxes on the value of the shares on the day they were received. If the shares are worth $20 million then the individuals would pay the taxes on that figure. If the shares increased in value the government would not be able to collect any more taxes on the shares. If the shares fell in value then the executive would just have to accept the fact that they were probably not performing their duties in the proper manner or the shares would not have gone down. It would lead to better performance by the executives and then more taxes that the corporation would have to pay due to higher profits.

It seems like when the government placed the $500 thousand limit on the cash remuneration that could be paid to executives they should have had some foresight into how the corporations would manipulate their payment structure to benefit their executives. It just goes to show that big business has a much better understanding of how the business world operates than the government. That is one reason why the government should stay out of business at all levels.

Let me propose a question to the government. Would it be better to receive $6 million in taxes during the current year or to receive the $3 million spread over a possible ten year period and take the chance of not receiving them at all? There something about a bird in the hand is worth several that are in the bush. This would increase the tax receipts in the current year and help reduce the budget deficit. Sounds like something we need to accomplish by contacting our representatives in Washington to pass this type of legislation. Until the bureaucrats that are representing us are inundated with correspondence to start implementing a new law to benefit the citizens of the United States.

We will try and be conservative with these numbers. The number of corporations that are rewarding executives with stock is estimated to be 800. The average number of executives that are receiving shares as compensation is about 10 per company. That would be a conservative number of 8,000 executives that are receiving shares as part of their compensation. We used the average compensation of $3 million per executive and that would translate into $24 billion dollars in executive compensation during a year. If these were to be taxed at the rate of 30% on average it would generate a total of $7.2 billion in income taxes for the government per year. That would be a good start on balancing the budget every year. These would be current taxes instead of deferred taxes in the hopes that the value of the shares would increase and be sold later to be taxed at capital gain rates.

This would not be a tax increase to the executives but it would be closing a major loop hole in our tax system. The government will not like having to pass legislation to enforce this policy since it will go against the grain of the big spenders that are lobbying and supporting the campaigns of the politicians.

CHAPTER FOURTEEN

Putting America to Work

When we create enough jobs to put Americans back to work we will take a major step in lowering the budget deficit. There are currently 15 to 20 million unemployed people in the United States. The federal government is reporting an unemployment rate of 9.8%. We will use the 9.6% that the federal government is reporting for our computations on the affect to the budget.

In our computation we will use 10,000,000 unemployed to make the numbers simple and that would leave an unemployment rate of about 4.8% to 5% which is the level that is should be. With the average income of the 10 million that are now employed the government will receive the following taxes:

These employees are going to make on average $35 thousand per year. The 10 million employees would be paid a gross wage of $350 billion per year. The tax revenue from the social security and Medicare deductions would provide the government with $53.55 billion. This includes the amount deducted from the employee and the amount that is matched by the employer. We are not going to make any calculations for the amount of income taxes that will be paid on the $350 billion due to the number of different family situations. Being very conservative the government could expect to receive $17.5 billion in revenue using only 5% of the wages paid.

The Congress needs to structure legislation that will make it a law to complete the fence on the border with Mexico. This work project could employ thousands of the unemployed Americans. Another great project that would employ several thousand unemployed would be to start drilling operations in the Rocky Mountain Region and the Alaskan wilderness. Both of these projects would be of the type that pays excellent wages.

The unemployment problem in the United States will not improve until the private sector can create at least 400,000 new job opportunities per month. This requirement is to compensate for the number of new workers that will be looking for employment.

One of the methods for helping the unemployment situation would be the accumulation and dissemination of information on available jobs and workers could be improved. There could be a national database in which job centers centralize the employment procedure. This database would be a central listing of all jobs, employers and available employees.

This type of database could reduce the time spent by an average worker on the unemployment roll and thus reduce the unemployment rate. Employment agencies could tighten their job search and job acceptance requirements. In addition, there could be improvements to the education and training provided to young people, with a greater focus on vocational skills.

Most importantly the country needs to ensure that our welfare systems do not provide disincentives to work. Making the unemployed do the labor in cleaning up America in order to receive their unemployment checks will have a positive effect on the unemployment rate. We will find out how many of the unemployed are actually in search of work instead of just getting more unemployment?

CHAPTER FIFTEEN
The Bailout AIG

The American International Group (AIG) has been making the news again. One thing is for certain if AIG is offering an exit plan it is not going to be good for the taxpayers of the United States. The following is copied from the Yahoo news information services. We are going to take the writers to task about some of the information in the article.

If this offer by American International Group is such a good deal for the government why doesn't the President's friendly banker Morgan Stanley do an offering to the public and their investment banking associates? They could do an offering for $55 billion earn an astonishing $5.5 billion in fees to reward their executive with great bonuses. This way Morgan Stanley could write a check to the government for the $49.1 billion that AIG owes. It is obvious why they won't do an offering to cover this debt is that Morgan Stanley knows that the offering would not work any more than the offer by AIG will work for the government.

Just how stupid is our federal government? Would you vote for the government purchasing 1.66 billion shares of an initial public offering of AIG stock? The offer from AIG is a great way so shoving their stock down the taxpayer's throats. We do not want the government to own 92.1% of your company especially since you have already shown in the past that you have no clue about how to run a successful company. The practices that AIG followed led it to the brink of disaster and now they want the government to purchase 1.66 billion shares of their stock. Pay the government with old fashioned cash just like the people bailed you out with. This plan of

AIG has to be rejected by the people's government. The Treasury Secretary that thinks this best for America needs to be replaced. This would not be good for America.

American International Group finally has a plan to exit the biggest of the Wall Street bailouts a month before midterm elections. But as much as embattled lawmakers might wish otherwise, the book on TARP won't close anytime soon.

The article states several facts that seem to be slightly misleading. The article states that AIG will give the Treasury a 92.1 percent stake in AIG before it begins to sell the shares. Later in the article it states that the government will receive about 1.66 billion shares of AIG common stock in exchange for the $49.1 billion investment. That would make the shares worth about $29.67 apiece. The stock did close on that day at $39.10 which is correct. The thought that the government would make a $15.8 billion profit on that part of the stake is absolutely insane. The only way you can have a profit on any stock position is to sell it and then subtract the cost of the position. Now let's get real just how these writers ever think that a position of 1.66 billion shares can be absorbed into the market without causing it to go severely lower. The financial reporting networks show that the average daily volume on AIG is 3.21 million shares per day.

Could the mainstream news media be peddling information to paint a brighter picture than there actually is? It wouldn't be the first time.

Wow!!! Treasury Secretary Timothy Geithner praised the agreement. He said it "puts taxpayers in a considerably stronger position to recoup our investment in the company." I think that the Treasury Secretary needs to take a very hard look at the rest of the information that we are going to give the taxpayers.

On September 30, 2010, American International Group had a total of 135,120,000 common shares outstanding.

Another thing to consider in looking at this transaction is that when an investor takes a sizable position in any company they usually acquire their shares at a deep discount since they will not be able to sell them for an extended period of time. The 52 week low price for AIG was $21.54 and that price would even be excessive. The thing that really concerns me is that the number of shares is going to go astronomically high and the price is definitely going to adjust to these additional shares. I do not believe there is any way that the price of AIG will not go down considerable and stay there. The company reported earnings of $3.985 per share on the 135.12 million shares. When you increase the number of shares to 1,795,120,000 shares those earning per share are going to drop to about $0.22 per share. There is absolutely no way that the price of AIG is going to stay at the current levels. Who is going to buy the stock?

What the taxpayers need to know is that if AIG is willing to give 1.66 billion shares for the government's $49.1 billion investments AIG is going to be the one that will benefit and not the taxpayers of the United States.

Another thing that needs to be checked out is the short interest in AIG. On September 30, 2010 there was a short interest of 20.05 million shares. That indicates that there are a lot of people that think the price of AIG is going to be much lower in the near future. Could it be the traders of AIG and Morgan Stanley know a lot more about what is going on than is provided to the taxpayers and the public? These investors know exactly what is going to happen. AIG is going to sell at 15 to 20 times earnings and that will be about $3.30 to $4.40. The investors with the short interest are going to make millions on this transaction. What about trying to sell 1.66 billion shares of AIG? The average daily volume has been about 3.21 million shares a day. Most reporting systems report both the purchase and the sell so there in reality are a lot less shares traded than the report shows. Does anyone realize how long it would take to unload 1.66 billion shares into any capital market? The markets are also very smart. As soon as they see large orders to sell the price is going to work lower at a very rapid pace. Could it be that Morgan Stanley is the firm that holds the 20.05 million share short position? Think about it. They could repurchase the shares that are shorted at a much lower price than they are today. If the short sales were executed in the $25.00 range to be conservative and they were replaced in the $10.00 range the short sellers would show a profit of $300 million. Not a bad haul considering who the government will be screwed.

The Treasury Secretary definitely needs to cancel this offer from the American International Group. There is no way this is good for the American taxpayer or the country. How about making them pay the government back in cash? That is how they received the money, wasn't it?

Or how about reporting that the 1.66 billion shares of AIG will more than likely be worth $7.304 billion instead of the $49.1 billion that the government would have invested in AIG? The end result probably will be a loss of $41.796 billion. That sure doesn't seem like a good deal for the taxpayers of the United States. Does it?

Maybe we need a new Treasury Secretary too.

CHAPTER SIXTEEN

The Bailout of General Motors

President Barack Obama celebrated the return of a reborn General Motors to the United States stock market, saying it shows some of the "tough decisions that we made" during the financial crisis were beginning to pay off.

"American taxpayers are now positioned to recover more than my administration invested in GM, and that's a good thing," Obama said, speaking of his administration's $50 million taxpayer-backed rescue of the venerable automaker.

The stock rose sharply at first, rising to nearly $36 per share from the $33 price GM set for the initial public offering before pulling back and closing at $34.19.

The trading of more than 400 million GM shares traded hands during its debut on the Big Board — helped reduce the federal government's stake in the company from 61 percent to about 36 percent. For the United States to break even on its investment, it must sell its remaining stake for about $53.00 a share.

Obama said estimates indicate that actions by his administration helped save more than 1 million jobs across 50 states.

The Center for Automotive Research estimated that aid to GM and Chrysler saved more than 1.1 million jobs in 2009 and 314,000 jobs this year. The third Big Three automaker, Ford Motor Co., did not accept federal assistance and stayed out of bankruptcy.

"We are finally beginning to see some of these tough decisions that we made in the midst of the crisis pay off," the president said.

House Republican leader John Boehner of Ohio, in line to become the House speaker in January, avoided a direct answer when he was asked whether the government's treatment of General Motors had saved any jobs.

He said he had favored allowing GM to go through bankruptcy, and said the episode "could have been handled without the heavy hand of the federal government in the midst of it." He said tens of thousands of people were punished as a result of the process that was used.

Those who held old GM stock were essentially wiped out when the company filed for bankruptcy.

Look this is all a sham! GM should have gone into bankruptcy and it would not have cost us tax payer's one penny. GM would have survived the bankruptcy but they wouldn't have paid off their creditors, that is what bankruptcy is for and it is a part of our system. However, the Democrats are tied to the financial folks who would not have been paid and so they made us tax payers pay the creditors off for GM. What a crock!

Obama and his Wall Street advisers screwed us and now he is trying to tell us that taking our money and paying off GM's debt was a great deal. What a liar!!

What a scam. Look at General Motors balance sheet. They are broke and will go broke again. If they were allowed to go broke in the first place they would have been in a better position now. The 50 billion was a payoff to the unions that pay dues to the union and then they send that money to the Democrats to run their campaigns. The unions ended up with approximately 4 million shares instead of being put out of business. We need to remove the unions from the automobile industry so that it can hire more qualified working Americans. That would benefit the country and improve our unemployment figures. When President Obama states that he saved millions of jobs by bailing out General Motors he did not indicate that all of the saved jobs were union jobs. We could hire two employees that are skilled for every one on the union payroll and decrease the cost of producing the automobile. That would be making progress but it would cut into the Democratic voting base and really make the unions unhappy. How about looking out for all of America and not just the unions?

The general public could not purchaser shares in General Motors until the stock opened at $35.00 per share. The Wall Street bankers placed all the stock with their favorite clients and foreign governments and were hoping the gullible American public would start buying the shares at a higher price. The typical underwriting where the preferred clients of the investment bankers are rewarded with the new issue and the general public gets stuck with the higher priced shares if they are stupid enough to purchase them. It also lets the preferred investors sell into the general public because they have the cheap stock. It makes the investment banking firm's loads of commissions in the process. Nothing changes on Wall Street. Wall Street will try and keep the price of General Motors at a higher price to entice more of the average Americans to invest in their stock. They will do this by reporting inflated earnings and buy recommendations to make it look like a wonderful opportunity for the smaller investors. This will allow all of their favorite clients to have a chance to sell their shares into the public. Same old scam.

Let's not forget the fact that the federal government took a $9 billion loss on the IPO. The President sure knows how to try and spin every thing to make him appear better than he is. Why doesn't President Obama spin the fact that all of the original shareholders and bond holders got nothing? Only Obama could spin this as a major success.

President Obama probably does think this was a success because it fits his socialist agenda and is working just as he planned. The government screwed the shareholders and bondholders out of their money when General Motors declared bankruptcy and now all my union buddies are rich, boy this is so easy when the sheep bury their heads in the sand.

Sorry no. The rise in General Motors stock does not validate the president despite his claim. Of course if the stock of GM sinks next week, he will then run, hide and then blame Bush and claim he had nothing to do with the bailout.

Obama your insane! You policy helped the unions. This is another Obama scam. Ask a GM bond holder or a retirement plan who had invested heavily how this helped them. Obama please take your lying liberal self and take a long walk on a short pier.

United States taxpayers will get back 25 cents on every dollar we gave General Motors. The UAW Union will get $4 billion dollars without having to invest any money into the company. Who is this a great deal for?

I'm not sure which is greater, President Obama's ignorance or his arrogance.

How is it that union auto workers average $55 per hour including pensions, insurance? No way that in a free market you can get $55 per hour average for what amounts to unskilled labor. If Obama wants to do something for America, abolish the UAW and let the auto manufacturers open up their doors to anyone without a union card willing to learn the trade.

Obama allowed Government Motors to forget about a $65 billion dollar tax obligation. It's so much easier to look like a success when you don't have to show a real accounting for what you have wrought, especially when it's on the taxpayer's dime. You need to wake up America. The President has pulled a bag over your head so you can't see the light.

Let's discuss this in 30 days. How did the UAW end up with 4.8 million shares of stock while the American people's value was diluted? What in the hell did they do for this gift; besides getting Obama elected? This stock in General Motors is expected to peak at $38-$40/share, institutions will sell off, individual citizens will get in and get end up holding the bag as usual. Do not buy this stock. If you want to invest in an automotive stock buy Ford. Then go out and buy a Ford Truck. Ford did it the American way; they bailed themselves out the old-fashioned way.

The government put $49.5 billion into GM in 2008 and 2009. Before the IPO General Motors ad paid back (or committed to pay back) $9.5 billion. The government sold about 412 million shares in the offering worth $13.6 billion, bringing the total returned to $23.1 billion. Taxpayers still own and are stuck with about 500 million shares of General Motors which is worth about $17 billion at current prices. So the IPO has brought cash into Treasury's coffers and establishes a mechanism for reducing the remaining stake over time. But for the taxpayers to be made whole, General Motors stock will have to rise significantly over the next few years. The United States government is still on the hook for $26.4 billion dollars.

Let me ask any reasonable minded American if they would invest in a company that had to increase in price by 80% to break even? I think Americans are smarter than that.

I believe that Sarah Palin has the common sense to keep the government out of private business. If they run their companies properly they will succeed. If they do not run their companies properly then they should be forced to pay the consequences for their stupidity. No business is too big to fail.

CHAPTER SEVENTEEN

Ethics in Congress

We should stop all funding and do away with the Committee on Standards of Official Conduct. It serves no purpose other than to spend money and protect its own. It does not set the House backward in the ongoing fight to combat corruption in Washington. Abolishing it would clean up some of the wasteful spending and corruption. That's why some of the members are against the abolishment.

Imagine if Charlie Rangel was a white Republican. CNN would go all the way back to grade school and highlight any flaws, perhaps showing that the perpetrator took someone's lunch money when he was in the third grade. MSNBC would have documentaries every hour on the hour highlighting any flaws they could find. Carville and Begalla would be on all the talk shows and spraying spit as they viciously spewed out their hateful rhetoric and doing the ultimate in character assassination. Keith Olberman would feature the culprit as the worst person of the day for several months and Chris Matthews would threaten to run for the senate.

After two years of investigation by the Committee on Standards of Official Conduct (the official name of the ethics committee), Rangel was sentenced to a slap on the wrist for 11 separate ethics violations. It's a humiliating blow to the vanity of a 20 term lawmaker, perhaps, but Rangel won't have to resign from the House of Representatives or face penalties beyond paying back taxes on the charges. Rangel, like those before him, will benefit from a system designed entirely by Congress to protect its own.

The fact that they are not even considering expulsion from the House of Representatives for Rangel or that he will ever have to fully pay for his crimes in a criminal court, shows how the crooked protect their own, while trying to give the false appearance of ethics enforcement. The potential sanctions that Rangel is facing are a slap in the face to the American people and real justice. How can they give a slap on the wrist to a proven felon? Does Congress really wonder why they have such low performance ratings from the American people?

The House of Representatives may recommend that a member be stripped of a committee assignment when a member's activities suggest the taint of corruption, but other than that, a lawmaker who appears to be connected to corruption usually just continues business as usual. The House, in short, protects its members.

Every two years around this time, a common mantra repeated by Democrats and Republicans alike makes its way through Capitol Hill: This will be the Congress that finally cleans up Washington.

"We're going to drain the swamp," Nancy Pelosi vowed in 2006, echoing congressional leaders before her. And just last week, Eric Cantor, the No. 2 GOP leader in the House, promised virtually the same thing as the Republicans prepare to take the House majority. "We will drain the swamp rather than learn to swim with the alligators," Cantor declared.

But the conclusion this week of the House Ethics Committee investigation of New York Democrat Charlie Rangel confirms what virtually everyone in Washington knows about the House's interest in cracking down on ethics: It's a joke.

Democrats and Republicans alike have worked for years to undermine the House ethics process. And as a result, the ethics committee has long functioned in a state of political stalemate--in part because both parties insisted on an equal number of representatives on the committee, which ensured a deadlock.

The committee has one more trial on its plate before the session concludes: A House proceeding opens November 29, 2010, for California Democratic Rep. Maxine Waters, who faces three ethics charges connected to her advocacy for a bank with ties to her husband.

Beyond that, however, the House ethics process seems likely to revert to the earlier status quo as the majority switches to Republican control.

Incoming Speaker John Boehner has already begun talk of dropping the funding for the Office of Congressional Ethics, which he opposed from the start, arguing it's an unnecessary expense and has been an ineffective body. Boehner's opponents argue his plans could move the House backward in the ongoing fight to combat corruption in Washington.

All indications are that the team of Reid, Obama, Pelosi and Holder are really not too concerned about draining the swamp as they have stated. Of course since Rangel and Waters are Democrats who happen to be black they should go lightly with them. After all they are above the rest of the American citizens and don't have to abide by the rules or ethics of government or civilian law.

The facts are that these should not be ethics hearings by Congress members but a Federal Grand Jury trial. The charges on these members are felonies and being under oath and sworn to uphold the laws they should be punished more like Madoff and serve jail time. The government needs to start living by the laws that are enacted for every citizen of the United States. There can be no exceptions to this policy. How can Charlie Rangel justify evading income taxes for 17 years and think it was an over sight on his part? After all, Rangel was the leader of the House Ways and Means Committee on Taxes.

Instead of having an Ethics Committee, why not have the federal and state prosecutors through the judicial system hold the hearings and trials just as they did in the case of Louisiana Democratic Rep. William Jefferson and former Majority Leader Tom DeLay. This would rid the government of the "we protect our own" mentality. Remember, illegal is illegal and persons no matter what their status are not exempt from being prosecuted for crimes.

Heard on Mark Levin that a caller from Beverly Hills spoke with a Justice Department lawyer and asked him if the IRS was going to be contacted to have Rangel investigated and brought up on felony charges. The lawyer's answer, in so many words, that Rangel has too much political clout in Washington and that any lawyer would be afraid to touch that case.

Can you believe it? This scum is going to walk free after fleecing the American public. Having a Senate committee yell at you for your wrong doings is nothing. This egregious lout is milking this thing to the hilt, acting like he's hurting and downfallen when he's laughing on the inside for getting away with it. This egregious slob needs to be put into prison and I don't mean one of those cushy federal institutions.

I believe that Sarah Palin has the leadership qualities and courage to change these policies in Washington and needs to be our next President of the United States. She will fight corruption at all levels of government and has done so in the past.

Who would you vote for right now to be President?

Sarah Palin would win in a landslide if she campaigns by telling the people what her programs are and how they are going to benefit the American people.

HARRY REID'S DREAM LEGISLATION IS A NIGHTMARE...

Harry Reid survived the 2010 election in great part due to the votes of Nevada Hispanics. As a thank you, he announced last week that he would reintroduce the so-called DREAM Act in the lame-duck session of Congress.

The DREAM Act cannot pass. It's not meant to pass. It's not meant even to come to a vote. It's meant to mobilize and excite Hispanic in advance of 2012. It's a ruse and a sham. But it's also an appalling, deceptive piece of legislation with very sinister consequences. So let's take it seriously for a minute and consider what it would do.

The DREAM act purports to be a humanitarian measure on behalf of young Hispanics who were brought to this country as children. Suppose your parents moved to America from Mexico without legal permission when you were five years old. You grow up in America. You graduate from high school in America. You're an American in every sense except the legal one. You want to go to college, but because your parents came into the country illegally, you don't qualify for government financial aid, and you can't get legal work. If caught by immigration authorities, you face the possibility of detention or deportation, even though this is, in every sense, your home. That doesn't seem fair. Every year, over 60,000 kids like you graduate high school in the United States. And unless something like the DREAM Act becomes law, you and they will become part of a growing class of marginalized and unprotected Americans without papers. Even then, the papers are no sure thing. You've got to serve in the military or get a couple years of college under your belt, and stay out of trouble. But at least you'll someday have the chance to enjoy the same rights and opportunities as your date to the prom. Well that seems compassionate! And it's only a small group of people we're talking about, right? That is just 60,000 illegals a year? Wrong. Hugely wrong.

Here are three alternative scenarios, all of which would become possible if the DREAM Act were passed into law.

Possibility No. 1: You are an illegal alien who entered the country at age 21, too old to qualify for DREAM. You've been apprehended and are threatened with deportation. What to do? Simple — using falsified papers, you file an application under DREAM anyway. Filing an application immediately halts deportation proceedings.

Wait a minute, you wonder: won't using false papers get me in trouble? Not in this case, it would be just opposite. Even if the fraud is detected and your application is refused, you simply revert to your previous status. In the process, however, you have gained a new legal advantage: DREAM forbids the Department of Homeland Security from using any information in a DREAM application in deportation proceedings. So now you argue that the deportation proceedings are fatally tainted because you have yourself provided DHS with information that they could now use against you. The ploy might fail. Still: what a great no-risk option!

Possibility No. 2: You're a 40-year-old illegal alien who entered the country as an adult. You have a third-grade education. You are barely literate even in Spanish. Your back is bothering you; you are not sure how long you can continue working. Quite frankly, no country on earth would regard you as a desirable immigrant. Don't despair. DREAM can offer you too an amnesty and gain you access to a lifetime of taxpayer-funded disability payments.

You have kids don't you? If they apply successfully under DREAM, they can sponsor you. While some talk about DREAM applicants as "skilled" immigrants, in fact the law's requirements are so lenient that your kids would have to mess up very seriously to forfeit the law's benefits. All they need to do is enroll in some institution of higher learning or the military and survive there for two years. Graduation is not required.

Does that sound expensive? Don't worry: your kids will receive in-state tuition rates and will be eligible for federal student aid. They're too young for university? Don't worry: They can file the papers at age 12. As soon as they give notice of their future intent to attend to college or join the military, they immediately receive safe haven.

They don't find military life attractive? If they can show "significant hardship," they can quit before their two years have been fulfilled. Honorable discharge is not a requirement under the DREAM law. They have had a little trouble with the law? They could have a history of moving violations that put people's lives at risk? So long as they have not been convicted of a serious crime, they're okay.

DREAM is an amnesty not only for the people described, but also for all their parents and siblings.

Possibility No. 3: I'm still living in Guatemala, but I'd dearly like to come to the United States. Can DREAM help me? Absolutely! DREAM sends a message to every teenager on planet Earth: Come to America. If you enter the United States before age 16, and if you can remain here for five years (or can buy papers that purport to show you have lived here for five years), you're as good as a citizen already. No deportation proceedings. No risk that your application will be used against you. The Dream act is lenient and subsidized requirements for permanent residency. What's not to love?

And best of all: DREAM stands as an ongoing invitation, forever and ever. The DREAM acts benefits extend not only to people who happen NOW to be illegally present inside the United States. The DREAM acts benefits will be extended to all those who may enter illegally in future. The DREAM acts message goes forth to Indonesia, to Egypt, to India, to China, to anywhere where teenagers find $7 an hour more attractive than $7 a day: come now and come early. Don't waste your time acquiring an education before you arrive. We'll subsidize your education right here in America.

It sounds too crazy to be true. That is why the law can not be passed. And why it's so very deeply cynical of Senator Reid to dangle this false hope before Nevada's and America's Hispanics. He is just positioning the Democrats for votes in 2012.

Obama, Reid, Pelosi and Holder are Democrats worst nightmares. Pelosi an airhead who should have retired was elected to be the minority leader. Reid should be run out of office or placed in jail for his actions. Now that we have the same leaders in the Democratic Party all the American people can look forward to is more of the same. If you are here illegally go back where you came from and take the right channels to get into this country we have to curb immigration. When you enter a country you follow that country's rules no head scarf's no burkas and no bi lingual pamphlets. Learn English if you want to be in the United States.

More political crap and attempts to pass law's to send this country into further depression and the taxpayer's would have to pay for it. Don't the politician's and the government know that you can't get blood out of a turnip, the well is almost dry? They better start taking care of our own because if they don't the United States of America is going to crumble out from under us, which has already started. The illegals are sucking our system dry. How many taxpayer dollars have been wasted on them just for the last ten year?

25% to 35% of the Hispanic gang membership is made up of illegal immigrants and the cost and consequences of their activities is more than the taxpayers can absorb. Politicians like Harry Reid are taking America down a road from which we may not be able to return. He and his peers will not suffer the consequences, but the rest of us will.

America can not allow dirty Harry's dream act to pass into law. Contact every representative possible and make sure that they vote for America.

The Republican Party has announced that will block all bills until the Bush tax cuts have been extended for everyone. In addition, a bill is passed to fund the federal government, vastly complicating the Democratic attempts to leave their own stamp on the final days of the post election Congress. The Democrats are going to try and get everything passed before the new House of Representatives in sworn in January.

"While there are other items that might ultimately be worthy of the Senate's attention, we cannot agree to prioritize any matters above the critical issues of funding the government and preventing a job-killing tax hike," all 42 GOP senators wrote in a letter to Majority Leader Harry Reid, (D-NV). The 42 signatures are more than enough to block action on almost any item he wishes to advance.

The threat does not apply to a new arms control treaty with Russia that is pending, since it would be debated under rules that differ from those that apply to routine legislation. President Barack Obama has made ratification of the pact a top priority.

Thank the Republicans for stopping the reckless attempts of the Democratic attempts to lift the Pentagon's ban on openly gay members of the military, a separate item to give legal status to young illegal immigrants who attend college or serve in the military, and a measure to expand first responders' collective bargaining rights. The tax and spending bills are likely to be the last to pass before Congress adjourns for the year.

"Republicans have pleaded with Democrats to put aside their wish list to focus on the things Americans want us to focus on. They've ignored us. The voters repudiated their agenda at the polls. They've ignored them. Time is running out. They're ignoring that," Senate Republican Leader Mitch McConnell of Kentucky said in remarks on the Senate

floor. "The election was a month ago. It's time to get serious. It's time to focus on priorities."

The Democratic to-do list also includes extending the expiring tax cuts although they and Republicans differ on particulars, as well as a measure to keep the government in operation. But the rest of their agenda marks an attempt to court voters Democrats need in 2012 to recapture the majority, including Hispanics, gay-rights activists and organized labor.

Take the so-called Dream Act, a measure to give young people whose parents brought them into the United States illegally before they were 16 a path to legal status by going to college or joining the armed forces.

The measure has enjoyed some degree of bipartisan support in the past, and Reid, the majority leader, vowed last month - in the thick of his tough re-election fight in heavily Hispanic Nevada - to hold a vote on it when Congress returned to finish its end-of-the-year business. He said Tuesday he'd move to overcome GOP objections and force a test vote, although it's unclear when one will occur.

Hispanic voters also played a major role in sparing other Democrats - including Senators Michael Bennet of Colorado and Barbara Boxer of California - from being toppled by a GOP wave.

"There was a firewall in the West where Latino voters turned out in big numbers to reward people who championed them," said Frank Sharry of America's Voice, an immigrant advocacy group. "We're going to try to make it painful" for those who oppose efforts to give illegal immigrants a path to legal status, he added.

Most Republicans vehemently oppose the Dream Act, saying it amounts to amnesty. And they decry the strategy of acting on such issues during the lame-duck session, accusing Democrats of playing politics and ignoring the message voters sent November 2, 2010.

But Democrats also face pressure from their left flank.

Gay-rights groups have criticized Reid for not pushing hard enough to repeal the "don't ask, don't tell" policy against openly gay soldiers, as the House has already voted to do.

Reid has promised to hold a Senate vote on the matter before year's end; after hearings can be held on a Pentagon report on the impact that openly serving gays would have on the military.

Republicans say they need to examine the report before acting. It concluded that getting rid of the policy might cause some disruption at first but wouldn't create widespread or long-lasting problems.

Obama seized on the conclusion to call on the Senate to act "as soon as possible" to repeal the ban, "so I can sign this repeal into law this year and ensure that Americans who are willing to risk their lives for their country are treated fairly and equally."

Reid also said he'd force action on legislation long sought by public safety worker unions to create federal rules guaranteeing first responders in every state and the District of Columbia have the right to organize and bargain on hours, wages and work rules, among other things.

The measure is seen by labor as a final chance before Democrats' Capitol Hill clout fades to accomplish a legislative goal, after its top priority - a bill to make it easier for workers to form unions - stalled in the Senate.

The International Association of Fire Fighters, which has pushed hard for the bill, gave nearly $2 million to congressional candidates in advance of last month's midterm elections, most of it to Democrats.

So basically after the voting public sounds off with a very loud blast against what the Democratic Party has been doing, rather than slowing down and listening to the public, instead they charge headlong a fool hardy into more of the same stuff that the public is furious about. Will someone refresh me on the definition of insanity again?

CHAPTER EIGHTEEN

The Immigration Policies

The US Constitution is a fluid document that is interpreted in light of prevailing customs and norms. 200+ years ago, what might have been acceptable criminal punishment is now deemed cruel and inhumane. Similarly, 200+ years ago, or indeed up until the 1920s, virtually anyone could immigrate to the United States. The times have changed and we have strong laws on our books. When the federal government chooses not to enforce each and every law for one group of people but not others, and that has an adverse impact on United States citizens' property and safety, states should be able to craft supplemental but non-conflicting legislation to protect its citizens. In every poll out there on the Arizona law, a minimum of 66% of United States citizens agree. This is not a race issue. If there were 20 million illegal Europeans in the United States they would need to go as well.

I wonder why there is so much commotion being made about airport security? I find it offensive to think that someone is going to pat me down if I choose to fly. They can use the detection devices that are at all airports and forget about imposing on individuals private parts in a pat down. The airport security systems have been used by the government to indicate that they are concerned about terrorists entering the United States. That is great but we can overdue the checking procedure.

Now let's get to the real problem that the United States should be worried about. It is just amazing that the Department of Homeland Security, the Justice Department, President Obama, Senator Reid, Nancy Pelosi and Eric Holder can not see or understand that our borders are not protected in any manner. When a state tries to implement a program to ease the threat the President and his lemmings start legal proceedings against the state. There are about 1 million illegals that enter into the United States every year through our southern borders. I would hate to know how many terrorists are among those that are walking freely into our country. Until the government becomes aware of the need for complete border security it seems rather foolish to worry about the airport security to the extreme. There is nothing happening along the southern border that will prevent terrorists from coming into the United States.

The major affect that the illegals have in America is to try and destroy our standard of living and turn our beautiful country into another third world country that does not seem to care whether it is kept clean and respectful. How dare they come into our country and demand the same rights as the American citizens and the legal immigrants. Americans work very hard to preserve our freedoms and protect our rights. We do not appreciate the fact that the illegals grab the Mexican flag and do protest marches against our country because we do not want to make them citizens.

There are thousands of illegals marching through our southern border every week. They do not have any fear of the border patrol and leave miles of garbage strewn all over the Arizona Desert. It is outrageous that our federal government does not enforce the laws of our country. We need to contact every representative and make sure that they vote to stop amnesty and finish the construction of the border fence. There can not be any amnesty if we want America to return to "America the Beautiful"

The following statistics have been presented by the local ranchers who observed the situation first hand. They did not use the government statistics but kept track of the local incidents. What the residents found was that they were involved in the capture on one bunch of illegals at one time. They did not bother with the countless small groups. They found loads of drugs and captured 213 illegals. They had dangerous encounters with illegals on 132 separate occasions. There were 16 dead illegals that were found by civilians in the area. In the last year there were 14 high speed chases between dope haulers and law enforcement. Fires that were started by these illegals happened 9 times and over 100,000 acres were burned costing the taxpayers $40 million dollars. One fire in Portal, Arizona in June 2010 cost the taxpayers $10 million to fight according to estimates of the forest service.

There also have been some outlandish incidents one of which was a bachelor in the Portal area was burglarized around 100 times. He finally took all his valuables and put them in a steel vault and welded the door shut. He then moved out of his house into a shed hoping the illegal aliens would leave him alone. They did not and he finally had to abandon his property. Another outlandish event was when outlaws stole a brand new Caterpillar motor grader on the Geronimo Trail east of Douglas, Arizona and drove south through the border fence never to be seen again. The grader belonged to Cochise County Hwy Dept.

It is estimated that the financial losses to private sector – exceed $100,000,000 in the value of real estate, personal property, loss of wildlife habitat among a few. We need to secure our border and deport all the illegals. We do not want to become a third world country.

The area we are reviewing is an area that covers approximately 17 or 18 townships with only 20 miles being adjacent to the US - Mexico Boundary. Within this area, there is a population of perhaps 600 people, 90% of which reside in Rodeo, New Mexico or Portal, Arizona 30 miles or so north of Mexico. No less than 80% of the people in this area have been burglarized or otherwise molested by illegal aliens.

Unless you have witnessed first hand what is going on at the borders of the Unites States you don't understand just how serious the problems of these illegals are. The photo below could help you understand who might be your new neighbor in a couple of days. I couldn't post the photo for copyright reasons. If you want a copy email meinders@aol.com or visit www.thomasmeinders.com.

There is a billboard close to the Arizona border that says it all about the feelings of the Arizona citizens.

> "Attention Illegal Immigrants"
>
> Arizona does not welcome you, but Los Angeles loves you.
>
> Free Housing, Free School, Free Food, Free Medical, and
>
> Free Hospital.
>
> No Insurance Costs, no taxes, and plenty of jobs.
>
> TURN LEFT ON I-8 AND FOLLOW YOUR ROAD TO PARADISE!

The illegal immigrant problem is not limited to the federal government. The state of California is facing a $19 billion deficit for the current fiscal year. If California was not supporting 10.8 million illegals they would have a balanced budget. There would not be rampant unemployment and the social services departments would not be overloaded with payments to these illegals. The amount that California is spending to support these illegals is much higher that the $1,759.30 that each of them would save the state of California. We all know that it is costing the state many times that amount to support each of these illegals. Anything over the $1,759.30 per individual that the state of California would save would contribute to a surplus. Why is it that the Governor of California is against deporting the illegals? Sure would make the state of California much better off financially and would improve the standard of living in many cities. After all we can't offend the poor Mexicans that are destroying our way of life. It might also offend the ACLU and the other special interest groups. Who would the Democratic Party have left to vote for them?

CHEAP TOMATOES

This information actually happened in a school in California and should be read and understood by as many Americans as possible. It does not matter if you are a Democrat, Republican or Independent

This explains about what is going on in our school systems under the Title 1 program. If we do not address these problems we will ultimately suffer because people just do not care. We need to get our heads out of the sands and take action.

As you listen to the news about the student protests over illegal immigration, there are some things that everyone should be aware of. This information comes from a teacher in charge of the English-as-a-second-language department The US Constitution is a fluid document that is interpreted in light of prevailing customs and norms. 200+ years ago, what might have been acceptable criminal punishment is now deemed cruel and inhumane. Similarly, 200+ years ago, or indeed up until the 1920s, virtually anyone could immigrate to the United States. The times have changed and we have strong laws on our books. When the federal government chooses not to enforce each and every law for one group of people but not others, and that has an adverse impact on United States citizens' property and safety, states should be able to craft supplemental but non-conflicting legislation to protect its citizens. In every poll out there on the Arizona law, a minimum of 66% of United States citizens agree. This is not a race issue. If there were 20 million illegal Europeans in the United States they would need to go as well.

at a large southern California high school which has been designated a Title 1 school, meaning its students average lower socioeconomic and income levels.

Most of the schools you are hearing about, South Gate High, Bell Gardens, Huntington Park etc are where these students are protesting are also Title 1 schools.

Title 1 schools are on the free breakfast and free lunch programs. These students receive a free breakfast that is not just a glass of milk and roll. They are full breakfasts served with cereal bars, fruits and juices that would make a Marriott proud. The amount of food that is wasted is monumental with trays and trays of it being dumped in the trash uneaten. The schools estimate that well over 50% of these students are obese or at least moderately overweight. The students are living off of the system and yet about 75% or more have cell phones. The schools also provide day care centers for the un-wed teenage pregnant girls. Some of these girls are as young as 13 so they can attend class without the inconvenience of having to arrange for babysitters or having family watch their kids.

The school where this teacher worked was ordered to spend $700,000 on the department or risk losing funding for the upcoming year even though there was little need for anything.

The budget was already substantial. They ended up buying new computers for the computer learning center, half of which, one month later, have been carved with graffiti by the appreciative students who obviously feel humbled and grateful to have a free education in America. They had to interview several times for young and substitute teachers whose classes consist of many illegal immigrant students, here in the country for less than three months, who raised so much hell with the female teachers, calling them "Putas" (whores) and throwing things at them to the extent that the teachers were in tears.

These illegals receive free medical, free education, free food, free day care, etc. etc. Is it any wonder they feel entitled to not only be in this country but to demand rights, privileges and entitlements?

To those who want to point out how much these illegals contribute to our society because they like their gardener and housekeeper and they like to pay less for tomatoes. People need to spend some time in the real world of illegal immigration and see the true costs to the American taxpayers.

Try these items on for size and see if you really want to continue supporting the illegals. The illegals cause higher insurance, medical facilities closing, lower standards of education in our schools, overcrowding, new diseases and the list goes on. Personally, I would rather pay a much higher price for my tomatoes.

Americans we need to wake up. It does have everything to do with culture: it involves a culture that is not the American way of life. We do not want our country to turn into a third-world.

This email that I received almost brings a tear to your eye, doesn't it?

MEXICO IS ANGRY!

Three cheers for Arizona.

Now that the shoe is on the other foot and the Mexicans from the State of Sonora, Mexico do not like it. Can you believe the nerve of these people? It's almost funny.

The State of Sonora is angry at the influx of Mexicans into Mexico. Nine state legislators from the Mexican State of Sonora traveled to Tucson to complain about Arizona's new employer crackdown on illegals from Mexico. It seems that many Mexican illegals are returning to their hometowns and the officials in the Sonora state government are ticked off. A delegation of nine state legislators from Sonora was in Tucson on Tuesday to state that Arizona's new Employer Sanctions Law will have a devastating effect on the Mexican state. At a news conference, the legislators said that Sonora, Arizona's southern neighbor that is made up of mostly small towns cannot handle the demand for housing, jobs and schools that it will face as Mexican workers return to their hometowns from the USA without jobs or money.

The Arizona law, which took effect January 1, 2010, punishes Arizona employers who knowingly hire individuals without valid legal documents to work in the United States. Penalties include suspension of or loss of their business license. The Mexican legislators are angry because their own citizens are returning to their hometowns, placing a burden on THEIR state government. "How can Arizona pass a law like this?" asked Mexican Rep Leticia Amparano-Gamez, who represents Nogales. "There is not one person living in Sonora who does not have a friend or relative working in Arizona," she said, speaking in Spanish. "Mexico is not prepared for this, for the tremendous problems it will face as more and more Mexicans working in Arizona and who were sending money to their families return to their home-towns in Sonora without jobs," she said, "We are one family, socially and economically," she said of the people of Sonora and Arizona. Wrong! The United States is a sovereign nation, not a subsidiary of Mexico, and its taxpayers are not responsible for the welfare of Mexico's citizens.

It's time for the Mexican government, and its citizens, to stop feeding parasitically off the United States and to start taking care of its/their own needs.

How many of the American citizens realize that there is over 10% of the Mexican population living on welfare in the United States illegally? If we ever want our country back we have to have the courage to deport all of the illegals that are destroying our country. It will take some time but we need to make our country beautiful again.

The immigration problem of the United States.

How it affects every American.

If I could have "My American Dream" with regards to the immigration problem that the United States of America is struggling with it would go something like the following:

"Close every border and access point into the United States of America. Should the Mexican, Canadian, Cuban or any other government be offended by our border policy that is fine? We can live with that much better than we can live with the illegal migrants into the United States."

"Locate every illegal person that is in the United States of America and take them back to the nearest border where they came from. The simple fact is that they are criminals and illegal and are not deserving of any type of protection by our laws."

"This is to include all the anchor babies born in the United States of America during the time that the illegal parents are living in our country."

"Current polls show that approximately 75% to 80% of the legal voting American Citizens are in favor of securing our borders. About the same percentages are in favor of adopting laws similar to the Arizona SB1070."

Is it just me, or does anyone else find it amazing that during the mad cow epidemic our government could track a single cow, born in Canada, almost three years ago, right to the stall where she slept in the State of Washington and they tracked her calves to their stalls? But they are unable to locate 20 million illegals when they wander around our country. Maybe we should give each of them a cow so that we can locate them?

Every American should be proud to salute our flag and be proud to be an American. Thank God for our military that will stand and fight for our freedom and the freedom of the rest of the world. If any one living in this wonderful country does not want to adjust to our way of life then they should go back where they came from.

The American people think that the war in Iraq was costing us too much? Read on: boy was I confused. I have been hammered with the propaganda that it is the Iraq war and the war on terror that is bankrupting the United States. I now find that to be ridiculous. I hope that the following 14 reasons are enough to provide an understanding for the American citizens. I have also included the URL's so that you can verify all of the following facts...

1. **$11 Billion to $22 billion is spent on welfare to illegal aliens each year by state governments. You can verify at:** *http://www.fairus.org/site/PageServer?pagename=iic_immigrationissuecenters7fd8*

2. **$2.2 Billion dollars a year is spent on food assistance programs such as food stamps, WIC, and free school lunches for illegal aliens. You can verify at:** *http://www. cis.org/articles/2004/fiscalexec.HTML*

3. **$2.5 Billion dollars a year is spent on Medicaid for illegal aliens. You can verify at:** *http://www.cis.org/articles/2004/ fiscalexec.HTML*

4. $12 Billion dollars a year is spent on primary and secondary school education for children here illegally and they cannot speak a word of English! You can verify at: http://transcripts.cnn.com/TRANscriptS/0604/01/ldt..0

5. $17 Billion dollars a year is spent for education for the American-born children of illegal aliens, known as anchor babies. You can verify at: http://transcripts.cnn.com/TRANscriptS/0604/01/ldt.01

6. $3 Million Dollars a DAY is spent to incarcerate illegal aliens. You can verify at: http://transcripts.cnn.com/%20TRANscriptS/0604/01/

7. 30% percent of all Federal Prison inmates are illegal aliens. You can verify at: http://transcripts.CNN.com/TRANscriptS/0604/01/l

8. $90 Billion Dollars a year is spent on illegal aliens for Welfare & social services by the American taxpayers. You can verify at: <*http://cnn.com/TRANscriptS/0604/01/ldt.01.HTML%3E;*> http://premium.cnn.com/TRANSCIPTS/0610/29/ldt.01

9. $200 Billion dollars a year in suppressed American wages are caused by the illegal aliens. You can verify at: *http://transcripts.cnn.com/TRANSC%20RI%20PTS/0604/*

10. The illegal aliens in the United States have a crime rate that's two and a half times that of white non-illegal aliens. In particular, their children are going to make a huge additional crime problem in the US. You can verify *at:* http://transcripts.cnn..com/TRANscriptS/0606/12/ldt..01

11. During the year of 2005 there were 4 to 10 MILLION illegal aliens that crossed our Southern Border also, as many as 19,500 illegal aliens from Terrorist Countries. Millions of pounds of drugs, cocaine, meth, heroin and

marijuana, crossed into the US from the Southern border. Verify at: *Homeland Security Report:*

12. The National policy Institute, estimated that the total cost of mass deportation would be between $206 and $230 billion or an average cost of between $41 and $46 billion annually over a five year period. You can verify at: *<http://transcripts.cnn.com/TRANscriptS/0606/12/ldt.01 http://www.nationalpolicyinstitute..org/PDF/ deportation.*

13. In 2006 illegal aliens sent home $45 BILLION in remittances to their countries of origin. You can verify at: *http://www/..rense.com/general75/niht.htm http://rense. com/general75/niht.htm%3E;*

14. "The Dark Side of Illegal Immigration: Nearly One million sex crimes Committed by Illegal Immigrants In The United States." You can verify at: *<http://www.rense.com/ general75/niht.htm%3E> www.drdsk.com/articleshtml <http://www.drdsk.com/articleshtml>*

This is a total cost of a whopping $338.3 billion a year. That amount would be enough to stimulate the economy for the citizens of the United States. Why are we this stupid? Why does our government get away with this? We need to correct this problem. NOW!!!

CHAPTER NINETEEN
The Amnesty Policies

I do not know what Sarah Palin's thoughts are on giving amnesty to the 20 million illegals that are in the United States. I would hope that she will have the courage to protect our great country and deport every one of them. Palin would be the first president since President Eisenhower to take the problem seriously and do what the majority of the Americans want. We can not afford to support 10% of the Mexican population with our welfare systems.

There has only been one President in the last 50 years that has had the courage to deal with illegals that were in the United States. President Eisenhower deported every one of the illegals that could be rounded up over a period of two years. This policy of deporting instead of providing amnesty provided several million jobs for the working people of the United States.

For centuries the American people have welcomed individuals from all over the world. The difference is that these immigrants did it legally. Does any one understand the difference? The legal immigrants tend to respect the laws of our great country while the illegals are criminals that have started their lives in America by breaking the law. For generations people have wanted to come to America and wanted to end up being citizens of the great country. They have waited the five year waiting period and taken the tests required to become citizens. These immigrants have been sworn in as citizens in front of the flag of the United States and appreciate with all their heart that America has let them become citizens.

On the other hand we have the illegals that cross over the border under the cover of darkness and in many cases carrying a backpack full of illegal drugs. The fact that our government has not enforced the laws of our country is an absolute disgrace to the citizens of the United States.

It is hard to understand why the federal government does not want to accept the fact that the Mexican's are actually in a war with the United States. They have invaded our country with 20 million people, many of whom carry weapons. We need to wake up America and start standing up for our rights. Does anyone really think that there is another country in the world that would let 20 million people invade their nations?

Then we see on the news that the United Nations is looking into the actions of our individual states. The report from a representative of the United Nations said "Arizona's new immigration law, passed to expel nearly half a million illegal immigrants from the state and stem the flow of human drug smugglers over the border from Mexico was certain to be raised at an international conference on migration in Mexico in November."

The South African jurist said the Global Forum on Migration and Development, an annual United Nations initiative, would discuss the measure, which United Nation officials have already denounced as discriminatory because it allows police to stop and search individuals on the suspicion they are illegal immigrants.

The people of the United States need to declare the war and let the United Nations know that when they show that one of their countries will allow 20 million illegal immigrants to enter without papers we will too. You can bet anything you own that there will be a different attitude when it comes to their countries.

On October 3, 2010 the Denver Post reported that a couple enjoying a lake on the Texas Mexico border had to dodge gunfire from pirates on the lake.

The wife was forced to make an impossible choice: risk her life by staying with her husband or return to land and seek help.

The couple was sightseeing on Jet Skis on the Mexican side of Falcon Lake when several boats of gunmen opened fire, striking her husband in the back of his head. According to the 911 call released reports from law enforcement officials detail the tragic incident.

The woman was seeing bullets hitting close to her in the water and realized that her husband had been hit behind the head. She went back trying to find, trying to help him. She went in the water trying to load up her husband to her Jet Ski trying to get his body and Jet Ski back to the United States side. She was being shot at so she finally had to let go of the body, climb back in her Jet Ski and head back over here to the United States. The woman said that the armed men believed to be pirates associated with a Mexican drug cartel, chased her into United States waters as she fled.

The lake is not secure, the border is not secure because the incident we were dreading the most has in fact happened. We cannot go to Mexico, we cannot recover that body, we cannot conduct an investigation and we have to tell the family we can't do anything about it.

Although it was only one couple of Americans it is still an act of war against the citizens of the United States and should be treated as such. We will have to wait and see what our President is going to do about this incident. More than likely he will scold the woman for enjoying the lake. To my knowledge the President has done nothing with regards to this incident.

Why the members of Congress are not proposing legislation to stop this insane policy of allowing the illegals to remain in our country is nothing more that lack of respect for the country that they represent. I published a list of the Congressional members that voted to allow the illegals to receive social security benefits and the members that voted against making English the official language of the United States. It seems to me that that was what the founders of America wanted and that the requirement is in the Constitution.

These illegals sneak into the United States under the cover of darkness and then feel that they have more rights and considerations than an American citizen. That is what the liberals of our once proud country have done to the good citizens. The politicians want to make these people legal instead of deporting them solely for the purpose of obtaining their votes. Why then are some of the Republicans looking out for the illegals? They should realize that the vast majority of the illegals will be voting Democratic.

The effect of the illegals in the United State can be measured in many ways. We are going to look at some of the problems that are caused by the 20 million illegals that are living in the United States of America.

The American people need to realize just how much the illegal population in the United States is costing us in terms of real dollars and supporting costs caused by the entitlement programs that have been provided by the government.

How about computing some real costs for the 20 million illegals in the country? First, if these illegals are working they will probably be earning in the $6 to $10 thousand range per year. Most of them will be supporting their families and have on average two children. OK?

We will use the $10 thousand per year income to make the numbers easier to work with. Let's assume that there are 3,000,000 families that would fall into this category. The fact that most of these are working illegally they will not be paying anything into the government such as social security and Medicare deductions from their wages. Then these 3 million families file a tax return because they know from all of their other illegals that the government will give them an earned income credit that will provide them with a refund of about $3,200 per family. That does not sound like a huge amount of money but how about multiplying it over the 3 million people. It is a cash outlay to the federal government of $9,600,000,000. That is right, $9.6 billion.

When we compute the average of the entitlement programs that these illegals are receiving the cost is going to go up by an astounding amount. These entitlements will cost the tax-payers on average $22 per illegal that is in the United States. That figure is for every one of the 20 million illegals and would cost the government $4,400,000,000. With just these two items we could cut our budget deficit by $14 billion dollars per year.

I recommend that the federal government pass legislation that would set up a super fund for deportation and construction of the fence to secure the borders in the amount of $20 billion. In the proposed federal budget for the year there is a provision for 20,000 troops. How many are we really expecting to see on the border? This fund would be used to hire as many employees as it needs to deport the 20 million illegals that are draining our resources. The government would save many times that amount during the first two years and we would have the problem solved. This fund would also be used to complete our border security so that we do not have the problem again. The Obama administration does not want the border secured is where the problem comes from. Going back to the 2011 proposed budget there are already funds allocated to hire an additional 20,000 border support personnel. Somewhere along the way these troops have been only a figment of Obama's imagination. They are no where to be seen on the border between Arizona and Mexico. These funds would be returned to the United States economy due to the fact that the 20 million illegals would not be able to send $35 to $50 billion in American money back to Mexico.

I know that this would create some government spending but it would also pave the way for balancing the budget in the next and future years. I am only for spending that can be recovered by the savings that will be generated by the legislation. This proposal is a situation where every American will benefit and the government will be saving money and resources for years to come. We will be balancing the annual budget and creating millions of jobs with the same legislation. A balanced budget and creation of jobs is what the American people want, isn't it?

You can already hear the ACLU and other organizations that are always screaming about these illegals civil rights. What about the civil rights of the American citizens? Of course the illegals are the only thing they care about and not the recovery of the United States. Why do they want to turn our beautiful country into a third world mess such as Mexico?

Now we will try to compute some of the resources that the government is spending because of these 20 million illegals. The cost of incarceration alone cost the government $1.095 trillion per year. Welfare and social services for these illegals is costing the government $90 billion per year. The American workers are being denied access to $200 billion per year in wages that are taken by these illegals. Trying to be conservative these expenditures are causing an increase in the federal deficit every year in the amount of $1.385 trillion. Not even taking into consideration the lost wages for the American people.

The following steps were recommended by others but they reflect my feelings accurately and should be those of the entire United States. We need to close the border with Mexico. The President's proposed budget has included 20,000 troops that could be utilized for that purpose. This will provide instant relief to our local communities, state social services, federal social services, hospitals, schools, jails and federal prisons. We need to make E-verify a universal law and the employers that do not verify must be held accountable and fined $50,000 per infraction.

Every illegal that is living in the United States should be given a 30 day grace period to get their possessions in order and go back over the border. Those that do not choose to leave will be arrested and prosecuted for violating the law of the United States by entering our country illegally. If they are arrested the government will be authorized to seize all of their property.

Any illegal that is receiving public money or any other kind of support from the federal, state, or local authorities will cease to receive any funds immediately. There are over 20 million illegals in the United States and we need to stop providing shelter, jobs and any other support. These illegals are taking over 10 million jobs from the American people.

Every legal citizen needs to prepare for the next new neighbor that comes parading across the southern border. They just might move in next door.

There are about 20 million illegals in the United States that are hoping that President Obama and the Democrats are going to give them amnesty.

The American people know how President Obama stands on the illegal immigration problem and by the actions of Senator Reid trying to slip

amnesty to 800,000 illegals through with an earmark to another piece of legislation.

When Sarah Palin endorses the above policies concerning amnesty the people of the United States will back her with a majority vote.

The latest polls that were available indicated that over 60 percent of Americans want our borders secure. Over 80 percent of the Americans want to stop the flow of illegals into the United States and 75 percent of Americans do not want any kind of amnesty for the illegals. If indeed Sarah Palin were to adopt the above policies our vote for the most qualified to be President of the United States based on their knowledge of these problems would be as follows. The vote on a scale of 1 to 10 "By the People, For the People"

Sarah Palin   10

Barack Obama`   2

There are illegals marching in protests carrying signs that are bragging about today we march and tomorrow we vote. The United States better get their act together and stop all amnesty.

The following are what the illegals think about the United States of America.

CONSTITUTION?
WE DON'T NEED
NO STINKIN'
CONSTITUTION!!!

Unfortunately that seems to be what most of the illegals that are in our country believe is the actual way of life in America.

AMERICA CAN RECOVER WHEN WE WAKE UP AND DEPORT ALL OF THE ILLEGALS AND THEIR FAMILIES THAT ARE IN THE UNITED STATES OF AMERICA!!! ABSOLUTELY NO AMNESTY FOR ANY OF THEM....

CHAPTER TWENTY

The Economic Policies

The most important thing that the new Congress can do would be to prepare legislation that makes it a law to have a balanced budget. We need to get this law passed before the current budget request is signed into law. The 2011 proposed budget that the President has developed has a deficit of $1.267 trillion dollars which is 8.3% of the GDP. What is amazing is that in the proposed federal budget there is discretionary spending that is $1.3 trillion which is 33.9% of the entire amount of $3.834 trillion expenditures for the year. Why are we giving these departments what is considered a blank check instead of itemizing what they are going to spend our money on?

We are concerned with the direction that the economy, unemployment, spending, immigration and lack of transparency with the current administration. It is time that the voting citizens voice their opinions and vote for representation that will vote for programs that are for "We the People, By the People and For the People".

The excessive federal spending programs have to stop. We need a balanced budget in the United States. We need to enact programs that will reduce the unemployment and stop the illegals from entering the United States. The United States needs to be firm on completing the border fence and enforcing the laws with regard to illegals. There can not be amnesty for the 20,000,000 illegals that are already in the United States.

We are hoping that America can reduce the size of the government and can get back to government for the people.

The federal government could cut into the deficit without sacrificing our security, services or dignity by reducing the discretionary spending in the 2011 proposed budget by only ten percent. (10%) The government could reduce the deficit by $130.068 billion by passing the balanced budget by this one austerity program for the year ending on September 30, 2011.

All of us citizens have had to reduce our budget by a whole lot more that the 10 percent. The government needs to stop the spending.

The United States is the greatest nation in the world and it needs to start acting like it deserves the respect of the rest of the world by setting an example of how to run a country. The United States needs to understand that the days of continued spending without any means of paying for the obligations except to borrow from other countries has to stop now.

The country will have to demand their representatives pass the law to have a balanced budget each and every year. This is going to require a lot of work from the citizens by writing or calling all of our representatives and demanding that we will not accept anything less. Hopefully, everyone has voted for representation that is going to start listening to the people of their districts. There has been too much of the back door policies that the Democrats have been practicing. Look at some of the votes; they were rammed down the people by having given away programs that the only ones that voted for them were the Democrats.

What is really difficult to understand is how our President can sign a bill into law that will provide $42 billion for the banks to control and lend to small businesses and provide tax incentives and ignore the rest of the American taxpayers? Incidentally the taxpaying citizens of the country did not want this law passed and should make sure it repealed. Anyway, there is a serious tax increase coming on January 1, 2011 if the Congress does not quit playing games. If the Bush Tax Cuts were renamed the Obama

Tax Cuts they would have been passed months ago. We are faced with a President that needs to get his ego out of the way and start looking out for the entire population. We need to forget about a class structure in the United States. From all reports to extend the entire Bush Tax Cuts would cost the government $3.7 trillion over 10 years. The cost to provide for the entire taxpaying population of the United States is cheap compared to the $42 billion second stimulus bill that the President just signed into law. This piece of legislation was another of the Democrats pet projects to appease the banking institutes so they could encourage loans to the small businesses and they could charge excessive loan fees. The only people that are going to benefit from this bill are the bankers. The small businesses are not interested in borrowing money that they don't have a method of paying back. That is only a practice followed by the government. The government needs to learn to stop spending until they can show how the spending is going to be repaid.

I know reading the proposed budget is rather long, boring and probably will make the average American want to throw-up. When you finish you will understand why we need to make changes in the direction of our government.

Budget of the United States Government, Fiscal Year 2011 contains the Budget Message of the President, and information on the President's priorities and budget overviews organized by agency. The President paints a great picture without any real specifics and a lot of rhetoric. His proposed budget message is below:

THE BUDGET MESSAGE OF THE PRESIDENT

To the Congress of the United States:

We begin a new year at a moment of continuing challenge for the American people. Even as we recover from crisis, millions of families are still feeling the pain of lost jobs and savings. Businesses are still struggling to find affordable loans to expand and hire workers. Our Nation is still experiencing the consequences of a deep and lasting recession, even as we have seen encouraging signs that the turmoil of the past 2 years is waning. Moving from recession to recovery, and ultimately to prosperity, remains at the heart of my Administration's efforts. This Budget provides a blueprint for the work ahead.

But in order to understand where we are going in the coming year, it is important to remember where we started just 1 year ago. Last January, the United States faced an economic crisis unlike any we had known in generations. Irresponsible risk taking and debt fueled speculation—unchecked by sound oversight—led to the near-collapse of our financial system. Our Gross Domestic Product (GDP) was falling at the fastest rate in a quarter-century. Five trillion dollars of Americans' household wealth had evaporated in just 12 weeks as stocks, pensions, and home values plummeted.

We were losing an average of 700,000 jobs each month, equivalent to the population of the State of Vermont. The capital and credit markets, integral to the normal functioning of our economy, were virtually frozen. The fear among economists—from across the political spectrum—was that we risked sinking into a second Great Depression. Immediately, we undertook a series of difficult steps to prevent that outcome. We acted to get lending flowing again so that businesses could get loans to buy equipment and ordinary Americans could get financing to buy homes and cars, go to college, and start or run businesses. We enacted measures to foster greater stability in the housing market, help responsible homeowners stay in their homes, and help to stop the broader decline in home values. To achieve this, and to prevent an economic collapse that would have affected millions of additional families, we had no choice but to use authority enacted under the previous Administration to extend assistance to some of the very banks and financial institutions whose actions had helped precipitate the turmoil. We also took steps to prevent the rapid dissolution of the American auto industry—which faced a crisis partly of its own making—to prevent the loss of hundreds of thousands of additional jobs during an already fragile time. Many of these decisions were not popular, but we deemed them necessary to prevent a deeper and longer recession.

Even as we worked to stop the economic freefall and address the crises in our banking sector, our housing market, and our auto industry, we also began attacking the economic crisis on a broader front. Less than 1 month after taking office, we enacted the most sweeping economic recovery package in history: the American Recovery and Reinvestment Act. The

Recovery Act not only provided tax cuts to small businesses and 95 percent of working families and provided emergency relief to those out of work or without health insurance; it also began to lay a new foundation for long term economic growth and prosperity. With investments in health care, education, infrastructure, and clean energy, the Recovery Act both saved and created millions of jobs and began the hard work of transforming our economy to thrive in the modern, global marketplace and reverse the financial decline working families experienced in the last decade. Because of these and other steps, we can safely say we have avoided the depression many feared, and we are no longer facing the potential collapse of our financial system. But our work is far from complete.

First and foremost, there are still too many Americans without work. The steps we have taken have helped stop the staggering job losses we were experiencing at the beginning of last year. But the damage has been done. More than seven million jobs were lost since the recession began 2 years ago. This represents not only a terrible human tragedy, but also a very deep hole from which we have to climb out. Until our businesses are hiring again and jobs are being created to replace those we have lost—until America is back at work—my Administration will not rest and this recovery will not be finished.

That is why this Budget includes plans to encourage small businesses to hire as quickly and effectively as possible, to make additional investments in infrastructure, and to jump-start clean energy investments that will help the private sector create good jobs in America. Long before this crisis hit, middle-class families were under growing strain. For decades, Washington failed to address fundamental weaknesses in the economy: rising health-care costs, a growing dependence on foreign oil, and an education system unable to prepare our children for the jobs of the future. In recent years, spending bills and tax cuts for the wealthy were approved without paying for any of it, leaving behind a mountain of debt. And while Wall Street gambled without regard for the consequences, Washington looked the other way.

As a result, the economy may have been working very well for those at the very top, but it was not working for the middle class. Year after year, Americans were forced to work longer hours and spend more time away from their loved ones, while their incomes flat-lined and their sense of economic security evaporated. Beneath the statistics are the stories of hardship I've heard all across America. For too many, there has long been a sense that the American dream—a chance to make your own way, to support your family, save for college and retirement, own a home—was slipping away. And this sense of anxiety has been combined with a deep frustration that Washington either didn't notice, or didn't care enough to act.

Those days are over. In the aftermath of this crisis, what is clear is that we cannot simply go back to business as usual. We cannot go back to an economy that yielded cycle after cycle of speculative booms and painful busts. We cannot continue to accept an education system in which our students trail their peers in other countries, and a health-care system in which exploding costs put our businesses at a competitive disadvantage and squeeze the incomes of our workers. We cannot continue to ignore the clean energy challenge and stand still while other countries move forward in the emerging industries of the 21st Century. And we cannot continue to borrow against our children's future, or allow special interests to determine how public dollars are spent. That is why, as we strive to meet the crisis of the moment, we are continuing to lay a new foundation for the future.

Already, we have made historic strides to reform and improve our schools, to pass health insurance reform, to build a new clean energy economy, to cut wasteful spending, and to limit the influence of lobbyists and special interests so that we are better serving the national interest. However, there is much left to do, and this Budget lays out the way ahead.

Because an educated workforce is essential in a 21st Century global economy, we are undertaking a reform of elementary and secondary school funding by setting high standards, encouraging innovation, and rewarding success; making the successful Race to the Top fund permanent and opening it up to innovative school districts; investing in educating the next generation of scientists and engineers; and putting our Nation closer to meeting the goal of leading the world in new college graduates by 2020.

Moreover, since in today's economy learning must last a lifetime, my Administration will reform the job-training system, streamlining it and focusing it on the high-growth sectors of the economy. Because even the best-trained workers in the world can't compete if our businesses are saddled with rapidly increasing health-care costs, we're fighting to reform our Nation's broken health insurance system and relieve this unsustainable burden. My Budget includes funds to lay the groundwork for these reforms—by investing in health information technology, patient-centered research, and prevention and wellness—as well as to improve the health of the Nation by increasing the number of primary care physicians, protecting the safety of our food and drugs, and investing in critical biomedical research.

Because small businesses are critical creators of new jobs and economic growth, the Budget eliminates capital gains taxes for investments in small firms and includes measures to increase these firms' access to the loans they need to meet payroll, expand their operations, and hire new workers. Because we know the nation that leads in clean energy will be the nation that leads the world, the budget creates the incentives to build a new clean energy economy—from new loan guarantees that will encourage a range of renewable energy efforts and new nuclear power plants to spurring the development of clean energy on Federal lands. More broadly, the Budget makes critical investments that will ensure that we continue to lead the world in new fields and industries: doubling research and development funding in key physical sciences agencies; expanding broadband networks across our country; and working to promote American exports abroad. And because we know that our future is dependent on maintaining American leadership abroad and ensuring our security at home, the Budget funds all the elements of our national power—including our military—to achieve our goals of winding down the war in Iraq, executing our new strategy in Afghanistan, and fighting al Qaeda all over the world. To honor the sacrifice of the men and women who shoulder this burden and who have throughout our history, the Budget also provides significant resources, including advanced appropriations, to care for our Nation's veterans. Rising to these challenges is the responsibility we bear for the future of our children, our grandchildren, and our Nation. This is an obligation to change not just what we do in Washington, but how we do it.

As we look to the future, we must recognize that the era of irresponsibility in Washington must end. On the day my Administration took office, we faced an additional $7.5 trillion in national debt by the end of this decade as a result of the failure to pay for two large tax cuts, primarily for the wealthiest Americans, and a new entitlement program. We also inherited the worst recession since the Great Depression—which, even before we took any action, added an additional $3 trillion to the national debt. Our response to this recession, the Recovery Act, which has been critical to restoring economic growth, will add an additional $1 trillion to the debt—only 10 percent of these costs. In total, the surpluses we enjoyed at the start of the last decade have disappeared; instead, we are $12 trillion deeper in debt. In the long term, we cannot have sustainable and durable economic growth without getting our fiscal house in order.

That is why even as we increased our short-term deficit to rescue the economy, we have refused to go along with business as usual, taking responsibility for every dollar we spend, eliminating what we don't need, and making the programs we do need more efficient. We are taking on health care—the single biggest threat to our Nation's fiscal future—and doing so in a fiscally responsible way that will not add a dime to our deficits and will lower the rate of health-care cost growth in the long run.

We are implementing the Recovery Act with an unprecedented degree of oversight and openness so that anyone anywhere can see where their tax dollars are going. We've banned lobbyists from serving on agency advisory boards and commissions, which had become dominated by special interests. We are using new technology to make Government more accessible to the American people. And last year, we combed the budget, cutting millions of dollars of waste and eliminating excess wherever we could—including outdated weapons systems that even the Pentagon said it did not want or need. We continued that process in this Budget as well, streamlining what does work and ending programs that do not—all while making it more possible for Americans to judge our progress for themselves. The Budget includes more than 120 programs for termination, reduction, or other savings for a total of approximately $23 billion in 2011, as well as an aggressive effort to reduce the tens of billions of dollars in improper Government payments made each year. To help put our country on a fiscally sustainable path, we will freeze non-security discretionary funding for 3 years. This freeze will require a level of discipline with Americans' tax dollars and a number of hard choices and painful tradeoffs not seen in Washington for many years. But it is what needs to be done to restore fiscal responsibility as we begin to rebuild our economy.

In addition to closing loopholes that allow wealthy investment managers to not pay income taxes on their earnings and ending subsidies for big oil, gas, and coal companies, the Budget eliminates the Bush tax cuts for those making more than $250,000 a year and devotes those resources instead to reducing the deficit. Our Nation could not afford these tax cuts when they passed, and it cannot afford them now. And the Budget calls for those in the financial sector—who benefited so greatly from the extraordinary measures taken to rescue them from a crisis that was largely of their own making—to finally recognize their obligation to taxpayers. The legislation establishing the Troubled Asset Relief Program (TARP) included a provision requiring the Administration to devise a way for these banks and firms to pay back the American taxpayer. That is why in this Budget we have included a fee on the largest and most indebted financial firms to ensure that taxpayers are fully compensated for the extraordinary support they provided, while providing a deterrent to the risky practices that contributed to this crisis.

Yet even after taking these steps, our fiscal situation remains unacceptable. A decade of irresponsible choices has created a fiscal hole that will not be solved by a typical Washington budget process that puts partisanship and parochial interests above our shared national interest. That is why, working with the Congress, we will establish a bipartisan fiscal commission charged with identifying additional policies to put our country on a fiscally sustainable path—balancing the Budget, excluding interest payments on the debt, by 2015.

This past year, we have seen the consequences of those in power failing to live up to their responsibilities to shareholders and constituents. We have seen how Main Street is as linked to Wall Street as our economy is to those of other nations. And we have seen the results of building an economy on a shaky foundation, rather than on the bedrock fundamentals of innovation, small business, good schools, smart investment, and long-term growth. We have also witnessed the resilience of the American people—our unique ability to pick ourselves up and forge ahead even when times are tough. All across our country, there are students ready to learn, workers eager to work, scientists on the brink of discovery, entrepreneurs seeking the chance to open a small business, and once-shuttered factories just waiting to whir back to life in burgeoning industries.

This is a Nation ready to meet the challenges of this new age and to lead the world in this new century. Americans are willing to work hard, and, in return, they expect to be able to find a good job, afford a home, send their children to world-class schools, receive high-quality and affordable health care, and enjoy retirement security in their later years. These are the building blocks of the middle class that make America strong, and it is our duty to honor the drive, ingenuity, and fortitude of the American people by laying the groundwork upon which they can pursue these dreams and realize the promise of American life.

This Budget is our plan for how to start accomplishing this in the coming fiscal year. As we look back on the progress of the past 12 months and look forward to the work ahead, I have every confidence that we can—and will—rise to the challenge that our people and our history set for us. These have been tough times, and there will be difficult months ahead. But the storms of the past are receding; the skies are brightening; and the horizon is beckoning once more.

Barack Obama

The White House,

February 1, 2010

Wow! After reading the Presidents message to the Congress it is perfectly clear why they have not passed the budget. They are still trying to recover from the load of garbage the President has tried to get them to swallow. According to the Presidents writers we can expect the waters to part and our savior will emerge carrying the world on his shoulders.

We are into December and the Congress had to pass special legislation for the government to operate for an additional 60 days so it would have time to pass a budget. Hopefully, there will be some people that have to make a decision on the budget will have more common sense than our President. All through the message the President is trying to lay the blame on the previous two years. How respectful of him to blame the exact people that were in control of both houses of the Congress at that time. I wonder how the Democrats feel being blamed

for what they actually created. By the way, Obama was a Democratic Senator during this same time frame.

The Congress needs to take responsibility for not taking any action on the budget. They received the Presidents message on February 1 and have had plenty of time to iron out the mistakes and cut the overall spending on pork projects and items that do not affect our national defense. Try cutting the salaries of the Congressional members by 25%.

One of the major problems with trying to eliminate an annual deficit is to stop the flow of foreign made products into the United States. What the government needs to realize is that if we import $1 million of products from China we need to sell at least $1 million of our products to China. That will be a balance of trade and eliminate part of the deficit. In addition, when we start placing a tariff on products that are shipped into America it is going to slow down the amount. By placing a tariff it will also raise the prices of the cheap goods close to the price of "Made in the USA" products. The following is information regarding shipments coming into the United States.

Every American should boycott Wal-Mart until they return to Made in the USA. The following information should wake up America and show why America needs to wean itself from China.

The Emma Maersk is part of a Danish shipping line that is transporting all of the goods from China to the United States.

What a ship the Emma Maersk is. No wonder "Made in China" is displacing North American made goods big time. This monster transports goods across the Pacific in just 5 days!! This is one of three ships presently in service, with another two ships commissioned to be completed in 2012.

These ships were commissioned by Wal-Mart to get all their goods and stuff from China. They hold an incredible 15,000 cartons and have a 207 foot deck beam!! The full crew is just 13 people on a ship longer than a United States Aircraft Carrier (which has a crew of 5,000) with its 207' beam it is too big to fit through the Panama or Suez Canals.

It is strictly transpacific. Cruise speed: 31 knots.

The goods arrive 4 days before the typical container ship (18-20 knots) on a China to California run. Over 75% of Wal-Mart products are made in China. So this behemoth is hugely competitive even when carrying perishable goods.

The ship was built in five sections. The sections floated together then welded.

The command bridge is higher than a 10-story building and has 11 cargo crane rigs that can operate simultaneously unloading the entire ship in less than two hours.

Additional information:

Country of origin - Denmark

Length - 1,302 ft

Width - 207 ft

Net cargo - 123,200 tons

Engine - 14 cylinders in-line diesel engine (110,000 BHP)

Cruise Speed - 31 knots

Cargo capacity - 15,000 TEU (1 TEU = 20 cubic feet)

Crew - 13 people!

First Trip - Sept. 08, 2006

Construction cost - US $145,000,000+

Silicone painting applied to the ship bottom reduces water resistance and saves 317,000 gallons of diesel per year.

A recent documentary in late March, 2010 on the History Channel noted that all of these containers are shipped back to China, <u>EMPTY</u>. Yep, that's right. We send nothing back on these ships. What does that tell you about the current financial state of this country? Just keep buying those imported goods (mostly gadgets) until you run out of money. Then you may wonder what the cause of unemployment (maybe even <u>your</u> job) in the United States might be?

Do we need to show you anything more to want you to stop purchasing that junk that is imported from China?

Buy products that are "Made in the USA".

CHAPTER TWENTY ONE

The Energy Policies

The President is promoting wind, solar and other clean energy technologies which he states are essential for the environment and economy of our country. We agree that these technologies are essential and will help but we can not ignore our trade deficit and the natural resources that are available in our own country. We are not saying to scrap these types of energy proposals. What we are saying is to take advantage of what is available in our country that will fight the astounding amount of crude oil, natural gas and finished petroleum products that are imported into the United States from the Middle East and other countries.

The President needs to realize that we are incurring unrealistic and uncontrollable deficits from his policies. The energy policies that the President insists have failed are caused by the importation of the petroleum products from other nations. What he fails to understand is that American oil companies are going to make profits and that is the free enterprise system. Don't blame companies for operating their businesses in the manner that the government should be copying.

Do we really want these all over killing the migratory birds?

The President is under the conclusion that it was the big oil companies that have ruined the economy of the United States because they were making profits. What is wrong with a company making profits? Does our President really think that any other type of energy program is going to operate with the assumption that they are not going to be allowed to make profits? When is our President going to get his head out of the sand and start thinking properly? Everything that the President says in his addresses to the nation is purely political and nothing more than attempts to raise some votes for the Democratic Party.

We agree that we need to spur innovation and help make our country economically sound again. That is the primary reason we need to use our natural resources and stop the insane amount of petroleum products that are imported.

The solar power plant that was opened in the Mojave Desert was basically funded by the federal government. What about having private enterprises do these projects and get the government out of every type of business in this country and start running the government? We definitely need to freeze the remaining spending on the stimulus bill that was passed by the Democrats without the basic support of the Republican Party.

The President and his Democratic administration have been spending without providing the people with information about how these spending bills are going to be repaid. The President has pushed legislation to provide his favorite banking industries with an additional $30 billion to increase lending to small businesses.

Why if our President is so willing to push legislation to spend $30 billion for his pet projects and is he so against providing $3.7 billion to the taxpayers of the United States? Who really cares if the rich get the advantage as well as the rest of the country? We are a country that is for all of the people.

Of course the President wants to promote green energy. If you were involved with the Chicago Climate Exchange, when you and your friends stand to make billions it would be a really great idea for those involved. When you admit that you want to help America stay the land of the free home of the brave and the envy of the free world you will recommend that the United States will recommend that exploration for crude oil will never cease. Promote the drilling for our natural resources so we can stop sending our money to the other countries that in most cases do not like America anyway. They just want us to support them by buying all their oil. Let them find out what it will be like when we don't purchase their crude.

What the environmentalist and the rest of the United States need to accept is that oil will remain the country's top energy source for decades to come, but an imminent decline in oil production could send prices soaring. What sounds like a dream come true for climate activists - the slow end of the Oil Age - could be a time wrought with tensions?

The question about whether to drill for oil in the Artic National Wildlife Refuge (ANWR) has been a political hot potato in the United States since 1977. A report that was prepared by the Department of Energy shows some of the following information:

The report argued that the oil and gas potentials of the coastal plain were needed for the country's economy and national security. Conservationists argued that oil development would unnecessarily threaten the existence of the Porcupine caribou by cutting off the herd from calving areas. The Caribou are wonderful animals and should not be ignored but the citizens of the United States are also wonderful animals for the most part and should not be ignored either. Sometimes we have to make difficult decisions concerning the different types of life on our planet. Exploring for our natural resources in the AWNR would not necessarily mean that the Caribou would not be able to breed. It simply means that they would also have to adapt as well as the people need to adapt and drill in this area.

The Department of Energy also expressed concerns that oil operations would erode the fragile ecological systems that support wildlife on the tundra of the Arctic plain.

Arctic National Wildlife Refuge drilling was again approved by the Republican controlled House of Representatives as part of the Energy Bill on April 21, 2005, but the ANWR provision was later removed by the House Senate conference committee. The Republican controlled Senate passed Arctic National Wildlife Refuge drilling on March 16, 2005 as part of the federal budget resolution for fiscal year 2006. That Arctic National Wildlife Refuge provision was removed during the reconciliation process, due to Democrats in the House of Representatives who signed a letter stating they would oppose any version of the budget that had Arctic Refuge drilling in it.

On December 15, 2005 Senator Ted Stevens, a Republican from Alaska, attached an Arctic National Wildlife Refuge drilling amendment to the annual defense appropriations bill. A group of Democratic Senators led a successful filibuster of the bill on December 21, 2005 and the language was subsequently removed. On Jun 18, 2008 President George W. Bush pressed Congress to reverse the ban on offshore drilling in the Arctic National Wildlife Refuge in addition to approving the extraction of oil from shale on federal lands. Despite his previous stance on the issue, President Bush cited the growing energy crisis as a major factor for reversing the presidential executive order issued by President George H. W. Bush in 1990, which banned coastal oil exploration and oil and gas leasing on most of the outer continental shelf. In conjunction with the presidential order, the Congressional moratorium banning drilling was first enacted in 1982 and has been renewed annually.

When we look back at a little history concerning drilling in the Arctic National Wildlife Refuge we understand that the Democratic

Party has blocked every effort to use our own natural resources and reduce the dependence of foreign oil as well as showing no concern for the welfare of the United States citizens by lowering the deficit. The Democrats are more concerned about letting the Caribou raise their calves than they are about the Americans raising their babies into a country that is not going to be taxing them and their children for the next 50 years. How about getting the Democrats heads out of the ANWR marshes?

Supporting views

Former President George W. Bush and his administration supported drilling in the Arctic Refuge, contending that it could "keep America's economy growing by creating jobs and ensuring that businesses can expand and it will make America less dependent on foreign sources of energy," and that "scientists have developed innovative techniques to reach ANWR's oil with virtually no impact on the land or local wildlife."

Sarah Palin, the former Governor of Alaska and 2008 Republican vice-presidential nominee, supports drilling. She has said "Of the 20 million acres (81,000 km^2) up there, we're looking at 2,000 acres (8.1 km^2) as a footprint, smaller than LAX (Los Angeles International Airport). With new technology, with directional drilling, maybe that footprint will shrink even more. Arctic Power, a lobbying group which supports drilling in ANWR, points out that while ANWR is over 19,000,000 acres (77,000 km^2), only 1,500,000 acres (6,100 km^2), or 8% of the total, would be available for exploration. In addition, less than 2,000 acres (8.1 km^2), would be occupied by drilling platforms. In addition, the state of Alaska contains 16.17% of all the land of the United States of America. Drilling should commence as soon as the Republicans get into office. We can not afford to keep purchasing foreign oil and sending our money out of the United States.

A June 29, 2008 Pew Research Poll reported that over 50% of Americans favor drilling of oil and gas in ANWR while 43% oppose (compared to 42% in favor and 50% opposed in February of the same year). A CNN opinion poll conducted in August 31, 2008 reported 59% favor drilling for oil in ANWR, while 39% oppose it. A large majority of Alaskans support drilling in ANWR, including every governor, senator, representative, and legislature for the past 25 years. In the state of Alaska, residents receive annual dividends from oil-lease revenues. In 2000 the dividend came to $1,964 per resident

The United States Department of Energy estimates that ANWR oil production between 2018 and 2030 would reduce the cumulative net expenditures on imported crude oil and liquid fuels by an estimated $135 to $327 billion (2006 dollars), reducing the foreign trade deficit.

The Green River Formation of Colorado, Utah and Wyoming "holds the equivalent of 800 billion barrels of recoverable oil—as much as the U.S. would use in 110 years, at current consumption levels, and three times the proven oil reserves of Saudi Arabia," according to a Nov. 13 2007 press release from the Bureau of Land Management.

"More than 70 percent of the Formation, including the richest and thickest oil shale deposits, lies under federally managed lands," the release said. The federal government has a critical role in determining the future of the United States oil shale reserve, and it has quietly taken steps to support oil companies in accessing this resource.

In 2005, the Energy Policy Act "liberalized the lease ownership provisions of the Minerals Leasing Act of 1920, thereby removing a major deterrent to private-sector investment in oil shale development," according to a 2005 study produced by the RAND think tank for the Department of Energy.

What the environmentalists need to understand and then they might be able to realize just how important it is to produce our own crude oil and refined products. The United States imported 4,267,110,000 barrels of crude oil during 2009. This crude oil could be produced in the territories of the United States. When you consider that the United States is paying over $80.00 per barrel it is not to difficult to see what a devastating affect it has on our economy.

Technology Helps Reduce Drilling's "Footprint"

Exploring and drilling for natural gas will always have some impact on land and marine habitats. But new technologies have greatly reduced the number and size of areas disturbed by drilling, sometimes called "footprints." Plus, the use of horizontal and directional drilling makes it possible for a single well to produce gas from much bigger areas than in the past.

Natural gas pipelines and storage facilities have a good safety record. This is important because when natural gas leaks it can cause explosions. Since raw natural gas has no odor, natural gas companies add a smelly substance to it so that people will know if there is a leak. If you have a natural gas stove, you may have smelled this "rotten egg" smell of natural gas when the pilot light has gone out.

What can be done to work with environmental groups so that we can develop the natural resources of the United States? When is the government going to start to realize that the environmentalists are causing major problems and massive deficits? The United States has huge quantities of natural resources within the borders of this country. We need to relax the regulations so that they can be utilized. What good are all these resources if we do not use them for the good of the entire nation? The time has come to start drilling for crude oil and natural gas in the Rocky Mountain Regions and the wilderness areas of Alaska. There are credible reports that there are enough resources in these regions to satisfy the needs of the United States for the next 30 to 40 years. The price of foreign oil will go to about $20.00 per barrel since there will not be any demand from the United States. Wake up America.

There needs to be legislation passed that will commence the exploration and production of the vast amounts of natural resources that are within our country. There can be safe guards implemented that will protect our environment. We can not afford to keep depending upon foreign countries to provide us with our petroleum requirements especially when we can be doing it. The policy of importing our petroleum products is creating a huge trade deficit and transferring the wealth of our great nation to the Middle East. I do not want to be dependent upon that area of the world.

The future tax revenues from the production of our own petroleum products will provide the United States with a huge surplus every year and the budget will always be in balance. The deficit spending will be gone and the trillions of accumulated deficit can be paid off. This can be done with our own resources and eliminate the debt of our children and their children.

The environmentalists need to take their heads out of the sand that they are desperately trying to protect. Why is it so hard for them to see that to save a tree might mean that they actually are going to be the largest contributor in destroying the United States of America? I agree that America is the most beautiful place on earth. We do not have to destroy that beauty to protect our nation from being destroyed by the massive deficits. If we are not careful we will not have to worry about our environment because we won't own our country any more. That would be the worst thing that could ever happen to America and we can not let that happen.

The potential revenue from exploring the Rocky Mountain Region and the Alaskan wilderness would be enough to solve our deficit problems for the next 30 years. The states in those regions would be financially sound and capital would be freed up to benefit other states as well. We just can not afford to sit on these resources and let the United States struggle with our deficits and economy. In addition, by opening up these areas we will create substantial employment not only in the exploration industry but others as well. It is just the right thing to do and the time is now.

There are billions of barrels of crude oil in the regions that would provide massive amounts of income for the United States. For example if 10 billion barrels of crude are located in the region it could generate $100 billion in revenues to the government by taxing it at $10.00 per barrel. That would sure beat paying the Middle East $80.00 per barrel for crude.

It is past the time to be "Politically Correct" and propose the proper legislation in Congress and start thinking about what is good for all of the people. We do not need to placate the environmental segment of our population at the sacrifice of the rest of the citizens and the country. Do this legislation now.

The government could raise several billion dollars by taking bids from the oil companies to drill and recover these vast amounts of reserves. The government will only be allowed to take bids from American companies that are paying their income taxes. Protection and clean-up clauses could be placed in all the contract bids so that the environment will be left in great shape.

With all the screaming by the environmentalists about drilling in these areas how about the massive wind farms that are springing up all over the country? These are ugly, noisy and are killing the avian that migrate every year. Have any of you ever driven into Oakland, California in the evening on Highway 5 and heard the weird sounds. It is like going into a Halloween three movie set. These wind farms are creating a much larger eye sore that any drilling activity will cause.

The environmental activists are damaging the future of the United States instead of protecting our future. This is just one issue that they need to get over and save America.

Here is another dirty Little Secret that the liberal media (CNN, ABC, NBC, CBS, AND MSNBC) are not telling the American taxpayers.

ABC News: reported that nearly $2 billion in money from the American Recovery and Reinvestment Act has been spent on wind power, funding the creation of enough new wind farms to power 2.4 million homes over the past year. But the study found that nearly 80 percent of that money has gone to foreign manufacturers of wind turbines. So Where Are the Jobs? What a great question. Most of the jobs are going overseas as it was disclosed at the Investigative Reporting Workshop. The program analyzed which foreign firms had accepted the most stimulus money. According to the estimates, about 6,000 jobs have been created overseas, and maybe a couple hundred have been created in the United States. The problem: A liberal socialist Marxist is in the White House. We as taxpayers need to put a stop to these hidden agendas that are being implemented by the president of the United States. We need to make sure that there will be change and it will be for the people of the United States and not the select few in Washington.

The environmental groups are going to be screaming bloody murder about this. We need to get our head out of the sand and start permitting the drilling for natural gas and crude oil in the United States. There are tremendous amounts of natural resources in the wilderness areas of Alaska and the Rocky Mountain states. The geology studies proclaim that there are enough natural resources to take care of the entire United States for the next thirty years without importing any crude oil from foreign countries. If you will be happy with gasoline at $5.00 per gallon then we need to continue with the current policy of importing the crude. Do we really care if the countries of the Middle East make trillions of dollars of our demand for crude? I for one am really tired of sending all of our dollars to foreign countries that really do not like us but want our money. Think about how the balance of trade will be in our favor when we stop this. The government could place an excise tax on all the natural resources that are produced in the United States and these funds would be targeted for the reduction of the deficit. They could not be used for any other purpose until the deficit is gone. Now we are doing something for the future generations of Americans instead of saddling them with enormous debt. I know that I am in favor of that. I hope everyone else is too. It would be better to have drilling instead of leaving the resources in the ground. Drilling does not have to disrupt the environment.

President Obama has placed a moratorium on deep-water oil drilling in the Gulf of Mexico. Due to the president's unwillingness to reverse or modify its policy that has halted all the deep-water and nearly all of the shallow-water energy exploration in the Gulf which has resulted in the loss of jobs that are so important to the working families across the Gulf Coast. The president has spun the loss of jobs to indicate that it was minimal but the reality of it is that he was counting the people that were working on the clean up as employed. They were getting temporary work at a fraction of the income that they would be making doing what they are trained to do. The moratorium needs to be abandoned.

Every rig should have been inspected and certified by now. The delay is costing the citizens of the Gulf Region their livelihoods for no logical reason. What has been going on during the moratorium to insure the quickest solutions?

The White House had no business halting all oil drilling everywhere in the Gulf. That was just another ploy to put more people out of work so that they can be more dependent upon the government. It is about time that the Democrats start standing up to the White House and for the best interests of the people instead of helping give the government what they want regardless of what the people want.

The government needs to pass legislation that will make it enjoyable and safe for every American to have the opportunity to go to the Gulf States for vacations to enjoy clean water and clean beaches without wondering just how much oil might be in the water and under the sands.

The government needs to make sure that BP is not given concessions in the short term that might prevent the United States from receiving complete and full payment for the damages caused by their carelessness. The mess in the Gulf caused by BP will not be understood or corrected for many years. We need to have assurances that BP will be paying in ten or fifteen years.

The government needs to take steps in the Gulf to make sure that any ban on drilling is lifted so that the oil companies that are working in the area will not have to lay off thousands of employees. Just implement some safeguards on the drilling process addressing safety concerns. This should have already been done.

Studies have indicated that there is a 22-mile-long invisible mist of oil that is meandering far below the surface of the Gulf of Mexico, where it will probably loiter for months or more, scientists reported the first conclusive evidence of an underwater plume from the BP spill.

The most worrisome part is the slow pace at which the oil is breaking down in the cold, 40-degree water, making it a long-lasting but unseen threat to vulnerable marine life, experts said.

Earlier this month, top federal officials declared the oil in the spill was mostly "gone," and it is gone in the sense you can't see it. But the chemical ingredients of the oil that persist more than a half-mile beneath the surface, researchers found.

The oil is at depths of 3,000 to 4,000 feet, far below the environment of the most popular Gulf fish like red snapper, tuna and mackerel. But it is not harmless. These depths are where small fish and crustaceans live. And one of the biggest migrations on Earth involves small fish that go from deep water to more shallow areas, taking nutrients from the ocean depths up to the large fish and mammals.

The oil did not dissipate or just dissolve as BP stated. The gusher was so deep and under such pressure there are undoubtedly much huge bubbled or pure oil the size of mountains floating around under the surface. Millions and millions of gallons of oil do not just go away no matter how much disbursing chemical you put out. How long is it going to take before the disbursing chemical will disappear? How come we've never been told exactly what was in the disbursing chemical?

IT WILL TAKE LITERALLY YEARS TO GET ALL THOSE MILLIONS OF GALLONS OF BP OIL CLEANED OUT OF THE GULF AND THE SEAFOOD THE GULF ONCE YIELDED WILL TAKE MANY YEARS TO PURGE ALL THAT CONTAMINATION, IF EVER.

A lot of oil went into the Gulf. It did a lot of damage and it will do more, but nature will gradually repair the damage. We should rejoice that we appear to have stopped the flow for now and should have a permanent fix in place soon. The jury is still out on whether our attempts at fixes like tons of toxic dispersants did more harm than good, but knowing the extent of the present day problem might give us a chance to design sound remediation measures. At the very least it should inspire caution about future drilling and lead to research on safer drilling methods. Unfortunately, we rely on these government officials to take care of things. They lied to us and now that lie was exposed. The government can not be trusted. They are out for their own agenda and that agenda has nothing to do with the people that put them in to office

I was skeptical to begin with when I herd the oil just magically disappeared I didn't believe it and I still don't believe it. I see it as BP trying to weasel out of responsibility for this by just not telling the entire truth about what is still out there. I don't feel the government of the United States is helping either.

What concerns me the most are the people who keep saying this is nothing and it will go away in a few months? BP and the administration really scare me. What would be your goal in telling such lies; none of you even have the basic knowledge or know anything about the problem when you are talking about this subject. The experts are wrong and you guys working in totally unrelated fields are right. Did BP and Obama really think that 40-50 million gallons of oil was just going to go away because you want it to? That way of thinking is just plain ignorant and very dangerous.

The Obama administration announced that the BP oil disaster in the Gulf of Mexico has prompted it to scuttle plans to open waters off Florida and along the Atlantic coast to offshore oil and gas drilling for at least seven years. What a lame excuse for not trying to become independent from the foreign oil producing countries. Our President does not understand that when we reduce the amount of imports of oil we also reduce the trade deficit.

The change reverses key components of a sweeping energy plan President Barack Obama announced last March. The administration is adjusting their strategy in areas where there are no active leases. Our most appropriate course is to focus on areas with existing leases and not expand to new areas. Naturally, why expand into new areas and develop our own sources of crude oil and natural gas?

The federal government is canceling plans to open waters off Florida and the Atlantic coast to offshore oil and gas drilling for at least seven years in the wake of the BP Deepwater Horizon oil spill.

In a speech on March 31, 2010, Obama announced he was ending a decades-old ban on oil and gas drilling along the Atlantic coast, the eastern Gulf of Mexico and northern Alaska as part of a comprehensive energy plan designed to reduce reliance on foreign oil.

The changes, which drew harsh criticism from environmentalists, would have allowed drilling on tracts as close as 50 miles from Virginia's beaches and would end a moratorium on drilling from Delaware to central Florida. A congressional ban on drilling in most of those areas ended in 2008, although a ban on drilling off Florida's gulf coast would have continued until 2022.

"There will be those who strongly disagree with this decision," Obama said in March in his speech at Andrews Air Force Base in Maryland. "But what I want to emphasize is that this announcement is part of a broader strategy that will move us from an economy that runs on fossil fuels and foreign oil to one that relies more on homegrown fuels and clean energy."

This is a typical flip flop of the President. When he finally does something that would benefit the entire country he changes his mind and goes in the opposite direction. When we get Sarah Palin in the office of President we will have a person that has enough courage to fight for what is right for the entire United States population and not just a few special interest groups.

Three weeks later, BP's Macondo well blew out, killing 11 men and setting off a spill that spewed 50,000 barrels of oil into the gulf for the next 87 days -- nearly 5 million barrels in all.

The President's announcement drew immediate praise from environmentalists and Florida lawmakers. Senator Bill Nelson, a Democrat, praised Obama in a statement for "listening to the people of Florida."

How about listening to the majority of Americans that want the United States to explore and develop our own natural resources? The last time I saw a survey indicated that over 60 percent of the citizens wanted to stop the idiotic use of foreign oil when we have the proven reserves in our country. All we have to do is develop them. Look at the thousands of jobs that will be created for the American unemployed when we start using our head. The environmentalists are so set on saving a few Caribou calves and they would rather have the United States be buried in debt for the next 50 years.

But Doc Hastings, (R-WA), the ranking Republican on the House Resources Committee said in a statement that the administration is "taking the wrong approach in responding to the BP spill. The answer isn't to give up and say, 'America can't figure it out; we'll rely on other countries to produce our energy.' The answer is to find out what went wrong and make effective, timely reforms to ensure that United States offshore drilling is the safest in the world."

Karen Harbert, the President and CEO of the United States Chamber of Commerce's Institute for 21st Century Energy, said in a statement, "The administration is sending a message to America's oil and gas industry: take your capital, technology, and jobs somewhere else."

REDUCING OUR PURCHASES FROM VENEZUELA:

Good news for America. The ambitious plans of Hugo Chavez will squeeze Venezuela's coffers at a time when oil earnings have slipped and Chavez is sending his foreign allies generous amounts of crude on credit. So he has raised a possibility that once seemed remote: selling off Venezuela's United States based oil company, Citgo Petroleum Corp. For Chavez, it's an idea driven both by hard money realities and by politics. Chavez thinks that getting rid of Citgo and its refineries in the United States would give Chavez billions of dollars for domestic spending as he approaches his 2012 re-election bid and seeks to remedy problems including an acute shortage of affordable housing. A sale would also fit with the leftist leader's interest in distancing Venezuela from the United States while building stronger ties with allies such as Russia, China and Iran. What Chavez is not considering is the fact that any American company that would pay one penny for Citgo would have to be insane.

Citgo has delivered oil to Venezuela's No. 1 client for two decades, but judging by Chavez's complaints about Citgo not turning a profit he seems more than ready to sell it, if a buyer can be found. Chavez is dreaming if any American company would purchase Citgo knowing that the company would have to deal with the Venezuelan government.

"Citgo is a bad business, and we haven't been able to get out of it," Chavez said in a televised speech late last month. He ordered his oil minister, to look at options for selling off the state oil company's assets in the United States.

If Chavez were to go ahead with a sale, Venezuela would likely seek to negotiate a supply contract with the United States to keep selling low grade crude to the United States refineries. Any company that would purchase crude oil from Venezuela should be hit with a tariff on the crude that would make it impossible for refining at a profit. The tariff would shut off the source of revenue for Venezuela.

Even so, Venezuela's oil exports to the United States have been declining while Chavez has sought to diversify the country's markets, shipping more crude under preferential deals to allies including Belarus, Cuba and other Caribbean islands. Some buyers are granted low-interest loans, decreasing upfront revenue.

Oil shipments to the United States declined from 49 million barrels in February 1999, when Chavez took office, to 31.9 million barrels during the same month last year. Think how difficult it would be for Venezuela to carry out any of Chavez's plans when the United States finally has a president that will cut off the purchases from Venezuela altogether. The United States could reduce the amount of money spent for foreign oil by $25.5 billion dollars per month. That will make a very nice dent in our balance of payments with foreign countries. That amounts to $306 billion per year which is about one third of the projected deficit per year.

Just think about this. When we become free from foreign oil altogether we will have just about balanced the federal budget.

Venezuela's overall oil output has also been declining due to lower OPEC quotas and inadequate maintenance at some oil fields. While Venezuela says it produces about 3 million barrels of oil a day, the United States Energy Information Administration estimates 2.2 million barrels a day in 2009, down about 190,000 barrels from 2008.

Venezuela bought Citgo, it was a good deal. Their government oil company purchased 50 percent of the company in 1986 from Southland Corporation for $290 million as part of a drive to have its own refineries and other facilities in its key markets of the United States and Latin America. The state oil company purchased the remaining 50 percent of Southland's shares in Citgo in 1990 for $675 million. Now after running Citgo into the ground with huge losses Chavez thinks that the Venezuelan government oil company can sell Citgo for between $5 and $10 billion. Chavez must really think that the American companies are totally stupid. Any purchase of Citgo should have to be approved by the government and all purchases of crude oil from Venezuela would have to be discontinued immediately.

Since then, Citgo has grown. It now operates three refineries in Texas, Louisiana and Illinois, and sells fuel through thousands of gas stations.

Another motive for selling Citgo could be to reduce Venezuela's exposure to United States court suits over Chavez's expropriations of United States company assets.

United States based Exxon Mobil Corp. has sought international arbitration to claim billions of dollars in compensation after it refused to accept the government's terms for a 2007 nationalization of an oil project that had invested heavily.

Citgo, for its part, took a $201 million loss last year, and issued $3.5 billion in bonds this year as its profits plummeted. Profits were battered by lower world prices and a declining flow of heavy, sulfur-laden crude.

There is not any interest in purchasing Citgo at the present time. Exxon and other major United States refiners such as Chevron Corp. and Phillips Petroleum might end up being interested in Citgo or some of its assets if their price was well below the market value. Citgo has the potential to be a good business if it's well managed. But it's not being well managed, and that's causing problems.

Remember all those emails about not buying Citgo gas because it's owned by Chavez! Well we all stuck together and it looks like its working. Citgo is not turning a profit. When Americans stick together we can accomplish things even though our government says the opposite. Now let's work on the economy and unemployment. Start buying American products. I know its hard but a least try and look. Quit shopping at Wal-Mart until they put back up the "Made in the USA" signs. It's a tough adjustment at first but its kind of fun to beat the giant. Once you get the hang of it its easy. You are actually not saving by buying the cheap junk at Wal-Mart because you will end up having to buy 2 to make them last as long as the products that are "Made in the USA". Do your research Wal-Mart caters to the poor and low income families and they do not seem to mind buying junk.

Citgo doesn't make a profit because the American people choose not to buy from them. If a company buys it and uses oil from Venezuela I will still not buy from them. Consumers of the world need to take action against nations that oppress their people (like China) buy not buying their goods.

Chavez has used Citgo to further his socialist agenda. He was never interested in it being a viable business. He must have been licking his chops when Obama was elected knowing that an Obama campaign staffer had leaked one of their goals was to nationalize the oil and gas industry. A staffer actually said that, of course it was later denied and the socialist main media didn't report it. Why does anyone think Maxine Waters would threaten an oil executive with nationalizing that industry if the administration was not for it?

Maybe that is why Chavez's political tool, Citgo is on the block, or does anyone actually believe that Chavez will not be reelected? Everyone knows he'll claim victory regardless of the election results.

Discontinuing the policy of importing crude oil from Venezuela would be another great reason to explore the Artic National Wildlife Refuge of the vast amounts of oil reserves that are within our own country. It would make the United States free from the dependency on a huge amount of foreign oil and reduce our trade deficit.

Sarah Palin has already made a stance that we should be developing our own resources including the ANWR in Alaska. Remember the famous quote. "Drill Baby Drill"

The government needs to understand that is better to let private business develop our resources than it is to try and mandate policies that get in the way of proper development. Having private companies make profits will increase tax revenues and provide jobs.

This section is an easy decision. Palin would win in a landslide.

CHAPTER TWENTY TWO

The English Language Policy

There have been several proposals to make English the national language in amendments to immigration reform bills but none of these bills has become law with the amendment intact. The situation is quite varied at the State and Territorial levels, with some states mirroring the Federal policy of adopting no official language in any capacity, others adopting English alone, others officially adopting English as well as local languages, and still others adopting a policy of de facto bilingualism.

The United States does not have a national official language nevertheless, English is the primary language used for legislation, regulations, executive orders, treaties, federal court rulings, and all other official pronouncements; although there are laws requiring documents such as ballots to be printed in multiple languages when there are large numbers of non-English speakers in an area.

As part of what has been called the English only movement, some states have adopted legislation granting official status to English. Currently, out of 50 total states, 27 have established English as the official language, while another, Hawaii, has established both English and Hawaiian as official languages.

States with official English

Alabama	Alaska
Arizona	Arkansas
California	Colorado
Florida	Idaho
Illinois	Indiana
Iowa	Kansas
Kentucky	Mississippi
Missouri	Montana
Nebraska	New Hampshire
North Carolina	North Dakota
Oklahoma	South Carolina
South Dakota	Tennessee
Utah	Virginia
Wyoming	

The rest of the states are without official English.

We need to contact our representatives and make them aware of our desire to have the English language as the only language of the United States of America. The following list of representatives voted against making English the official language of America.

Akaka (D-HI)	Bayh (D-IN)

Biden (D-DE)

Bingaman (D-NM)

Boxer (D-CA)

Cantwell (D-WA)

Clinton (D-NY)

Dayton (D-MN)

Dodd (D-CT)

Domenici (R-NM)

Durbin (D-IL)

Feingold (D-WI)

Feinstein (D-CA)

Harkin (D-IA)

Inouye (D-HI)

Jeffords (I-VT)

Kennedy (D-MA)

Kerry (D-MA)

Kohl (D-WI)

Lautenberg (D-NJ)

Leahy (D-VT)

Levin (D-MI)

Lieberman (D-CT)

Menendez (D-NJ)

Mikulski (D-MD)

Murray (D-WA)

Obama (D-IL)

Reed (D-RI)

Reid (D-NV)

Salazar (D-CO)

Sarbanes (D-MD)

Schumer (D-NY)

Stabenow (D-MI)

Wyden (D-OR)

Additionally, here is a list of the Senators who voted to give illegal aliens social security benefits.

Alaska :   Stevens (R)

Arizona :   McCain (R)

Arkansas :   Lincoln (D)   Pryor (D)

California :   Boxer (D)   Feinstein (D)

Colorado :   Salazar (D)

Connecticut :   Dodd (D)   Lieberman (D)

Delaware :   Biden (D)   Carper (D)

Florida :   Martinez (R)

Hawaii :   Akaka (D)   Inouye (D)

Illinois :   Durbin (D)   Obama (D)

Indiana: Bayh (D)   Lugar (R)

Iowa: Harkin (D)

Kansas: Brownback (R)

Louisiana: Landrieu (D)

Maryland: Mikulski (D)   Sarbanes (D)

Massachusetts: Kennedy (D)   Kerry (D)

Montana: Baucus (D)

Nebraska: Hagel (R)

Nevada: Reid (D)

New Jersey: Lautenberg (D)   Menendez (D)

New Mexico: Bingaman (D)

New York: Clinton (D)   Schumer (D)

North Dakota: Dorgan (D)

Ohio :   DeWine (R)   Voinovich(R)

Oregon: Wyden (D)

Pennsylvania : Specter (D)

Rhode Island : Chafee (R)   Reed (D)

South Carolina: Graham (R)

South Dakota: Johnson (D)

Vermont: Jeffords (I)   Leahy (D)

Washington: Cantwell (D)   Murray (D)

West Virginia: Rockefeller (D)

Wisconsin :   Feingold (D)   Kohl (D)

As you can see the vast majority of the representatives that have voted against policies that went against the will of the people were Democrats. Not really surprising as the people that they are trying to cater too is usually voting Democratic.

The entire population of the United States needs to know this information. That is unless you don't mind sharing your Social Security with foreign workers who didn't pay a dime into the program. If we are to be serious about America recovering from our past policies we need to take action.

The United States needs to make English the official language and quit printing documents in other languages. It is a requirement of citizenship to be able to read and write the English language.

CHAPTER TWENTY THREE

The Unemployment Problem

With government reporting that the unemployment rate is hovering around the 10% mark it is one of the most serious problems facing the United States. When the Democrats took control of both houses of Congress on January 3, 2007 the unemployment rate was 4.8%. That indicates that the rate of unemployed has increased a little over 100% in a twenty-five month period under the Obama administration. When you take into consideration the fact there are millions of Americans that have accepted part time work, have given up or have been unemployed for a period longer than their benefits and are no longer counted the real rate is more like 20% unemployed.

The nationwide increase in unemployment claims suggests the economy is creating even fewer jobs than in the first half of this year, when private employers added an average of about 100,000 per month. That's not enough to keep the unemployment rate from rising. The jobless rate has been stuck at 9.6 percent for two months.

Private employers added only 71,000 jobs in July. But that increase was offset by the loss of 202,000 government jobs, including 143,000 temporary census positions.

July marked the third straight month that the private sector hired cautiously, and economists are concerned that the unemployment rate will start rising again because overall economic growth has weakened significantly since the start of the year.

After expanding at a 3.7 percent annual rate in the first quarter, the economy's growth slowed to 2.4 percent in the April-to-June period. Some economists forecast it will drop as low as 1.5 percent in the third quarter

Does anyone really believe that we are in a recovery? The government keeps revising DOWN the past GDP numbers and jobs reports, sometimes by substantial amounts as well. The April-June quarter is apparently about to get revised down from a GDP of 2.4% to around 1.2% after having taking in to account more recently available data. Similar downward revisions have been on going since the so called recovery began. Now they're revising down future projected growth rates for next year as well.

When you build an economy on a house of cards and provide free benefits to 20%-30% of the populace including illegal migrants what do you really expect. Building on the European model was doomed from the beginning.

Like Jack Nicholson said in an old movie, "Keep telling me how good it is...." The 9.6% unemployment figure is a joke. We know the real numbers are more like 20% -25%. Our future generations are saddled with a debt that can never be paid and now the baby boomers are retiring. Where is the golden goose now? Have you ever heard that the golden goose is cooked?

There was never a recovery, just a delay in the inevitable. The government borrowed money to bail out banks, Wall Street, General Motors, Chrysler, Fannie Mae, Freddie Mac and others, to keep the unemployed eating and with a roof over their head and funding two wars. The United States government has amassed a staggering amount of debt. California, Arizona, Nevada and many, many more are on the verge of default. A nation cannot leverage itself by intentionally moving millions of jobs out of the country

I look at small children and wonder just how difficult life will be for them with all the debt that is being incurred that they will have to someday repay. I know it won't be easy because the current generation has made a mess of what was the greatest nation in the world. We have left the Constitution in ashes as the federal government usurped more and more power from the States in order to be all things to all people. We have created enormous future financial obligations by putting in place entitlement programs which we should have realized were not sustainable.

The government announced more news about their failed economic policies. The private sector is tanking big time. About the only jobs that are created are government funded jobs paid by the taxpayers. Private employers are afraid to hire or expand as they are waiting to see what's in store with the health care and the new financial reform regulation.

While the current administration pretends it has saved millions of jobs that would have been lost if not for the stimulus, there is good reason to believe that in fact millions of people are now unemployed because the stimulus plan has delayed the recovery. The rest of the world is recovering from the global recession far faster than the United States. I suspect this is because their governments eschewed stimulus and many in fact instituted austerity programs - the opposite of stimulus. If we do in fact get the double dip recession that looks increasingly likely, it will be obvious where to lay the blame fro the second dip.

I remember just a few of the statements that were made by the President, Vice President and Mr. Gibbs.

"We are beginning to see glimmers of hope." -- BO - 4/14/2009

"We are seeing the corner turn on the economy growing again." -- BO - 2/7/2010

"The worst of the storm is over. ... We are beginning to turn the corner." – BO 4/3/2010

"The economy is getting stronger by the day." -- BO - 6/4/2010

Vice President Joe Biden dubs the months ahead "Recovery Summer," and David Axelrod adds that "this summer will be the most active Recovery Act season yet." -- 6/17/2010

"The economy is getting stronger." -- Robert Gibbs - 7/8/2010

The mainstream news media reported that the recession ended in June 2009. What were they smoking anyway?

We have to experience the market correction before things will ever get better. The politicians don't want to be the ones on duty when it happens so they're going to delay the inevitable and keep trying to spend they're way out of the problem all the while compounding the problem so when the correction does occur it will be ten times worse. We need a leader in the White House that has the guts to tell the American people we're in for some really hard times and it's going to be rough for awhile until things get corrected. Instead, we have the government telling us things are getting better. Things are not getting better, all sectors of the market are on life support and the government is trying to save the economy that needs to have the plug pulled on it. Political affiliation does not matter, we need someone who sincerely cares about the country and isn't afraid to finally tell all the lobbyists the days of controlling and buying off politicians are over and seriously reel in the size of government and its spending by cutting entire departments across the board and cutting taxes drastically and let the people save and spend their money instead of wasting citizens money on failing stimulus bills to try and prop up a broken market.

It is funny that the current administration blames Bush, liberals blame Bush, and everyone blames Bush. But it all comes down to the Democrats for blame and failure. They took the congress back in 2004 and got a super majority in 2006. They caused this mess no matter what the administration says and lies about. Mr. Obama was part of the Senate when the Democrats started ruining this country. So if you want blame forget Bush. This is all a Democrat mess we are in. Only if you believe their lies will you see otherwise.

The majority of the economist predicted this back in February 2009, when the President and the Democrats rammed their stimulus package down America's throat. If they were going to spend 787 billion dollars that we did not have they should have given it directly to small business owners in the form of very low interest loans so those businesses could keep and hire more employees. Instead they threw it all at wasteful government spending while they were passing new laws (Healthcare) that did nothing but add to costs for many businesses.

Our economy is in the quick sand and the President and Chairman of the Board of General Motors are going to be spending $500 million to expand a General Motors plant in Mexico. This is a company that we bailed out to the tune of $50 Billion and that the government owns 61% of the company. How does this administration explain a company it owns taking taxpayer money to expand its foreign operations. Why isn't General Motors going to expand in Detroit? Jobs are leaving the United States because of moves like this and the governments anti-business mentality. General Motors should have their payroll in Mexico taxed a rate of 75% of the gross wages paid.

It should be noted that when the Democrats took over Congress in January 2007, gas was $1.89 a gallon, the rate of unemployment was 4.8%, the national debt was $9 Trillion and the largest deficit in history at that time was $400 Billion.

Yes, I'll take a 3/5 majority in Congress to raise the National Debt any day over this disgusting, wasteful and intolerable spending that is an insult to the American Taxpayer, the American people, the American economy and all free people of the world.

My Fellow Americans, the challenges that our nation faces are not rocket science, we just need leadership that can explain those challenges in a little more detail, with a little more explanation about the struggle that we will endure and the ultimate outcome that will make our nation strong and prosperous.....simply, logically and with a little Common Sense. Shucks, I forgot these people are educated with degrees from the highest learning institutions. To bad they are lacking in common sense.

Once the Balanced Budget Amendment is enacted, I will guarantee you that everyone's attention will be focused on finding solutions, and quickly, because Congress, in its infinite wisdom, will no longer be able to borrow money without a 3/5 majority in both houses of Congress to raise the National Debt.

Maybe if our government would stop giving away money we don't have to foreign countries whenever they fail to handle their own crisis situations. We have our own crisis here at home. Our Citizens and States need that aid money that the government is sending abroad. Why should America borrow money from China just to give it away overseas? Let someone else be the world's deep pockets for a change. You don't see China giving much money to the United Nations, Pakistan, etc even though they could afford it.

The Democrats are also not off the hook. Bill Clinton signed into law the Gramm-Leach-Bliley act in 1999 and the vast majority of Democrats voted for it. Barney Frank and friends pushed so hard for more bad loans to be written to the indigent and minorities who did not have a prayers chance of making payments full term. This created more bad derivative products and more leverage and more trouble placing positions well over the edge. Believe it or not President Bush tried to warn and stop this but was beaten down as being against the under privileged. The immigration problem is largely to be blamed on Democrats who pander to ethnic lobbyists against the needs of the United States.

The current administration has been working very hard for the last twenty-five months. They have blamed the prior administrations for all the current problems. It is time that the present administration steps up to the plate and admits that they have a majority in both houses and are just trying to cram programs down the American citizens throat that the majority do not want. The current administration has increased our federal deficit by approximately $4 trillion all while going on extended vacations and sending their family to foreign countries. Their plan to pass job destroying plans is working very successfully since we have a real unemployment figure in the range of 20% to25% when we count everyone whose unemployment benefits have expired, those that do not qualify for unemployment benefits, and those Americans that have just given up.

The current elevated level of claims is a sign employers are reluctant to hire until the rebound is well under way. When companies need people they will only hire if they are able to show investors a profit for several consecutive quarters. Earnings have been spotty for many companies and reductions in employees are one way they can reduce their expenses. If you have a bad quarter and it looks like the same for the next quarter then you have layoffs. Companies need to show a profit for investors to invest and to get bank loans. Companies do not wait for a rebound. They respond to their needs and the needs of their customers when they hire. Right now the demand of products and services is low. Until the public and companies start spending again, we are in for a long haul.

The current administrations policies will never work. The government has spent $787 billion of the taxpayer's money on a stimulus program that has been a total disaster. Wake up and admit that the government can not spend us out of this current recession. I think it is really a depression.

The administration has to develop legislation that does not punish business expecting to achieve favorable results. We need to extent the Bush tax cuts for at least 5 years until this current financial mess is resolved.

Some changes that could be made to improve the unemployment problems in the United States would be. The changes will take time and effort by the government.

The first major legislation that I would recommend would be to place a payroll tax on every corporation that is exporting jobs to Mexico, Canada, China, Russia, Japan or any other country. This payroll tax would be paid to the Treasury on a monthly basis the same as the normal payroll taxes are paid. The rate of the payroll tax should be 75% of all the wages paid to employees in a foreign country. This would place a very large demand upon the corporations to bring the jobs back into the United States and would be a major factor in improving the unemployment picture as well as the economy.

The unemployment picture will change very quickly when the United States starts enforcing the laws regarding illegal migrants that are taking 12,000,000 to 15,000,000 jobs. Approximately 2% – 3% of these jobs are in farming and the rest are jobs that most Americans are trained and able to fill.

The real unemployment in the United States is more like 20% -25% when you factor in the unemployed that have finished receiving their checks, the part time workers that are unable to locate a full time job, those that were self employed and had their business closed do to lack of business.

I would like to see the unemployment figures drop to the 5% range by implementing the tax on foreign labor and sending the illegal migrants back to their home country.

We could start employing temporary workers to implement the transfer and deportation of all the illegal migrants and their families.

I have based these decisions upon reviewing some of the information that has been gathered from news articles written by the media. I have taken information that I collected and tried to explain in a manner that I believe meets my expectations for the United States.

It is not now, nor should it ever be the government's job to provide, pay for, stimulate financially or create jobs. The only way the Government should stimulate jobs should be with reduced or eliminated taxes that are caused during job creation such as investment tax credits for research and development, acquiring capital items for production and lowering barriers to employment. When United States companies are able to fairly compete against each other they make some of the best products and services in the world. When China subsidizes its entire manufacturing sector and keeps its prices low by forcing its labor force to work for substandard wages then they should be penalized by tariffs to sell their goods here.

CHAPTER TWENTY FOUR

The Deficit Problem

At this time in America's history we need a President that understands the 21st century economic policies and one that will uphold the Constitution and the laws of the United States of America. The American people can not settle for anything less. Contact your representatives and make sure that they vote for the policies that are critical to the country and ones that will vote on what the citizens want.

How serious is the trade deficit to the United States? What can we do to reduce or eliminate the amount of goods that are shipped into the United States?

The most important thing that the United States can do is reduce the amount of petroleum products that are imported into the country every year. Stop importing goods that can and should be "Made in USA" I find it hard to believe that the citizens of America can not make their own clothes instead on importing them from third world countries. The trade deficit would go down and the Americans could be put back to work.

The President advocates the support of building more wind energy systems. Does he realize that the propellers for all of these are being shipped in from China? Why not support building facilities in the United States that can make the propellers? It would reduce the trade deficit and have an added benefit of creating jobs in our own country.

There are too many individuals that are waiting for the federal government to resolve our economic problems. We all need to understand that the federal government can not continue to subsidize our countries over consumption of goods and services which will eventually bankrupt the government. Our economy will not return to normal until we reinstate manufacturing in America. By restructuring the manufacturing system in America it will automatically provide for growth in the economy.

In the last recessions the trade deficit has played a major role in the recessions. The current trade deficit reached $4.2 trillion. This was a very large amount of money that has disappeared from the United States economy. This was a major contributing factor in the economic failure of 2008. The continued increase on the trade deficit is going to cause a reduction in economic gains instead of improving them. We well see more unemployment and more Americans are going to loose their homes. This is going to happen time and time again until the manufacturing sector of our economy is reinstated.

The number one long term economic crisis for our economy is the trade deficit and the illegal immigrations. If they are left unchecked they will reduce America to a second rate power and a third world underclass society saddled with a very large federal deficit. Economically over the long term illegal immigration will destroy community safety nets unless something is done to correct the problem. It is already out of control.

The long term strategy of corporate America is to increase profit and jobs outside of America and reduce jobs in the United States. Economically, America's middle class is at severe risk of slipping backward. The downsizing in America started with outsourcing of our manufacturing jobs.

Outsourcing and the trade deficit are parts of an economic puzzle hidden behind import cost, shipping cost, insurance cost, wholesale and retail mark-up. The trade deficit is a direct subtraction from the GDP. The larger the trade deficit is each year the more it will drive the GDP into a negative growth.

The economic clock is ticking faster in the 21st century and we can not afford the luxury of having individuals in offices who do not understand 21st century economics. The illegals and the trade deficit will cause irreversible harm to our system if left uncheck. We need an overhaul of the federal, state and local governments. If history is of any value the New York Times in 1929 printed probably the number one reason for the stock market crash and eventually the depression was started when foreign investors pulled their investments out of the stock market. There are other similarities to the 1929 crash too. The Federal Reserve borrowed money for two years and poured it into the economy. The stock market crashed; there was a decline in GDP, the number of new jobs decreased, and the dollar declined worldwide.

According to the latest statistics from the United States International Trade Commission, United States imports of crude oil amounted to $60.4 billion for the first 4 months of 2010. That figure represents a 65.4% increase over the $36.5 billion that America spent on crude petroleum imports from January to April 2009. If that pace continues, total crude oil imports will cost an estimated $181 billion for 2010 which would be America's second highest expenditure on imported crude over the past 10 years. The total oil bill for 2010 will have been exceeded only by the $259.3 billion bill spent on imported crude oil during 2008.

These crude oil purchases would not be required if we developed the natural resources that are in our own country. How can we Americans be so stupid as to let one group of citizens have so much control over our country? The number of jobs that would be created would include: trucking, construction, engineering, housing, service, accommodations, refining, manufacturing, and many others to support the exploration industry. When the government starts to produce its own crude to eliminate the need for imported oil we will be able to install a reasonable tax increase per gallon of 10 cents and we will generate $17.922 billion in revenue. Take the 4,267,110,000 barrels of crude oil during 2009 times the 42 gallons per barrel and the tax it at 10 cents a gallon. When you figure that the average American uses 100 gallons per month the cost per individual is only $10.00. I would rather pay the extra few dollars and help get my country back to respectability and eliminate the deficits. That sure would be a lot better than sending $181 billion to the foreign countries around the world.

That would be in addition to the amount saved by not having to purchase crude oil from the Middle East and other countries. A great start to create a balanced budget. That would be a major improvement to our economic system and our balance of trade deficit.

Further benefits to the United States economy would be the natural gas that is captured during the process of extracting the crude oil. The United States utilizes 3,981 billion cubic feet of natural gas per day. The average cost per 1,000 cubic feet of natural gas was $7.00 in 2008. You can figure out how much money we are wasting by not producing our own natural gas. When this amount of natural gas is produced from our natural resources it will produce $1.453 billion in tax to the government.

The Congress needs to take control of our country and initiate legislation that will open up the exploration into all parts of the United States. The country just can not afford to waste our resources to save a few trees. We can build additional sections of our beautiful parks after the exploration has been completed. This will provide more usable recreation areas instead of just vast wildernesses.

Another aspect of the exploration is the amount of income tax that would be generated and the American companies would be paid the $372,646 billion instead of sending it to the foreign countries. If the production companies return a 15% net operating profit that they have to pay income tax on it will generate $19.565 billion. The production companies could pay to their employees 20% of the revenue to cover expenses which would generate $74.529 billion that would go directly into the economy. The social security and Medicare tax deductions along would generate an additional $11.179 billion in tax revenue for the government. We are not even taking into consideration the capital expenditures and the benefits to the local economies. This part of the equation will generate a total of $30.744 billion in revenue to the federal government.

Fuel taxes in the United States vary by state. For the first quarter of 2009, the mean state gasoline tax is 27.2 cents per US gallon, plus 18.4 cents per US gallon federal tax making the total 45.6 cents per US gallon. For diesel, the mean state tax is 26.6 cents per US gallon plus an additional 24.4 cents per US gallon federal tax making the total 50.8 cents US per gallon. There are also a few states that charge sales tax on top of the excise taxes and the retail price.

The Presidents proposed federal budget for 2011 shows the following items as receipts for the federal government.

I know that the figures do not add up. The correct total should be $2,565 billion from the numbers that they included in the budget. Maybe this is some kind of new math. Oh well, what's a couple of billion? Page 151 of the federal budget.

Receipts:	Amount in billions:
Individual Income Taxes	$1,121
Corporate Income Taxes	297
Social Security Payroll Taxes	674
Medicare Payroll Taxes	192
Unemployment Insurance	60
Other Retirement	8
Excise Taxes	74
Estate and Gift Taxes	25
Customs Duties	27
Earnings Federal Reserve System	79
Allowance for Jobs Incentives	(25)
Allowance for Health Reform	16
Other Miscellaneous Receipts	17
Total Receipts	$2,567

Since the tax receipts from petroleum products do not show up in the federal budget it makes one wonder just where they show up and who is accounting for them? When we consider that the United States uses 4,271,110,000 barrels of crude oil per year. Each barrel produces 42 gallons of gasoline. That would be 179,386,620,000 gallons of gasoline. The federal government is charging the consumers of the gasoline 18.4 cents per gallon. The revenue could be in the range of $3.3 trillion. I would like to know where these funds are accounted for and who is making the decisions on how this money is allocated? This is almost as much as the entire federal budget. Something smells a little fishy here.

In the United States, the fuel tax receipts are often dedicated or hypothecated to transportation projects so that the fuel tax is considered by many a user fee. In other countries, the fuel tax is a source of general revenue. If these are user fees they should be for the improvement of our roads, bridges and other federal projects that are for the transportation sector of our economy. Then I must ask why did the government $787 billion stimulus need to be primarily for road, rail and airport improvements?

I believe that with Sarah Palin's stance of exploring for the natural resources in the ANWR and other regions that she would be a much better President. Palin's stance on energy is what the country needs to stop the flow of capital from the United States and improve the employment picture by creating energy jobs.

CHAPTER TWENTY FIVE

Respect for America

I want to start this chapter by letting the American people know that there are places in the world that still say thank you for the freedoms they enjoy due to the valor of our American troops. There is a memorial that is a thank you to our troops and has been worshiped every year for 65 years in the town of Pilsen, Czech Republic. America should honor our troops the same way with total respect and gratitude.

A True American Hero

This is what a true American hero is all about. Colonel "Bud" Day served 30 months in the South Pacific during WWII as an enlisted member with the United States Marine Corps. He served as an Army reservist, and Army guardsman between WWII and Korea, and then in the Air Force during the Vietnam War (3 different services over a span of 3 different wars.) After being shot down on August 26, 1967, and serving 7 years in captivity, Colonel Day was repatriated in 1973. Colonel Day is the only man to earn both the Medal of Honor and the Air Force Cross. Colonel Day is the recipient of virtually every other available combat decoration. Colonel Day is widely considered the most decorated Airman in history.

I have included the text of this Medal of Honor winner so that the American people can see exactly what torture is all about. Not what our wimpy President and his lemmings are all about.

"Bud" Day, Medal Of Honor Recipient George Everett "Bud" Day (born February 24, 1925) is a retired U.S. Air Force Colonel and Command Pilot who served during the Vietnam War. He is often cited as being the most decorated U.S. Service member since General Douglas MacArthur having received some seventy decorations, a majority for actions in combat. Day is a recipient of the Medal of Honor. These are his comments.

I got shot down over North Vietnam in 1967, a Squadron Commander. After I returned in 1973 I published 2 books that dealt a lot with "real torture" in Hanoi. Our make believe president is branding our country as a bunch of torturers when he has no idea what torture is.

As for me, I was put thru a mock execution because I would not respond. Pistol whipped on the head....same event.

Couple of days later... Hung by my feet all day I escaped and a couple of weeks later, I got shot and recaptured. Shot was OK...what happened afterwards was not.

They marched me to Vinh...put me in the rope trick, trick...almost pulled my arms out of the sockets. Beat me on the head with a little wooden rod until my eyes were swelled shut, and my unshot, unbroken hand a pulp.

Next day hung me by the arms...re-broke my right wrist...wiped out the nerves in my arms that control the hands....rolled my fingers up into a ball. Only left the slightest movement of my Left forefinger. So I started answering with some incredible lies.

Sent me to Hanoi strapped to a barrel of gas in the back of a truck. Hanoi ..on my knees....rope trick again. Beaten by a big fool. Into leg irons on a bed in Heartbreak Hotel.

Much kneeling hands up at Zoo. Really bad beating for refusing to condemn Lyndon Johnson. Several more kneeling events. I could see my knee bone thru Kneeling holes.

There was an escape from the annex to the Zoo. I was the Senior Officer of a large building... Because of escape...they started a mass Torture of all commanders.

I think it was July 7, 1969...they started beating me with a car fan belt. In the first 2 days I took over 300 strokes...then stopped counting because I never thought I would live thru it. They continued day-night torture to get me to confess to a non-existent part in the escape. This went on for at least 3 days. On my knees... Fan belting...cut open my scrotum with fan belt stroke. Opened up Both knee holes again. My fanny looked like hamburger. I could not lie on my back.

They tortured me into admitting that I was in on the escape...and that my 2 room-mates knew about it. The next day I denied the lie.

They commenced torturing me again with 3- 6- or 9 strokes of the fan belt every day from about July 11 or 12th to 14 October 1969. I continued to refuse to lie about my roommates again.

Now, the point of this is that our make-believe President has declared to the world that we (U.S.) are a bunch of Torturers...Thus it will be OK to torture us next time when they catch us...because that is what the U.S. Does.

Our make-believe president is a know nothing fool who thinks that pouring a little water on some one's face, or hanging a pair of women's pants over an Arabs head is TORTURE.. He is a meathead.

I just talked to MOH holder Leo Thorsness, who was also in my squadron, In jail...as was John McCain...and we agree that McCain does not speak for the POW group when he claims that Al Gharib was Torture...or that "water boarding" is torture.

Our president and those fools around him who keep bad mouthing our great country are a disgrace to the United States. Please pass this info on to

Sean Hannity. He is free to use it to point out the stupidity of the claims that water boarding...which has no after effect...is torture. If it got the Arab to cough up the story about how he planned the attack on the twin towers in NYC ... hurrah for the guy who poured the water.

God bless this truly great American. Wish we had a President that we could be equally as proud of. Oh I forgot that he has absolutely no inkling about any part of the United States military and what they are all about. What a damn shame. No wonder the foreign nations do not have any respect for the current government in Washington.

President Obama should take lessons on the behavior of a President from Sebastian Pinera the President of Chile. We endured the worst oil spill in the history of the world and we didn't see our President at the site. I watched most of the recovery from the San Jose Mile in Chile which lasted over 22 hours. All through the rescue the President of Chile and the First Lady of Chile were there to hug and congratulate each and every miner as they came out of the rescue capsule. Do you think our President would have stood through that amount of time and thank an American as they were saved?" I do not believe we will ever witness such a touching site from Obama.

Then we have a President trying to ban a song from being played on radio stations across America. The song "Here in America" contains the following words at the ending "In God We Still Trust".

The song has been performed at the Diamond Rio concerts in Las Vegas, Nevada and has received a standing ovation every time is has been performed. The major radio stations have refused to play the song because it was considered "politically incorrect".

President Obama is saying that it is not fit for release because it offends so many. Where does this idiot think he has the right to censor any song? What ever happened to the freedom of speech in America? The song was never released to the public and it should be. It will become one of the highest played song along with "America the Beautiful".

Reports are that the Congress is going to get involved and there should be a release date of the song in the future. The American people need to contact their representatives and stop the abuse of power that the President is exercising. He must be reminded that he is supposed to be for the people of the United States and was not elected to support his Muslim friends and our enemies.

When Urzua the last miner to be rescued stepped out of the capsule, he hugged Chilean President Sebastian Pinera and the First Lady and shook hands with him and said they had prevailed over difficult circumstances. With the last miner by his side, the president led the crowd in singing their national anthem.

One by one throughout the day, the men had emerged to the cheers of exuberant Chileans and before the eyes of a transfixed globe. The operation picked up speed as the day went on, but each miner was greeted with the same boisterous applause from rescuers and the President of Chile.

I have no idea who wrote this article but it is the thought that counts and hopefully it will touch you in the heart. Think about this the next time you see one of our service members and say thank you. Every American should stand at attention and salute the military personnel when you see them on the street.

I was sitting alone in one of those loud, casual steak houses that you find all over the country. You know the type--a bucket of peanuts on every table, shells littering the floor, and a bunch of perky college kids racing around with long neck beers and sizzling platters.

Taking a sip of my iced tea, I studied the crowd over the rim of my glass. My gaze lingered on a group enjoying their meal. They wore no uniform to identify their branch of service, but they were definitely "military:" clean shaven, cropped haircut, and that "squared away" look that comes with pride.

Smiling sadly, I glanced across my table to the empty seat where my husband usually sat. It had only been a few months since we sat in this very booth, talking about his upcoming deployment to the Middle East. That was when he made me promise to get a sitter for the kids, come back to this restaurant once a month and treat myself to a nice steak. In turn he would treasure the thought of me being here, thinking about him until he returned home.

I fingered the little flag pin I constantly wear and wondered where he was at this very moment. Was he safe and warm? Was his cold any better? Were my letters getting through to him?

As I pondered these thoughts, high pitched female voices from the next booth broke into my thoughts. "I don't know what Bush is thinking about. Invading Iraq! You'd think that man would learn from his old man's mistakes. Good grief. What an idiot! I can't believe he is even in office. You do know that he stole the election?"

I cut into my steak and tried to ignore them as they began an endless tirade running down our President.

I thought about the last night I spent with my husband, as he prepared to deploy. He had just returned from getting his smallpox and anthrax shots. The image of him standing in our kitchen packing his gas mask still gives me chills.

Once again the women's voices invaded my thoughts.

"It's all about oil, you know. Our soldiers will go in and rape and steal all the oil they can in the name of 'freedom'. Hmmm! I wonder how many innocent people they'll kill without giving it a thought. It's pure greed, you know."

My chest tightened as I stared at my wedding ring. I could still see how handsome my husband looked in his "mess dress" the day he slipped it on my finger I wondered what he was wearing now. Probably his desert uniform, affectionately dubbed "coffee stains" with a heavy bulletproof vest over it.

"You know, we should just leave Iraq alone. I don't think they are hiding any weapons. In fact, I bet it's all a big act just to increase the president's popularity. That's all it is, padding the military budget at the expense of our social security and education and, you know what else? We're just asking for another 9-11. I can't say when it happens again that we didn't deserve it."

Their words brought to mind the war protesters I had watched gathering outside our base. Did no one even appreciate the sacrifice of brave men and women, who leave their homes and family to ensure our freedom? Do they even know what "freedom" is?

I glanced at the table where the young men were sitting, and saw their courageous faces change. They had stopped eating and looked at each other dejectedly, listening to the women talking.

"Well, I, for one, think it's just deplorable to invade Iraq, and I am certainly sick of our tax dollars going to train professional baby-killers we call a military."

Professional baby-killers! I thought about what a wonderful father my husband is, and of how long it would be before he would see our children again.

That's it! Indignation rose up inside me. Normally reserved, pride in my husband gave me a brassy boldness I never realized I had. Tonight one voice will answer on behalf of our military, and let her pride in our troops be known. Sliding out of my booth, I walked around to the adjoining booth and placed my hands flat on their table.

Lowering myself to eye level with them and smiling I said, "I couldn't help overhearing your conversation. You see, I'm sitting here trying to enjoy my dinner alone. And, do you know why? Because my husband, who I love with all my heart, is halfway around the world defending your right to say rotten things about him."

"Yes, you have the right to your opinion, and what you think is none of my business. However, what you say in public is something else, and I will not sit by and listen to you ridicule MY country, MY president, MY husband, and all the other fine American men and women who put their lives on the line, just so you can have the "freedom" to complain. Freedom is an expensive commodity, ladies. Don't let your actions cheapen it."

I must have been louder than I meant to be, because the manager came over to inquire if everything was all right "Yes, thank you," I replied.

Then, turning back to the women, I said, "Enjoy the rest of your meal."

As I returned to my booth applause broke out. I was embarrassed for making a scene, and went back to my half eaten steak. The women picked up their check and scurried away.

After finishing my meal, and while waiting for my check, the manager returned with a huge apple cobbler ala mode. "Compliments of those soldiers," he said. He also smiled and said the ladies tried to pay for my dinner, but that another couple had beaten them to it.

When I asked who, the manager said they had already left, but that the gentleman was a veteran, and wanted to take care of the wife of "one of our boys."

With a lump in my throat, I gratefully turned to the soldiers and thanked them for the cobbler. Grinning from ear to ear, they came over and surrounded the booth.

As I drove home, for the first time since my husband's deployment, I didn't feel quite so alone. My heart was filled with the warmth of the other diners who stopped by my table, to relate how they, too, were proud of my husband, and would keep him in their prayers.

As for me, I have learned that one voice CAN make a difference.

Maybe the next time protesters gather outside the gates of the base where I live, I will proudly stand on the opposite side with a sign of my own. It will simply say, "Thank You!"

To those who fought for our nation, freedom has a flavor the protected will never know.

GOD BLESS AMERICA!

The government needs to rebuild the respect for America that has greatly deteriorated over the past several years. We have to stop bowing down to our enemies and return to supporting our allies. We have to regain our status of the greatest country in the world. Nothing else is good enough. The American people do not want our beautiful country to turn into a third would nation.

11 countries seek voice in Arizona immigration appeal

This should make every American extremely disgusted with our current administration. We need to make sure that all of the countries that are trying to interfere with the Constitution of the United States know where they can take their opinions.

The Associated Press printed the following information for the Americans to see. Mexico and 10 other Latin American countries want a federal appeals court to consider their viewpoints in Arizona Gov. Jan Brewer's appeal of a ruling that put parts of her state's new immigration law on hold.

The countries are asking the 9th U.S. Circuit Court of Appeals for permission to file so-called friend-of-the-court briefs in Brewer's appeal of the ruling, which arose from a lawsuit by the U.S. Justice Department.

The 11 countries say they have an interest in ensuring they have reliable relations with the United States that aren't frustrated by Arizona. Mexico is joined in the request by Argentina, Bolivia, Brazil, Chile, Costa Rica, Ecuador, El Salvador, Nicaragua, Paraguay and Peru.

Supporters of the law say it's intended to confront the state's vast illegal immigration woes that Washington is confronting adequately. The President is causing this kind of unrest in the world by his policies to sue the state of Arizona for doing the job the federal government is required to do by the law of the land.

There will not be any respect for the United States when our President does not provide the leadership required to enforce our Constitution.

Recent articles and speeches are indicating that some of the world actually hates America. That is alright because we can not expect everyone to accept our beliefs and culture. It is not alright to have world leaders from other countries get in front of the United Nations and insinuate that the American government actually plotted the 911 attacks. That kind of behavior is absurd. There used to be respect for our country.

This is information from an article that was printed by the Associated Press in early October 2010. Never in the history of the United States has there been such blatant disrespect for the United States and its President.

Iran's president called for the United States leaders to be "buried" in response to what he says are American threats of military attack against Tehran's nuclear program. Mahmoud Ahmadinejad is known for brash rhetoric in addressing the West, but in his speech he went a step further using a deeply offensive insult in response to United States statements that the military option against Iran is still on the table.

"May the undertaker bury you, your table and your body, which has soiled the world," he said using language in Iran reserved for hated enemies.

Several top U.S. officials including Adm. Mike Mullen, chairman of the U.S. Joint Chiefs of Staff have said in recent months that the military option remains on the table and there is a plan to attack Iran, although a military strike has been described as a bad idea.

The crowd of military men and clerics in the town of Hashtgerd just west of the capital chuckled at the president's insult and applauded.

The speech was broadcast by both state television and the official English-language Press TV, but the latter glossed over the insult in the simultaneous translation.

Ahmadinejad's remarks come in sharp contrast to ones he made to Al-Jazeera Arabic news channel in August in which he offered the U.S. Iran's friendship.

In his speech, Ahmadinejad also questioned once more who was behind the September 11 attacks in the U.S. and said they gave Washington a pretext for seeking to dominate the region and plunder its oil wealth.

During his speech in front of the United Nations General Assembly in New York, he said a majority of people in the U.S. and around the world believe the American government staged the attacks, drawing a strong rebuke from President Obama.

Ahmadinejad often resorts to provocative statements to lash out enemies. He has already compared the power of Iran's enemies to a "mosquito," saying Iran deals with the West over its nuclear activities from a position of power and he has likened the United States to a "farm animal trapped in a quagmire" in Afghanistan.

Iran also condemned the latest U.S. sanctions slapped on eight Iranian officials Wednesday, saying they show American interference in Tehran's domestic affairs.

Washington this week imposed travel and financial sanctions on the eight Iranians, accusing them of taking part in human rights abuses during the turmoil following Iran's June 2009 presidential election.

One of the major problems that the United States is facing with regard to gaining the respect of the other nations of the world starts here with our President. Let's take a look at some of the things that are destroying our respectability around the world and quite frankly embarrassing the United States. Some of these actions are actually disgusting as well as disrespectful of America and our troops abroad.

There are photos of President Obama with the President of Afghanistan and he has his hands in his pockets. In the Muslim world hands in your pockets is a sign of weakness. This is humiliating, emasculating, embarrassing to our country and a disgrace to the sacrifice of our brave and heroic military personnel.

We should have known that there would be a grave amount of disrespect when the President's backers were in total violation of the laws by desecrating the American Flag during his campaigns. How does this President expect to gain the respect of the American public and the rest of the world? Copies of these photos can be provided upon request.

<u>US Code, Title 4, Chapter 1, Section 8, "Respect for the flag"</u>: The code is provided below.

No disrespect should be shown to the flag of the United States of America; the flag should not be dipped to any person or thing. Regimental colors, State flags, and organization or institutional flags are to be dipped as a mark of honor.

(a) The flag should never be displayed with the union down, except as a signal of dire distress in instances of extreme danger to life or property.

(b) The flag should never touch anything beneath it, such as the ground, the floor, water, or merchandise.

(c) The flag should never be carried flat or horizontally, but always aloft and free.

(d) The flag should never be used as wearing apparel, bedding, or drapery. It should never be festooned, drawn back, nor did up, in folds, but always allow falling free. Bunting of blue, white, and red, always arranged with the blue above, the white in the middle, and the red below, should be used for covering a speaker's desk, draping the front of the platform, and for decoration in general.

(e) The flag should never be fastened, displayed, used, or stored in such a manner as to permit it to be easily torn, soiled, or damaged in any way.

(f) The flag should never be used as a covering for a ceiling.

(g) The flag should never have placed upon it, nor on any part of it, nor attached to it any mark, insignia, letter, word, figure, design, picture, or drawing of any nature.

(h) The flag should never be used as a receptacle for receiving, holding, carrying, or delivering anything.

(i) The flag should never be used for advertising purposes in any manner whatsoever. It should not be embroidered on such articles as cushions or handkerchiefs and the like, printed or otherwise impressed on paper napkins or boxes or anything that is designed for temporary use and discard. Advertising signs should not be fastened to a staff or halyard from which the flag is flown.

(j) No part of the flag should ever be used as a costume or athletic uniform. However, a flag patch may be affixed to the uniform of military personnel, firemen, policemen, and members of patriotic organizations. The flag represents a living country and is itself considered a living thing. Therefore, the lapel flag pin being a replica should be worn on the left lapel near the heart.

(k) The flag, when it is in such condition that it is no longer a fitting emblem for display, should be destroyed in a dignified way, preferably by burning.

In one of the Presidents recent speeches while using his teleprompter he used the term Corpsemen. We truly hope that he was not wishing our men and women in the uniform of the United States to become corpses. This is just another of the disgraceful statements that have been made by our President. Sometimes we wonder about his rhetoric.

During the 2008 campaign Obama stood without holding his right hand over his heart in a sign of saluting our flag and the people elected this disrespectful man president.

There are photos of the President taken during the playing of our beautiful song, "The Star Spangled Banner." From the time we were small children we were taught to respect the flag and the United States. We need to put respect and God back into the educational systems of America. There was never any intent by our founding fathers to remove God from our country. Take a look at any dollar bill in your wallet and you will see "In God We Trust". Is it any wonder that there seems to be a lack of respect among some of the citizens of the United States when the President doesn't display respect?

In other photos President Obama was once again using the troops to burnish his image and he couldn't even muster up the respect to give them a proper military salute. The President is supposed to salute troops when addressing them as the Commander in Chief. He prefers to ignore this military custom of respect for our courageous troops.

Respect for the office of President of the Unites States? Yes.

Respect the Man in the Office? No, I am sorry to say.

I have noted that many elected officials, both Democrats and Republicans, called upon America to unite behind Obama.

Well, I want to make it clear to all who will listen that I am not uniting behind President Obama.

I will respect the Office which he holds, and I will acknowledge his abilities as an orator and wordsmith and pray for him, but that is it. I have begun today to see what I can do to make sure that he is a one-term President.

I am doing this because I do not share the majority of his beliefs. I do not agree with Obama on his abortion beliefs. I do not share Obama's vision or value system for America. I do not share his radial Marxist's concept of distributing from the wealthy and giving to the poor. I believe every individual should earn his keep and contribute to the society they live in. I do not share his beliefs that we should raise the taxes on some Americans just because they were successful. I do not think that America is arrogant. I believe that America is a Christian nation under God. I do not want to reduce the size of our military. They have protected our great nation for over 200 years. Instead we should salute any member of the military every time we meet one. I certainly do not agree that amnesty should be given to any illegal. Each and every illegal in the United States needs to be deported and not given any type of amnesty.

I do not believe that radical Islam is our friend and that Israel is our enemy who should give up any land under any circumstances. I did not like the way Obama crammed the healthcare program down the throats of the citizens without any concern for what they wanted. I definitely do not share the President's plan to sit down with Iran or any other terrorist regime. We have enough terrorists coming across the southern borders of the United States because Obama will not do anything to secure them.

The Democrats have not moved toward the center in their beliefs and their philosophies, and they never came together nor compromised their personal beliefs for the betterment of our Country. They have portrayed my America as a land where everything is tolerated except being intolerant.

I am sure many of you who read this think that I am going overboard, but I refuse to retreat one more inch in favor of those whom I believe are the embodiment of Evil. President Bush made many mistakes during his Presidency, and I am not sure how history will judge him. However, I believe that he weighed his decisions in light of the long established Christian principles of our Founding Fathers.

Majority rules in America. I will honor the concept; however, I will fight with all of my power to be a voice in opposition to Obama and his goals for America. I am going to be a thorn in the side of those who, if left unchecked, will destroy our Country. Any more compromise is more defeat. I pray that the results of this election will wake up many who have sat on the sidelines and allowed the crowd to slowly change so much of what has been good in America. God bless you and God bless our Country.

Why is Obama, the Illinois Democrat, the worst president in history, far surpassing the previous record holder -- Jimmy Carter, the Georgia Democrat? Unfortunately, history does seem to repeat itself. The people elected Jimmy Carter who did not have any experience in government and then repeated the process by electing Barrack Obama who did not have any business or government experience. For the record, being a community organizer does not count as business experience. Don't you think it is about time that the American people try to elect people that have some experience and are qualified?

Obama likes to blame the Republicans for everything. The Democrats had the majority for over two years and they still did nothing. All they were worried about was pushing through Obamacare that the majority of the American people did not want. The reason he is making appointments during a recess is because they would not pass through otherwise.

They are probably more Czars and even the public is sick of them. Something needs to be done before this President destroys America. Has any thought been given to the fact that he snubbed Israel because his true Muslim attitude is starting to show? He bows to Muslims kings but treats the Prime Minister from Israel like scum. Israel has been America's friends for decades. He demands that Israel stop building homes for their people but lets Iran keep building nukes. I believe he has his priorities backwards. In November, the American people voted to replace some of these corrupt politicians. We need to demand that President Obama show his birth certificate and his college records. All other Presidents have had too. Why is he getting shown special treatment? After all, The President is working for the American People, or is he?

The reasons that I believe Mr. Obama is going to be the worst President that has ever held the office in the United States are:

Obama promised to close Gitmo, it is still in operation.

He has treated terrorists as petty criminals. He hasn't tried them in military tribunals for their war crimes. Obama is inexperienced.

Obama policies have tripled the American debt creating obligations that will be taxing children who aren't yet born (remember no taxation without representation? – maybe politicians should not be able to place debt on future generations). Obama is incompetent.

The President from Illinois has supported programs that have lost 2 million jobs, permanently, according to Joe Biden, the Delaware Democratic Vice President. "It's the economy stupid." President Obama is a clueless concerning unemployment.

Obama promised an open and transparent debate on his policies. A great example is the Obamacare program, but delivered gangster-style, heavy-handed Chicago politics instead. There was not any transparency.

The President has bungled the economy.

Obama talked down America in foreign speeches. Obama is incompetent and reacts to foreign policies before the American peoples desires.

He promised an open and transparent administration. Instead we have back door Chicago politics.

Obama has failed to create jobs. Obama is incapable of supporting business programs to develop more jobs.

The President from Illinois gave a $1 trillion bailout to big business and banks, those who contributed the most to his election.

He has failed to hold unemployment to 8%, as promised: "It's the economy stupid." Obama is incompetent.

The President has bowed to every dictator he met. Obama is inexperienced.

Obama botched the management of the worst environmental disaster in history. Watch, he will take credit for capping the well.

He met in closed session with BP to get $20B. Maybe he could have gotten $100B if the meeting was in the open. Who was paid off?

Obama treats the American people with contempt. Obama does not listen to the will of the people he should have sworn to protect.

Obama has spent more time on vacationing and playing golf wasting his administration away during the oil spill and Christmas bombing attempt in Detroit. Obama is incompetent.

KKK leader Senator Byrd gets a state funeral that Obama attended. Obama honored and eulogized Byrd. Too bad Stalin, Mao Zedong, and Hitler didn't die on his watch Obama would have loved those three.

Obama is an embarrassment to America

President Obama has proven by his actions that he is failing in providing the leadership that America needs and wants. The President has had time to show improvement and it is time for a change. Sarah Palin will not make the mistakes that Obama has made in his two years in office.

With a lot of support and hard work we can make this the home of
Sarah Palin for several years.

CHAPTER TWENTY SIX

The Right to Bear Arms

Constitution of the United States.

We, the people of the United States, in order to form a more perfect union, establish justice, insure domestic tranquility, provide for the common defense, promote the general welfare, and secure the blessings of liberty to ourselves and our posterity, do ordain and establish this Constitution for the United States of America.

The document embodying the fundamental principles upon which the American republic is conducted. Drawn up at the Constitutional Convention in Philadelphia in 1787, the Constitution was signed on Sept. 17, 1787, and ratified by the required number of states (nine) by June 21, 1788. It superseded the original charter of the United States in force since 1781 (see Confederation, Articles of) and established the system of federal government that began to function in 1789. The Constitution is concise, and its very brevity and its general statement of principles have, by accident more than by design, made possible the extension of meaning that has fostered growth. There are seven articles and a preamble; 27 amendments have been adopted. The wording of the Constitution is general, necessitating interpretation, and any short summary is only rough and approximate. From its very beginnings, the Constitution has been subject to stormy controversies, not only in interpretation of some of its phrases, but also between the loose constructionists and strict constructionists. The middle of the 19th century saw a tremendous struggle concerning the nature of the Union and the extent of states' rights. The Civil War decided the case in favor of the advocates of strong union, and since that time the general tendency has been toward the centralization and strengthening of federal power.

The Preamble

The Preamble does not confer power, but its first words, We the People of the United States, describe the source of the powers conferred by the rest of the Constitution and have been used by the advocates of a strong union arguing against the proponents of states' rights. The Preamble also states the purpose of the document. One of the statements of purpose, to … promote the general welfare, has been of great importance in the 20th century in upholding social legislation, for which no warrant could be found in the enumerated powers of Congress.

The right to keep and bear arms—adopted with reference to state militias but interpreted (2008) by the Supreme Court as essentially an individual right—is guaranteed by the Second Amendment, while freedom from quartering soldiers in a house without the owner's consent is guaranteed by the Third Amendment. The Fourth Amendment protects people against unreasonable search and seizure, a safeguard only more recently extended to the states.

Cities like Chicago, Illinois have passed local laws that prevent their citizens from bearing arms. This is the worst kind of abuse to the constitution of the United States. Every citizen should revolt and purchase arms to protect themselves against any possible act against the United States. This is Illinois back door policies at work.

CHAPTER TWENTY SEVEN

Transparency Policies

The leaders of the Democratic Party promised that there would be transparency in the operation of the federal government. Now that Obama has been elected it would be difficult to see where any transparency has been by Reid, Pelosi, Holder or any of the other leaders has been.

This is a good example of the lack of transparency in the federal government. The attempt to repeal the "Don't Ask Don't Tell" legislation that was enacted in 1993 was shot down this month. Then a few days later a federal judge in San Diego is going to decide if she is willing to halt the military's ban on openly gay troops. Since the administration could not get the bill repealed through Congress they have asked the Department of Justice attorney's to prepare a legal filing for a federal court in Riverside, California. This follows government procedure by defending an act of Congress that is being challenged, but it does not detract from the President's efforts to get 'Don't Ask, Don't Tell' repealed. "This filing in no way diminishes the President's firm commitment to achieve a legislative repeal of "Don't Ask, Don't Tell' indeed, it clearly shows why Congress must act to end this misguided policy," White House Press Secretary Robert Gibbs said in a statement e-mailed to The Associated Press.

It is very sad and disappointing that the government would take this type of action just days after the bill was defeated in Congress. Part of the reason for the defeat was the attachments that were made by the Democrats.

Military laws prevent certain items from being brought in or mailed to Muslim nations because it is either against their law, the Koran, or their moral standards. If the gays/lesbians are allowed to openly serve in the military the next un-constitutional right they'll demand is that they shouldn't be ordered to serve in a Muslim nation. After all, homosexuality is a crime punishable by death. And believe it they will be will be exempt from serving in those countries. Obama and his liberal judges will soon decide that gays/lesbians are exempt from combat or police duties in the Middle East. Our children can be put at risk while Obama wants to protect his minority of perverts. It only indicates how fearful he is about the elections in 2012. The gays make up less than 3% of our population. The president needs any vote he can get at this time.

What I would like to see is that only active duty service members would be allowed to decide the fate of "Don't Ask Don't Tell" instead of the members of Congress, judges, and civilians. Have the military take a secret ballot and send the results to Congress and then let them vote according to the wishes of the members serving in the military. They should be the ones to decide since they have to live and fight together for our country. Get the politics out of the process. Every member of all the military services should be required to vote.

The Obama administration invoked the state secrets privilege which would kill a lawsuit on behalf of United States born cleric Anwar al-Awlaki, an alleged terrorist said to be targeted for death or capture under a United States government program.

In a court filing, the Justice Department said that the issues in the case are for the executive branch of government to decide rather than the courts.

The department also said the case entails information that is protected by the military and state secrets privilege.

The courts have sufficient grounds to throw out the lawsuit without resorting to use of the state secrets privilege, the Justice Department said in its filing.

"The idea that courts should have no role whatsoever in determining the criteria by which the executive branch can kill its own citizens is unacceptable in a democracy," "the American Civil Liberties Union and the Center for Constitutional Rights said in a statement. "In matters of life and death, no executive should have a blank check."

It appears that the President is not concerned with anything except trying to dictate what can be done in the United States. These types of policies just have to stop.

E-mails link him to the Army psychiatrist accused of the killings at Fort Hood, Texas, last year. Al-Awlaki has taken on an increasingly operational role in al-Qaida in the Arabian Peninsula, the Justice Department filing said, including preparing Umar Farouk Abdulmutallab in his attempt to detonate an explosive device aboard a Northwest Airlines flight from Amsterdam to Detroit on Christmas Day 2009.

One tends to wonder just what the motivation of our President is that would remove this case form the court system.

The lawsuit filed on the cleric's behalf seeks to have a court declare that the Constitution and international law bar the government from carrying out targeted killings; seeks to block the targeted killing of al-Awlaki; and seeks to force the United States government to disclose the standards for determining whether United States citizens can be targeted for death.

What al-Awlaki's father is seeking would be "unprecedented, improper, and extraordinarily dangerous," said the Justice Department filing, which neither confirmed nor denied the existence of a targeted killings program.

The lawsuit would necessarily and improperly inject the courts into decisions of the President and his advisers about how to protect the American people from the threat of armed attacks, including imminent threats, posed by a foreign organization against which the political branches have authorized the use of necessary and appropriate force, said the Justice Department filing.

When the President was campaigning to be elected he promised that there would be total transparency in his legislation. There was to be open discussions and debate about the policies that were presented for passage. We are still looking for that to happen after 26 months. A prime example of this is the healthcare package that was passed in spite of opposition by the Republicans and the public. This bill was crammed down the throats of the people of the United States.

We actually have a civil war going on in this country between the liberal extremists, led by Obama and his cohorts and staffed with foot soldiers from the public service unions, against the rest of Americans. These people want more and more tax money that they can distribute to their friends who keep them in power, they want bigger government and government control so that they can stay in power, they want to control private companies

One percent transaction tax is proposed by President Obama's finance team is recommending a transaction tax. His plan is to sneak it in after the November election to keep it under the radar. This is a 1% tax on all transactions at any financial institution including the banks, credit unions, etc. Any deposit you make, or move around within your account will have a 1% tax charged. If your pay check or your social security or whatever is direct deposit this 1% tax will be charged. If you hand carry a check in to deposit, 1% tax charged, if you take cash in to deposit, and 1% tax charged. This is from the man who promised that if you make under $250,000 per year, you will not see one penny of new tax. Keep your eyes and ears open, you will be amazed at what you learn. The bill would tax 58 million seniors more than the annual amount of money that they were hoping to receive in their annual increases in social security.

Some will say aw it's just 1%... remember once the tax is there they can raise it at will.

Pelosi: Transaction Tax Has "Great Deal of Merit"

A proposed tax on financial transactions "has a great deal of merit" and would help Congress raise needed revenue, U.S. House of Representatives Speaker Nancy Pelosi said.

"I believe that the transaction tax still has a great deal of merit," Pelosi said at a news conference.

The tax would have a "really minimal impact on the transaction, but a tremendous impact on helping us meet our needs," Pelosi said.

Now that you have seen what the Pelosi has said about this tax why don't we look at the bill that the Democrats are trying to shove down our throats?

The bill is HR-4646 introduced by US Rep Peter DeFazio D-Oregon and US Senator Tom Harkin D-Iowa. It is now in committee and will probably not be brought out until after the November elections. Suggest that you pass this along to everyone you know and also to your state senator and representative and United States Congressman and Senators.

H.R. 4646

The bill proposed a One percent transaction tax. You can go to into THOMAS (Library of Congress and print out and read the entire bill. It contains 15 pages. The bill has been given the short title of "Debt Free America Act." It is the most socialistic bill that could ever been proposed. It needs to be stopped.

Just think if you deposit $5,000.00 into your checking account or savings account the bank has to take out 1% or $50.00 of that money and send it to Washington. Then, any checks or cash you take out of your bank they will deduct 1% from what is still in the bank and send it to Washington. Total put in the Bank $5,000.00. $100.00 of that you give to Washington. Isn't this triple + Taxation?

This bill, spells it out that everyone will pay the Government 1% of their gross income.

Page 9 states the House and Senate shall convene not later than November 23, 2010 and Page 11 states the vote on passage shall occur not later than December 23, 2010.

I believe that Palin would not try and cram such a piece of legislation down the throats of the American citizens. This is an outrageous tax increase that targets the lower income Americans. We need to make sure that it does not get passed into law. Wake up America.

CHAPTER TWENTY EIGHT

Smaller Government

The United States needs to reduce the size of the federal government. We can accomplish this by eliminating many of the departments that have very little or no useful purpose in our current society. These departments have become drags on the economy and have out lived the purpose that they were established for.

When the government implements the policy of reducing every government employee's salary by 25% there will be enough attrition from the unhappy employees that will reduce the number of employees and payroll at the same time.

Fannie Mae and Freddie Mac should be forced out of the mortgage guarantee program and let the lending institutes be responsible for making loans on the merits of the home buyers credit rating, earnings record, proper down payment and availability of emergency funds. As hard as it is there is just not any reason to believe that every American should be able to own a home. The practice of lending to unqualified buyers has been the major contributing factor to the mortgage crises. The government does not know how to run any business not alone guaranteeing mortgages that they have no idea who are the homeowners.

The federal government could eliminate 20% of the employees on the payroll and the efficiency of the government would probably improve. The remaining workers would understand that they must produce at certain levels or they will be the next ones that are given pink slips. There should not be any unions involved with the government employees. The unions are not interested in the welfare and interests of the American citizens.

The government needs to eliminate the Department of Education and return all educational policies back to the state and local level. The government does not have any idea about running a school system. Each local school district has its own set of problems and can't be solved by a blanket directive from the federal government. This would eliminate a huge bureaucratic department and the schools would be able to educate in the proper manner. The states should make it a requirement that there will be no child held back instead of no child left behind. If the student can't keep up they should be held back a year. The states should all pass legislation that the only language in the school systems will be English. If a student does not know how to speak and write English they need to be put into a special English class until they can perform up to the level of the Americans in the school. This will not set well with most of the teachers but the unions should be abolished from all educational programs. If the teachers want a raise then produce exceptional results. Another benefit would be that if the teachers do not get a raise they will not be able to strike and the students unable to attend school.

The student loan division of the Department of Education would be transferred to the banking industry. There are way too many student loans that have not been repaid and the government will probably never see these loans paid.

On page 37 of the Presidents proposed budget for the year ending September 30, 2011 he states that the government is laying a new foundation for economic growth and prosperity for working families will take a change in policies and programs to unleash the creativity and hard work of the American people. But to prevent our country from backsliding into the irresponsibility of the past, we need to change how Washington works. We have seen the consequences of fiscal recklessness, of tolerance for programs that no longer work or are outdated, and of a government that is most open to those with access and influence. The deficits, wasted resources, and special treatment squandered funds that could have been used to help Americans gain or retain a foothold in the middle class and enjoy what every family wants: a good job, a roof over their heads, excellent schools for their children, affordable and high-quality health care, and a secure retirement.

Wow! The President must be smoking some really powerful cigarettes. The President's writers are completely out of touch with what has happened to America since Obama became the President. Has anyone noticed anything in this rhetoric that has actually happened? The next paragraph is also from the budget and guess where the blame is going to be placed?

Restoring Fiscal Discipline

When the President took office he faced a deficit of $1.3 trillion for that first fiscal year, a far cry from the budget surpluses predicted at the start of the previous administration. Since the 2010 Budget was released in February of 2009, unfavorable economic conditions and technical re-estimates have worsened the deficit outlook by $2 trillion through 2019—the equivalent of 1 percent of GDP per year—with a deterioration of about $200 billion in 2015 alone. Looking out over the next decade, we are $12 trillion deeper in debt than we were in 2001 because of three specific developments. The national debt is $7.5 trillion larger by the end of this decade because of the failure to pay for two large tax cuts, primarily for the wealthiest Americans, and a new entitlement program. An additional $3 trillion in debt is the result of inheriting the worst recession since the Great Depression. Our response to this recession, the Recovery Act, which has been critical to restoring economic growth, added an additional $1 trillion to the debt— only 10 percent of the total. Now, as we turn the corner from rescuing the economy to rebuilding it, it's time to once again take responsibility for our fiscal future. While it's essential that we do not stifle the momentum of our recovery from the current recession, we also cannot adequately grow the economy and spur job creation in the long term if we allow these deficits to persist. That is why, as the economy recovers, the Administration will take the steps necessary to restore discipline to our Nation's finances to put our country on firm fiscal footing.

The President sure knows how to spread the donkey dung. In what part of the United States has this recovery started? The recovery has started only in the minds of the Democrats and their lemming economists. The American people sure have not seen any real signs of recovery. The rhetoric above does not agree with the numbers that most of the country is seeing. The deficit at the end of the budget year discussed will be more like $13.5 to $14 trillion. The President has instigated policies that have increased the budget more in two years that the rest of the Presidents of the United States combined.

MY AMERICAN DREAM

Newsletter   December 1, 2010

Volume 2010-49   www.my-american-dream.org

What is Happening in Washington?

I have been listening to the Fox news this morning. It appears that the federal employees are outraged over the proposed 2 year salary freeze. They are really going to be upset with my proposal for the federal employees. The Congress should pass legislation that reduces the pay of every federal employee by a minimum of 25%. The only exclusions would be for military, border security, FBI and other agencies that are for the purpose of protecting the United States.

This 25% salary reduction would be effective immediately. Any federal employee that is backed by the union and wants to strike will be fired immediately. Anyone that does not want to take the pay cut will be removed from the federal payroll. When it becomes time to cut bait and fish the losers will leave the federal employment rolls and the true Americans that are concerned about our country will remain and become more effective. I can hear the whining all the way to Colorado.

During all the freezing of the Social Security benefits to 58 million senior citizens these federal employees have enjoyed salary increases. You will probably hear the roar of approval all the way to Washington. That would include all federal employees throughout the United States.

What is upsetting the majority of Americans is the illegal immigration problem and not passing legislation that will deport all of the 20 million that are ruining our country. Declare a state of war against these illegals and ship them back to where they came from. Due to the fact that they are criminals they do not have the right to be protected by our Constitution. Let ACORN and all the other rights groups go to the border and protect the American citizens instead of the illegals.

In all the bickering about the deficit the President and Congress fails to look at one of the major problems facing our great country. Deport the illegals and it will free up close to 10 million jobs for American citizens. Putting these Americans to work will generate billions of dollars in revenue for the United States. In addition, it will eliminate about $50 billion per year in welfare and incarceration costs. Not to mention the estimated $30 - $50 billion that is sent to Mexico from the illegals that are taking our American jobs.

WAKE UP CONGRESS AND DO WHAT IS RIGHT FOR AMERICA.

CHAPTER TWENTY NINE

The Stimulus Programs

It is a slow day in the small Minnesota town of Marshall, and the streets are deserted. Times are tough, everybody is in debt, and everybody is living on credit.

A rich tourist visiting the area drives through town, stops at the motel, lays a $100 bill on the desk and says he wants to inspect the rooms upstairs before selecting one for the night.

1.. As soon as he walks upstairs, the motel owner grabs the bill and runs next door to pay his debt to the butcher.

2. The butcher takes the $100 and runs down the street to retire his debt to the pig farmer.

3. The pig farmer takes the $100 and heads off to pay his bill to his supplier, the Farmer's Co-op.

4. The guy at the Farmer's Co-op takes the $100 and runs to pay his debt to the local prostitute, who has also been facing hard times and has had to offer her "services" on credit.

5. The hooker rushes to the hotel and pays off her room bill with the hotel owner.

6. The hotel proprietor then places the $100 back on the counter so the rich traveler will not suspect anything.

At that moment the traveler comes down the stairs, states that the rooms are not satisfactory, picks up the $100 bill and leaves town.

No one produced anything. No one earned anything. However, the whole town is now out of debt and looks to the future with a lot more optimism.

And that, folks are how Stimulus works.

The snake oil salesman in the White House does not mention that he has increased those in poverty in the last year more than any prior President. You can choose to believe his imaginary numbers about how many jobs that he 'saved', but just ask your neighbor, and ask him if he/she is able to make their house payments. Obama must take us all for fools. The economy is in terrible shape and his solution is to spend the United States into oblivion.

This administration has passed legislation amounting to $2 to $3 trillion of new debt. The United States has only lost another 2.5 million jobs, the unemployment rate increased over 110% from 4.6% on January 3, 2007 until the current rate of 9.8%, which is not the real unemployment rate. Try about 20% if everyone out of work was counted. Barack Obama voted for the 2007-8 spending bills so he should understand what was happening. Well we guess he still thinks the Great Depression looks like it worked out alright.

"We can't give away $700 billion to folks who don't need it" is a comment that is disturbing on many levels. It sounds like the President and the Democrats believe that the American people are working and earning money in order to serve their government, not the other way around. Also, there seems to be an administration belief that all the solutions to our financial problems are going to come from Washington, which is why we should send all our earnings there and let them perform their magic on our behalf. Nobody outside the Democrat party believes this.

As for stabilizing the economy... let's be honest, it was going to stabilize eventually no matter who was President. Home prices weren't going to drop to zero. A guy jumping out of a 20 story window eventually "stabilizes" his fall too. That by itself is not necessarily a positive indicator. Has anyone seen the report on what is in the new Obama healthcare plan? If you haven't it is not surprising, most of the Democrats that voted the bill down our throats have not read the bill or seen it either. You now have to pay a 7% sales tax on property sold and that is in the healthcare bill he passed and you get penalized $364 for each child and $675 for each adult annually for not getting a government approved Health care plan. Like the economy can afford that.

Let's take a few minutes to study the problem and have a brief history lesson:

▶ In 1977, Jimmy Carter (D) signs the Community Reinvestment Act, guaranteeing home loans to low-income families.

▶ In 1999, Bill Clinton (D) puts the CRA on steroids by pushing Fannie Mae & Freddie Mac to increase the number of sub-prime loans.

▶ In September 1999, The New York Times publishes an article "Fannie Mae Eases Credit to Aid Mortgage Lending" which warned of the coming crisis due to lax lending policies of the Clinton (D) administration.

▶ In 2003, The White House calls Fannie and Freddie a 'systemic risk" Bush administration pushes Congress to enact new regulations.

▶ In 2003, Barney Frank (D-CN) says "Freddie Mac and Fannie Mae are not in a crisis" and bashes Republicans for crying wolf and calls F&F "Financially Sound" the Democrats block Republican sponsored regulation legislation.

▶ In 2005, Federal Reserve Chairman Alan Greenspan voices warning over F&F accounting "We are placing the total financial system of the future at a substantial risk".

▶ In 2005: Senator Charles Schumer (D-NY) says "I think F & F over the years have done an incredibly good job and are an intrinsic part of making America the best-housed people in the world".

▶ In 2006, Senator John McCain (R-AZ) again calls for reform of the regulatory structure that governs Freddie Mac and Fannie Mae.

▶ In 2006, the Democrats again block reform legislation.

▶ In 2008, the housing market collapses. Democrats blame the Republicans!

▶ In 2010, Barney Frank says to abolish Fannie Mae and Freddie Mac, and replace them with what.....???????

This is unbelievable. The Democrats are the ones who insisted that the government had to make it possible for everyone to own a home. It is their constitutional right. It wasn't fair if they weren't in a house. Everyone has a right to have a house. How many times has he said that these companies were operating in great shape? Barney Frank and other members of Congress tried to use them as social engineering tools. Now that it has failed Barney Frank wants to scrap them and replace them. He probably wants it abolished before anyone has an opportunity to conduct an investigation into his and other people's meddling into how these companies were run and misused by people of his kind. Never replace Freddie Mac and Fannie Mae with any government sponsored proposal. Let the private business sector run their business and make the loans with proper documentation and risk factors as they should.

For the tax year 2006, 353,000 Americans reported incomes exceeding $1,000,000. The people that make $250,000 to $999,000 live in our communities own the local Dairy Queen, McDonalds, Burger King, Tire store, Hallmark or most of the other small business. These people support youth basketball, baseball, community projects, and churches. These businesses provide local jobs that produce local taxes, state taxes and federal taxes. They and their employees buy homes, cars, gas, groceries and clothes locally. We think that money is better spent locally than shipped to Washington to be redistributed by Congress. It is terrible that our country vilifies these people that pay (top 5% of earners) 62% of the federal taxes as greedy do nothings. Most of this money was earned through hard work and sound decisions. They should be applauded. Class war fare is wrong for this country. As the president said it is all of us that make up the country.

If you took the $4 Billion Dollars that extending this tax cut and sent a check to everyone not in this tax bracket it would be less than $20 per person.

What is even more amazing about the Democrats refusal to extend the Bush tax cuts to every American is that they say it will mean the government will have their revenue reduced by an extra $700 billion over the next ten years. That would amount to $70 billion a year for the next ten years. Didn't this administration pass legislation to the tune of $787 billion that produced very little if anything that benefited the citizens of the United States? It is about time that the President and administration started passing legislation that benefits the taxpayers.

Well, the Democrats have succeeded in putting it to the American tax payer again. Passing their latest $30 billion will not have any positive effect in lowering the unemployment in the United States. When will they ever learn that spending does not create jobs? The primary focus on this bill is to provide funds to independent community banks to encourage lending to small businesses. When is Obama going to learn from the previous stimulus bills that it does not increase employment or lending to small businesses or individuals.

This bill will work exactly as the previous bill. The independent community banks will not use the funds to loan to small businesses. That is just a ruse to get more of their voters in line because they are looking very bleak with the upcoming election on November 2, 2010. The $12 billion in tax breaks in the bill will not benefit 1% of the small businesses in the United States. Small businesses do not sell their stock so the tax break is nothing but some more wind being blown by Mr. Obama. The current rules for depreciation and expanding business are more than adequate.

Passing this bill was just another way that the Democrats are trying to fool the American taxpayer and try to salvage to some of the losses that are projected in November. We have known many small businesses and they can tell you that there is nothing in this bill that will help them. When you operate a small business you will not be willing to borrow money because they are already struggling and the last thing any of them will want to do is go further into debt. Businesses will hire more employees when their demand for products or services require. Only a fool would hire unless there was positive indications that these employees would be providing enough profits to justify the costs. Businesses pay payroll taxes, Medicare, insurance and other benefits that are incurred for each employee they hire. It is not just the cost of the salary or wages that affects the businessman. You can figure that it takes about 20% in addition to the salary or wages.

To give everyone a summary of what this $30 billion program will cost divide the number by the 500,000 jobs that it is speculated to provide and you have a very large cost per job created of $60,000? It seems that there are much better ways of creating jobs than spending $60,000 each. That figure might be considerably low because this bill will not stimulate the creation of that many jobs. Once again the President and his lemmings are trying to create the impression that they are doing something to influence more voters to vote Democrat in November. What a crock. When are we as voting taxpayers going to take back our country?

Let's explore what the major cause of why jobs are going to keep being lost in America.

Here's the deal. You're going to start a business or expand the one you've got now. It doesn't really matter what you do or what you're going to do. I'll partner with you no matter what business you're in – as long as it's legal. But we can't give you any capital – you have to come up with that on your own. We won't give you any labor – that's definitely up to you. What we will do, however, is demand you follow all sorts of rules about what products and services you can offer, how much (and how often) you pay your employees, and where and when you're allowed to operate your business. That's my role in the affair: to tell you what to do. Now in return for my rules, we're going to take roughly half of whatever you make in the business each year. Half seems fair, doesn't it? We think so. Of course, that's half of your profits. You're also going to have to pay me about 12% of whatever you decide to pay your employees because you've got to cover my expenses for promulgating all of the rules about who you can employ, when, where, and how. Come on, you're my partner. It's only "fair." Now... after you've put your hard-earned savings at risk to start this business, and after you've worked hard at it for a few decades (paying me my 50% or a bit more along the way each year), you might decide you'd like to cash out – to finally live the good life. Whether or not this is "fair" – some people never can afford to retire – is a different argument. As your partner, We're happy for you to sell whenever you'd like... because our agreement says, if you sell, you have to pay me an additional 20% of whatever the capitalized value of the business is at that time.

We know that you put up all the original capital. You took all the risks. You put in all of the labor. That's all true. But we've done our part, too. We've collected 50% of the profits each year. And we've always come up with more rules for you to follow each year. Therefore, we deserve another, final 20% slice of the business.

All in all, if you're a very successful entrepreneur... if you're one of the rare, lucky, and hard-working people who can create a new company, employ lots of people, and satisfy the public... you'll end up paying us more than 75% of your income over your life. Thank you so much. I'm sure you'll think our offer is reasonable and happily partner with us... but it doesn't really matter how you feel about it because if you ever try to stiff us – or cheat us on any of my fees or rules we will send the Internal Revenue Service after you and harass you the rest of your life. That's how civil society is supposed to work, right? This is America, isn't it? That's the offer America gives its entrepreneurs. And the idiots in Washington wonder why there are no new jobs?

Here is an example of the incredible spending sprees that the Obama and his lemmings have splurged on. House Republicans are collecting photos from the citizens all over the country. These photos are showing that the program has wasted an idiotic sum of $192 million in taxpayer money to plaster every possible highway with signs touting how the stimulus cash is "Putting America to Work" with infrastructure projects. This is a total waste of the taxpayer's money. About the only jobs it created were to Mr. Obama's union buddies. Did it really create any new jobs that were not for the benefit of the unions?

Unfortunately, the vast majority of people in this country have never experienced first hand what it's like to try and start a business, and is completely and totally clueless about the harsh reality. The United States government isn't the solution, it's the problem.

What about the amazing way that Obama and Democrats can continue with these phony policies. The $26 billion bailout money to "save" teachers jobs was not really for that. Almost none of the school districts who got the money "rehired" any teachers. By the time they passed this bill, the districts had already made adjustments and their school year had already started. We are guessing it went to the teacher's pensions and unions. The really sad thing is that the Democrats don't even have a clue what is really in any bill... if Obama says "pass it".... they blindly obey him. Two good examples of this are.......Obamacare where Pelosi said "we have to pass it to know what's in it." The Financial "reform" bill - Dodd said "we won't know the impact of this bill until we pass it and apply these regulations."

CHAPTER THIRTY

Fannie Mae and Freddie Mac

The Real Estate problems in the United States. What can be done to improve the market?

The real estate market will finally correct itself when people start to buy homes that they can afford. The market will fall until the price of homes will be where the homeowner can make the payments; have the proper down payment and credit history to justify the mortgage.

As much as it would hurt the economy, the United States should let Freddie Mac and Fannie Mae go through a complete liquidation and then force them into bankruptcy. I agree it would create a short term burden on the taxpayers but in the long run it will force the mortgage companies and other lending institutions to make mortgages to qualified individuals

Every American would like to own their home. We have to be practical with regards to purchasing a home. Lending institutions need to do due diligence to make sure that the buyer has an adequate down payment, verified income to support the payments, a credit history of making payments on time and purchasing a home that they can afford.

The lending institutions that made the loans to the unqualified home purchasers should be required to incur the losses from these improper loans. The made the loans knowing that the purchaser would not have the means to pay the mortgage after the ARM kicked in. It was not their concern so they processed a loan that they knew they were going to sell to another mortgage company and then to a Freddie Mac and Fannie Mae guarantee.

On September 15, 2010, the Associated Press published an article stating that ("Government say banks should share Fannie, Freddie costs") please excuse them for their lousy English in their headline.

The institution that packaged these mortgages to Freddie Mac and Freddie Mae need to share in these loses. When these institutions incur losses that could put them out of business that is the way it should be. There will always be lending institutions that operate in a manner to make profits without taking undue risk. These institutions really loved the easy profits that were made illegally. It is time to make them realize what they did and make them suffer the consequences.

I believe that the real estate market collapsed due to excessive amounts of greed on the part of the banks, real estate salesmen, real estate appraisers and mortgage companies. I believe that the United States government, Freddie Mac and Fannie Mae were the primary people that fueled the greed of everyone.

I have based these decisions upon reviewing some of the information that has been gathered from news articles written by the media. I have taken information that I collected and tried to explain in a manner that I believe meets my expectations for the United States.

What caused some of the problems?

Did Edward DeMarco, the acting director for the Federal Housing Finance Agency read our website? We have stated all along that the banks have an obligation to pay the cost for bailing out mortgage buyers Fannie Mae and Freddie Mac because they sold them the bad mortgages that the Carter and Clinton administrations requiring the policy to make homes available to every American. That in it self did not tell the banks and mortgage institutions to loan to people regardless of their credit rating and ability to repay the loan.

Instead of caring what will happen to the taxpayer if the banks are not held responsible for the loans that they sold to Fannie Mae and Freddie Mac the government and Wall Street are concerned about what will happen to the banks. Quite frankly, who really cares what happens to the earning of the banks or Wall Street? Reports are that the banks could incur book losses of up to $42 billion if they are forced to repurchase the bad loans they sold to Fannie Mae and Freddie Mac. Wouldn't it be better for the banks that made the bad loans suffer the losses they forced upon Fannie Mae and Freddie Mac? Sources indicate that J. P. Morgan, Chase & Co., Citigroup, Inc., Bank of America and Wells Fargo & Co. could record $17 billion in losses if they repurchase a quarter of the mortgage giant's seriously delinquent loans.

Just think how big these company's losses are going to be when they actually report how many delinquent loans are on their books on real estate that they have not reported. It is not any wonder that the mortgage lending has been so futile. The institutions do not want to show the losses that they would have to take to refinance most of their loans. Could that underscore the fact that only 400,000 loans have been refinanced out of the 10,000,000 foreclosures?

It could all be a conspiracy on the banks part. If they do not loan money to purchase the houses that they have in their foreclosure portfolio then they can drive the prices down further. When they feel like the prices can not go any lower they will start buying these properties back and make the real estate market go higher again. Why is it that history always repeats itself? Isn't what the banks did during the depression of 1929?

One of the things that can be done to stop this is to force every bank to make a full disclosure of the loans in their portfolio. This disclosure will be required to show how many of them are underwater, past due on the payments, in foreclosure, current on the payments and current ration of loan value to the value of the property. The banks must report how many loans that are delinquent and that they have not started foreclosure proceedings on and when they intend to start. The banking industry must be required to make full disclosure on the value of their portfolios. They are currently reporting huge profits but if they were honest about their real estate situation would they be making these profits. If they are they can afford to accept the responsibility for the bad loans that they sold to Fannie Mae and Freddie Mac.

Freddie Mac reports loss seeks another $1.8 billion in taxpayer bailout. The mortgage giants Freddie Mac and Fannie Mae, between them, have needed $148.2 billion in bailout money since late 2008 to stay afloat. The aim is to ensure that mortgage credit remains available.

All the windows and doors are boarded up on houses all across the United States that are listed as foreclosure sales on a HUD website. The mortgage-finance company Freddie Mac reported a $4.7 billion net loss for the second quarter Monday, due to a rise in home loans that ended in default.

The report, following a similar loss at sister company Fannie Mae last week, underscores that the United States housing market remains a central trouble spot in the economy. Because these government-sponsored enterprises (GSEs) sit at the heart of the housing market, it also means the taxpayer tab is rising for keeping these firms afloat.

In reporting the loss, Freddie Mac also said that the Federal Housing Finance Agency will ask for $1.8 billion in additional Treasury funds to support the firm. The FHFA has held Fannie Mae and Freddie Mac with a conservator, to keep them from failing, since they collapsed during the 2008 financial crisis.

The FHFA made a similar request for new aid for Fannie Mae ($1.5 billion) last week. The new requests mean the two mortgage companies have needed $148.2 billion to stay afloat, according to the Associated Press. About $63.1 billion of that is being used by Freddie Mac.

The infusions of cash are designed to maintain a positive net worth at both firms. The goal is not simply to prop up the firms, but to avoid a collapse in the availability of mortgage credit at a time when the housing market is already weak.

Although both firms reported some positive trends, the taxpayer costs could climb much higher. In one recent survey of federal recession-fighting policies, economists Mark Zandi of Moody's Economy.com and Alan Blinder of Princeton University estimated that the GSE bailouts will ultimately total $305 billion, a bit more than double the current tally.

Losses at the GSEs could persist because America's great foreclosure wave appears to be continuing. Fannie and Freddie together end up owning or guaranteeing most of the new home loans made in the US by banks or other finance companies. The role the GSEs play, which is based on a congressional charter and implied federal backing, has helped to keep the market for mortgage-related securities alive, even amid the financial crisis.

But their enormous scale, and the guarantees they make, also means the mortgage giants are very exposed to housing-market risks. At Freddie Mac, for instance, charge-offs of bad loans hit $3.9 billion in the second quarter, up from $2.8 billion in the first quarter and $1.9 billion in the second quarter of 2009.

If the Zandi-Blinder forecast proves to be accurate, the rescue of the GSEs will be the largest of all the government bailouts – larger than the ultimate cost of the Troubled Asset Relief Program or the various actions by the Federal Reserve combined. The only larger cost, in their list of actions designed to revive the economy or to avert a depression, is the Obama economic stimulus package of tax cuts and new federal spending on things like highway projects.

Freddie Mac said some housing trends may be starting to shift in a positive direction. In the second quarter, the firm set aside a bit less money for future loan losses than it did in the first quarter, because of a small downshift in the percentage of mortgage holders who are delinquent.

"We recognize that high unemployment and other factors still pose very real challenges for the housing market," Freddie Mac chief executive officer Charles Haldeman Jr. said in a statement accompanying the financial report. "With that in mind, we continue to focus on the quality of the new business we are adding to our book to be responsible stewards of taxpayer funds as we support the nation's housing market."

His statement and the losses to taxpayers come as Congress is about to take up the question of so-called GSE reform, or what to do with Fannie and Freddie in the long term. The Obama administration has scheduled a public conference on the topic on Aug. 17, 2010.

The administration bailed out the banks at the expense of delinquent homeowners. Hundreds of thousands used the last of their life savings making modified mortgage payments only to be disqualified for permanent modification and kicked out on the street anyway.

These homeowners were destroyed at a time when they had no more money or credit left.

Homes for sale: New home sales rebound, prices keep falling. Homes for sale: New home sales rose in October, suggesting that the housing market is beginning to recover.

The housing market is finally seeing a rebound of sorts: Sales of new single-family homes rose in the current month.

But how builders achieved those new home sales is less encouraging. The average selling price of a new home dropped to $242,900, the Commerce Department reported. That's the lowest selling price for a new home since 2003 and the biggest year-over-year decline since the depths of the great recession in April 2009.

The surge in sales "is the first good piece of news for the housing market in a number of months," writes Paul Dales, an economist with Toronto-based Capital Economics, in an analysis. "Nonetheless, it doesn't alter our belief that high unemployment, tight credit conditions and low confidence will mean that housing activity will remain uncomfortably weak for some time."

The rebound to a seasonally adjusted annual rate of 330,000 homes surprised analysts on the upside. Consensus estimates were closer to 310,000. But the Commerce Department also revised the previous months figure down from 300,000 to 267,000. So the total for the two months was on par with estimates, which suggests that the housing market is finally emerging from the weakness after home buying tax incentives expired in April, analysts said.

Also positive was the drop in inventory of new homes for sales, down from 9.6 months of supply in May to a more normal 7.6 months in June.

The challenge is that the supply of new homes and the much larger pool of existing homes is still weighing on the price of homes, which could still fall further, analysts say.

Barney Frank sure changed his position from: "These two entities — Fannie Mae and Freddie Mac — are not facing any kind of financial crisis," said Representative Barney Frank of Massachusetts, the ranking Democrat on the Financial Services Committee. "The more people exaggerate these problems, the more pressure there is on these companies, the less we will see in terms of affordable housing." Aug 10, 2010 Las Vegas Review-Journal.

Wow! Barney Frank doing a complete 180 from what he did 10 years ago, when he and Chris Dodd and Acorn forced banks to do business with Fannie Mae and Freddie Mac in the first place. What a lying, arrogant, hypocritical crook. Fannie Mae and Freddie Mac have now cost the taxpayers over a trillion dollars, thanks, specifically to the Democrats and Liberals that hoisted it upon us. Today the comment made by Barney Frank is "I think we should, particularly, stop this assumption that you put everybody into homeownership."

Barney Frank and Chris Dodd are the men most responsible for Fannie Mae and Freddie Mac. Barney Frank and Chris Dodd should be in jail where they belong. The FDIC testified in front of Franks' congressional committee several years before the mortgage meltdown telling them exactly where it was headed and that Fannie Mae and Freddie Mac needed to be reined in before there was a meltdown. The committee dismissed their advice and did nothing and now the rest of us are paying for it.

Barney Frank and Chris Dodd are two of the biggest idiots that ever served in the United States Congress.

The Federal Government should have never been in the business of guaranteeing or subsidizing mortgages. They have already proved they have no concept of how to do it, and they are too liable to political manipulation. We don't need any replacements for these agencies. Look how much money we would save by eliminating all those overpaid administrators who lined their pockets at everyone else's expense.

An article from the Wall Street Journal reported that Rep. Barney Frank (D., Mass.): I worry, frankly, that there's a tension here. The more people, in my judgment, exaggerate a threat of safety and soundness, the more people conjure up the possibility of serious financial losses to the Treasury, which I do not see. I think we see entities that are fundamentally sound financially and withstand some of the disaster scenarios. . . Rep. Frank: I do think I do not want the same kind of focus on safety and soundness that we have in OCC [Office of the Comptroller of the Currency] and OTS [Office of Thrift Supervision]. I want to roll the dice a little bit more in this situation towards subsidized housing. . . Rep. Frank: I believe there has been more alarm raised about potential un-safety and un-soundness than, in fact, exists.

I suppose it would make sense that Barney Frank wants to replace Freddie Mac and Fannie Mae with another entity. Barney Frank is married to Fannie and Freddie and video footage is out there with Barney telling the world there was no housing bubble, and he would continue to push Fannie and Freddie to underwrite mortgages for the credit challenged.

If we abolish Fannie Mae and Freddie Mac we will sweep under the carpet all the bad decisions Barney Frank made in administering this financial fiasco. Someone needs to check out how many special loans were made for properties that our elected officials and their families were buying. What we need to do is abolish Barney Frank and Chris Dodd. We must not let the records be destroyed so that we can find out just how much corruption was involved in these organizations.

What is amazing to me is that Barney Frank and Democratic Senators like Chris Dodd prevented investigations of Fannie Mae and Freddie Mac before the real estate crash when republican senators like John McCain were warning that Freddie Mac and Fannie Mae were houses of cards.

We can not allow these to be replaced with anything that the government will be running. Get out of the mortgage business and send it back to the private sector.

Prominent Democrats ran Fannie Mae and Freddie Mac, the same government-sponsored enterprise (GSE) that donated campaign cash to top Democrats. And one of Fannie Mae's and Freddie Mac's main defenders in the House – Rep. Barney Frank, D-Mass., a recipient of more than $40,000 in campaign donations from Fannie since 1989 – In 1991, Frank and Rep. Joe Kennedy, D-Mass., lobbied for Fannie Mae and Freddie Mac to soften rules on multi-family home mortgages although those dwellings showed a default rate twice that of single-family homes, according to the Nov. 22, 1991, Boston Globe.

Frank opposed giving the Bush administration the right to approve or disapprove business activities that "could pose risk to the taxpayers." He told the Post he worried the Treasury Department "would sacrifice activities that are good for consumers in the name of lowering the companies' market risks." "Freddie Mac and Fannie Mae would not have prospered as long as they did without the help of Senators Frank, Schumer and Dodd. Unfortunately, the working taxpayers did not prosper.

This is the same Senator Frank that said before the housing bubble burst that Fannie Mae and Freddie Mac were in fine shape and told Bush and the Republicans that there was no reason to reform these two? Senator Frank along with good old Chris Dodd and Maxine Waters were in these deceptive policies together. And didn't Senator Frank have a big argument with Bill O'Reilly about none of the busting bubble being his fault? What the? Oops! We're not supposed to be smart enough to remember all of that as he Senator Frank tries to pull the wool over our eyes one more time.

Unqualified home buyers were not the only ones who benefited from Massachusetts Representative Barney Frank's efforts to deregulate Fannie Mae and Freddie Mac throughout the 1990s. Now that Fannie Mae and Freddie Mac are at the epicenter of a financial meltdown that threatens the United States economy, some are raising new questions about Frank's relationship with Herb Moses, who was Fannie Mae's assistant director for product initiatives. Moses worked at the government-sponsored enterprise from 1991 to 1998, while Frank was on the House Banking Committee, which had jurisdiction over Fannie Mae and Freddie Mac. Both Frank and Moses assured the Wall Street Journal in 1992 that they took pains to avoid any conflicts of interest. Critics, however, remain skeptical. "It's absolutely a conflict," said Dan Gainor, vice president of the Business & Media Institute. "He was voting on Fannie Mae at a time when he was involved with a Fannie Mae executive. How is that not germane? "If this had been his ex-wife and he was Republican, I would bet every penny I have - or at least what's not in the stock market - that this would be considered germane," added Gainor, a T. Boone Pickens Fellow. "But everybody wants to avoid it because he's gay. It's the quintessential double standard."

Barney and his Democrat buddy Dodd are the reason for the housing crisis! Rep. Barney Frank (D-MA) is Chairman of the Financial Services Committee in the House of Representatives. In 2003, he said of Fannie Mae and Freddie Mac: "These two entities – Fannie Mae and Freddie Mac – are not facing any kind of financial crisis. The more people exaggerate these problems, the more pressure there is on these companies, the less we will see in terms of affordable housing." In the late 1980s and early 90s, Frank was engaged in a sexual relationship with Herb Moses, who was Fannie Mae's assistant director of product initiatives! Bill O'Reilly exposed Frank's involvement in the mortgage crisis: YouTube - O 'Reilly - Barney Frank Had Affair with Fannie Mae Exec. Frank looked the other way, while our economy was being destroyed by federal policies created in Clinton and Carter Administrations.

Under President Jimmy Carter, the Community Reinvestment Act (CRA) was passed. It required federal financial institutions to encourage banks to give home loans to persons with little credit and low income. Economist Russell Roberts said that the CRA played a major role in creating the sub-prime mortgage crisis in the U.S.

Under President Bill Clinton, the CRA was expanded and Clinton set targets for low-income home ownership at the Department of Housing and Urban Development and at Fannie Mae and Freddie Mac. Banks were forced by the federal government to provide bad loans to the unqualified.

Barney Frank and Christopher Dodd received thousands of dollars in contributions from Fannie Mae and Freddie Mac over the years. Dodd has received $133,900 since 1989; Frank received $40,100. (While in the Senate, Barrack Obama received $105,849).

LOVE IT OR LEAVE IT

Q: Which Political Party took Social Security from the

independent 'Trust Fund' and put it into the

general fund so that Congress could spend it?

A: It was Lyndon Johnson and the democratically

controlled House and Senate.

Q: Which Political Party eliminated the income tax

deduction for Social Security (FICA) withholding?

A: The Democratic Party.

Q: Which Political Party started taxing Social

Security annuities?

A: The Democratic Party, with Al Gore casting the

'tie-breaking' deciding vote as President of the

Senate, while he was Vice President of the US

Q: Which Political Party decided to start

giving annuity payments to immigrants?

A: That's right!

Jimmy Carter and the Democratic Party.

Immigrants moved into this country, and at age 65 began to receive Social Security payments!

The Democratic Party gave these payments to them,

even though they never paid a dime into it!

Fannie Mae and Freddie Mac reform: Would it add $5 trillion to US debt? The Obama administration held a conference about how to reform mortgage giants Fannie Mae and Freddie Mac. Reform could involve adding Fannie and Freddie's roughly $5 trillion in obligations, in effect, to the federal balance sheet.

The Obama administration turned its focus squarely on a $5 trillion question. What to do with Fannie Mae and Freddie Mac, the giant financiers of United States home mortgages that fell into a bankruptcy-style conservator two years ago.

These two corporations together own or guarantee about half the mortgage debt in America. What happens to them will affect the ability of the economy and the housing market to recover. It also has big implications for US taxpayers, who could foot even higher bailout bills if the mortgage-insurance business isn't fixed.

"We will not support a return to the system where private gains are subsidized by taxpayer losses," said Treasury Secretary Timothy Geithner, in remarks that opened a day-long conference on how to reform these so-called government sponsored enterprises (GSEs).

Mr. Geithner cited the possibility of giving Fannie Mae and Freddie Mac an "elegant funeral." But that wouldn't mean a government exit from its prominent role in America's housing market. In fact, it could mean that the government agrees to stand explicitly behind the GSEs' obligations, while also putting in place a new system designed to ensure that mortgage credit is available even during recessions or a banking crisis.

"'Without such support, the risk is that future recessions could be more severe because the financial system would not have the capital to support mortgage lending on an adequate scale," Mr. Geithner said in his prepared remarks.

Other panelists at the conference echoed that view.

"The hit to the economy [from the recession] would have been measurably greater" without the GSEs and the Federal Housing Administration, said economist Mark Zandi of Moody's Analytics. By guaranteeing or insuring mortgages, these agencies enabled credit to keep flowing for typical home loans even as home values were falling and the private-sector channels of mortgage finance had dried up.

The Obama administration hasn't outlined its approach to GSE reform, which was notably missing in the financial-reform law the president signed recently. The conference represents a first step, at least in public view, toward developing a proposal.

The battle in Congress, expected to ramp up early in 2011, will reflect a sharp partisan split that's existed for years. Republican lawmakers emphasize the importance of scaling back government's role in the housing market and limiting taxpayer exposure to losses. Many Democrats emphasize the risks of providing too little support for the housing market, given housing's prominent role in family wealth and in the economy's ups and downs.

Both sides of this debate were represented in panel discussions. Many participants from the private sector – including Mr. Zandi – said the government should eventually scale back its role in the housing market significantly.

At the same time, many said government mortgage guarantees should continue to be available in some carefully managed forms.

At least one participant, bond-fund manager Bill Gross of the investment firm PIMCO, suggested that government guarantees should apply to virtually all mortgages. He said this resulted in mortgage interest rates that are about 3 percentage points lower than if the only mortgage insurance came from the private sector.

Whatever role the government takes in the future, policymakers must also decide on a transition plan to get there.

Many panelists urged that Fannie and Freddie should not be reconstituted in something similar to their pre-crisis form: profit-seeking private corporations that, at the same time, have a government-chartered mission and implicit taxpayer backing.

An exit strategy could involve adding Fannie and Freddie's roughly $5 trillion in obligations, in effect, to a federal balance sheet that already includes $13.3 trillion in federal government debts. The GSE obligations would be a different animal, because those liabilities would need to be covered by taxpayers only if things went bad in the housing market. But the nation has just seen things go bad in the housing market.

During the financial panic of 2008, investors who held GSE debts became increasingly worried about the solvency of those corporations. The Bush administration felt impelled to put Fannie and Freddie into a mortgage conservator, to avert a possible bankruptcy and to keep mortgage markets moving.

The companies weren't holding enough capital in reserve to cover likely losses.

As of March 31 this year, 6.3 percent of mortgages held by Fannie and Freddie are either seriously delinquent or in foreclosure. Although that's down slightly from the figure three months earlier, it represents a big one-year rise (from 3.9 percent in early 2009).

In the end, losses to Fannie and Freddie related to the financial crisis may cost taxpayers $305 billion, according to one estimate recently published by Mr. Zandi and Alan Blinder of Princeton University. But that figure could rise or fall depending on what happens with the economy – and with government policies on housing.

I'm so tired of those that see everything as a right. Home ownership isn't a right. While I agree that Fannie Mae and Freddie Mac need be abolished, the knee jerk reaction of liberals to immediately replace it with another subsidizing scheme is a mistake. What needs to be done

is to end government guarantees and government support of housing. Home loans will require far greater down payments and far better FICO scores than the government was allowing. FHA was allowing for a 3.5% down payment if an applicant has a FICO score as low as 500. My dog has a FICO score of 520. Requiring a score as low as 500 reminds me of the NCAA that decades raised their requirement for student/athletes to achieve an SAT score of 700 out of 1600. You can get 700 without reading the questions and just a random pick. That allowed the black student athletes to qualify to participate in sports and the people that could not buy groceries unless they had food stamps to qualify for a mortgage

This is only smoke and mirrors. The Democrats are still pulling the cranks, levers and buttons. Barney Frank really intends to destroy Freddie Mac and Fannie Mae because they have become "corrupt" and they should not be doing this (even though we all know at this point that they are run by the government) the next move is for Barney and the rest of the minions of evil to simply put it to you this way "as Freddie Mac and Fannie Mae are unable to continue on the current course we will now enact a single government run entity to do all the mortgages in the USA and with the oversight that "we" the government will know what to do.

We the government will decide from now on who can own a home and who can not." That sounds OK right - well what if you are not a card carrying member of the government - now they have the right to deny you for any reason they wish - conservative, middle class, tea party member - heck now they can deny you. Don't ever trust a politician like this to start sounding conservative it's all a big ugly lie. Remember that they are up for reelection on November 2012. They are running scared.

Continued policies driven by people like Senator Dodd and Senator Frank are the primary reason we are in a terrible recession. We don't have a manufacturing base any longer, thanks Mr. Clinton, so we rely on things like housing and consumer spending to drive the economy. The economic fortunes of the middle class begin to dry up. We are a country of consumers, not producers. Let's get back to our roots and bring our manufacturing back to the United States. The leaders in

Washington don't get that so they keep handing out money we don't have to other nations, unions and political backers to keep at least some people well oiled on the taxpayer money.

I cannot believe the voice of reason is coming from Barney Frank. He advocated "build affordable rental housing," "not everyone should be a homeowner," "recognize housing subsidies in the budget." He should also point out that subsidizing housing has inflated prices way above where they should be, causing our debt to explode and affordability to plummet. These are indeed interesting times when one of the most egregious housing cheerleaders recognizes the mistake of this failed policy

Barney Frank wants to destroy the evidence of his incorrect assertion that we didn't have a mortgage problem back in 2006 - 2007. Congress was warned and Barney Frank very famously challenged the assertion that the bubble was going to burst. Of course, Bush gets the blame for that although it was Barney's head where the sun doesn't shine that allowed the disaster to happen.

You comprehend the mess that our Federal government is in, when you see Frank, Dodd, Reid, Pelosi and the others who oversee it. None of these people would hack it in the private business sector, yet they're wheeling and dealing with the hard-earned taxpayers' money. Term limits, please. No more career idiots in Washington. Some examples of how our Stimulus money was spent: University of Florida: $325,000 (cactus bugs mating decisions study). University of California: $233,000 (why Africans vote study). $3.4 million turtle tunnel in Florida: Syracuse: $219,000 (sex patterns of college women study). Amtrak: ($850 Million) Hollywood: ($246 "million") - Hollywood Producers can buy movie film. There is plenty more of this waste of our money. New requirement for Congress: Term limits, age limits, qualification, no criminals and no tax cheats.

I have not read anything about where Sarah Palin stands on the Fannie Mae and Freddie Mac problems. I do believe that she will have the courage to face the problem and do what is right for the taxpaying citizens of the United States. I do not have the same feeling about the President.

CHAPTER THIRTY ONE

The Drug Cartels

There was information on the drug cartels on the news that provided a list of the eight most wanted drug cartel leaders. If the Mexican government does not have the military power to take out these individuals there must be some underlying reasons. Could it be that the Mexican government really needs and likes the amount of money that the drug cartels provide for the economy of Mexico?

The United States has the military power and the type of weapons that could eliminate these drug cartels in a few days. Why doesn't our President show some concern for the problem and tell his buddy Calderon that he needs to move out of the way because we are going to destroy the cartels in the next few days. These cartels have more weapons than the Mexican military and need to be dealt with now.

The supersonic B-1 was designed almost a half-century ago to attack deep into the Soviet Union with thermonuclear bombs. Surprisingly, the "Bone" has emerged as one of the most effective weapons of the counterinsurgency fight in Afghanistan, a turn of events that should humble today's analysts confidently predicting the shape of conflicts and weapons in the year 2060. Although the plane is not a B-1 you can get the picture.

We recently had a crisis on Falcon Lake which straddles the border between Texas and Mexico.

How long does the United States stick their head in the sand and condone the lawless mess in Mexico and the lawless mess in this country. How do 20 million illegals parade around, leech off the taxpayer, and our government does very little. Liberals have ruined this country.

The search for an American tourist reportedly shot dead on Falcon Lake has led Texas Governor Rick Perry to tangle with the Mexican government over the investigation and efforts to recover the body.

Perry said that Mexico needs to use every resource available to find the body and have it returned to the United States. Mexican President Felipe Calderon has not made any effort to contact the United States authorities concerning the homicide.

The District Attorney there, Marco Antonio Guerrero Carrixales, also told the paper authorities "are not certain that incident happened the way that they are telling us." That is as much as saying the widow of the slain man was lying about how he was slain. How lame can the Mexican government get?

Governor Perry also used the incident to renew his demand that the federal government do more to secure the United States - Mexican border as northern Mexico sinks deeper into drug and gang violence. The violence has spread in the last few months from Ciudad Juarez, the epicenter of Mexico's drug war across from El Paso, Texas, to the Mexican side of the Rio Grande Valley. Two drug gangs, the Gulf Cartel and the Zetas, are battling for supremacy there and fighting the Mexican military. Perry also said he spoke to Homeland Security Secretary Janet Napolitano's chief of staff and again asked for an additional 1,000 National Guard troops on the Texas-Mexico border, a request that has been repeatedly denied. "How many more American citizens have to die?" Perry said.

When are the President and the Department of Homeland Security going to start protecting our border?

Would anyone care to guess why the government is silent on illegal immigration? Why the government is afraid to tackle this issue? Why Obama is suing Arizona? It's really simple, politicians are so afraid of upsetting the Hispanic voters with such nonsense like securing our borders. Politicians are more concerned with loosing the Hispanic voters then actually doing what is right for the United States, and I don't see it changing any time soon. Since this latest death happened we need to ask Janet Napolitano who overseas the border security just why aren't you doing your job?

I am glad that the Governor of Texas is taking steps to resolve this dispute with the Mexican government. My question to every American is why isn't the President of the United States getting involved and demanding the Mexican government to secure their side of Falcon Lake? The President is too busy campaigning for his loosing Democratic candidates to worry about anything that has to do with protecting the United States. His only objective is to try and protect his majorities in both houses of Congress. If he fails to do that he will become the DDD president.

The Falcon Lake occurrence has become almost a daily activity along the entire border between the United States and Mexico. Why is it that the President does not take appropriate action and secure the border?"

The time has passed for the federal government to take action. The governors of the Border States need to take the proper action now. Every state on the border needs to activate their National Guard troops and send them to the border to protect all the citizens of the United States. Protecting your state should be the number one priority of each governor.

The federal government could send a United States Marines Corps expeditionary force to Falcon Lake immediately with orders to kill on sight any drug lords that were involved. It appears that the Mexican government lacks the will or power to maintain the activities of a civilized world and the drug cartels activities. Americans should demand Obama to deal with this threat but liberals seem to care more about illegal Mexican rights than then American citizen

If this had been a Mexican tourist killed in America, our President would be apologizing to the victim's family, and assuring the Mexican government that he will find and prosecute the perpetrators. We would have thousands of Mexicans marching in the streets of the United States protesting and demanding justice for "the racist killing". Obama would be assuring the victims family that he will get justice for them and issuing an advisory to Americans traveling to Mexico, instead, he says nothing.

Falcon Lake is on the border between the United States and Mexico and is about 25 miles long and 3 miles wide and was created by damming the Rio Grande River which is the border between the countries.

The violence that is currently happening on the Mexican side of the border is making it very dangerous to use this facility. The latest development on Falcon Lake was the killing of a Mexican investigator that was probing the shooting of an American on the lake.

That part of Tamaulipas state is overrun by violence from a turf battle between the Gulf Cartel and the Zeta drug gang, made up of former government and military officials.

I'm sick and tired of all these thugs who are screaming about how we "stole" the land from the Mexicans. We didn't steal the land. We won it through war, purchasing it and by forgiving debt. Perhaps these people need a quick history lesson:

The territory comprising of 545,783 square miles which includes the present states of California, Nevada, Utah and a large part of Arizona and New Mexico and part of Colorado came to the United States as a result of the Mexican War, through conquest and purchase. The treaty known as The Treaty of Guadeloupe Hidalgo was signed Feb. 2, 1848 and ratified by the Senate March 10, 1848 with the United States paying $15,000,000 in addition to assuming the payment of claims of American citizens against Mexico amounting to $3,250,000 for a total of $18,250,000. In 1853 the United States bought from Mexico a strip of land, now forming that part of Arizona and New Mexico lying South of the of the Gila River and expanding from the Rio Grande, near El Paso on the East, to the Colorado River on the West. It consisted of 45,535 square miles. General Sana Ana, captured at the Battle of San Jacinto, signed a treaty recognizing the independence of the Republic of Texas. In 1845 Texas was admitted as a state. So quit the whining that it belongs to Mexico and get on with your miserable lives. It's our land. We own it fair and square so get over your whining.

Let's examine the immigration laws of Mexico and determine what a wonderful country it really is? In Mexico there will be no special bilingual programs in the school systems. All of the nation's ballots will be in their nation's language. All of the governments business will be conducted in their language. Non-residents will not have the right to vote no matter how long they are living in Mexico. Non-citizens will never be able to hold political office. Foreigners will not be a burden to the taxpayers. There will be no welfare, no food stamps, and no health care or other government assistance programs. Any one who is a burden will be deported immediately. Foreigners can invest in this country, but it must be an amount at least equal to 40,000 times the daily minimum wage. If foreigners come here and buy land their options will be restricted. Certain parcels including waterfront property are reserved for citizens naturally born into this country. Foreigners may have no protests, and no demonstrations, no waving of a foreign flag, no political organizing, no bad mouthing our President or his policies. These will lead to deportation. And if you do come to this country illegally you will be actively hunted and when caught sent to jail until your deportation can be arranged. In addition all of your assets will be taken from you. Those are the current immigration laws of Mexico. Furthermore, Mexico enforces their immigration laws.

I wonder what the Mexican government is going to do when these people start heading south instead of north? Hopefully, they will all have their Mexican identification documents with them. The trash will just look like old Mexico so it will not create a problem.

This is an example of how qualified our President and his sidekick Vice President really are. "Vice President Joe Biden, asks for six months of retraining for Cattle Guards!"

CATTLE GUARDS, THIS IS ABOUT AS GOOD AS THEM WANTING TO CHANGE THE LAW OF PHYSICS!

You will love this one, I haven't stopped laughing yet. For those of you who have never traveled to the west, or southwest, cattle guards are horizontal steel rails placed at fence openings, in dug-out places in the roads adjacent to highways (sometimes across highways), to prevent cattle from crossing over that area. For some reason the cattle will not step on the "guards," probably because they fear getting their feet caught between the rails.

A few months ago, President Obama received and was reading a report that there were over 100,000 cattle guards in Colorado. The Colorado ranchers had protested his proposed changes in grazing policies, so he ordered the Secretary of the Interior to fire half of the cattle guards immediately.

Before the Secretary of the Interior could respond and presumably try to straighten President Obama out on the matter, Vice-President, Joe Biden, intervened with a request that before any cattle guards were fired, they be given six months of retraining for Arizona border guards. 'Times are hard', said Joe Biden, 'it's only fair to the cattle guards and their families!"

Do we really want these two guys are running our country?

The photo above is the type of cattle guards that were being discussed in the article. They really do need six months training. Our Vice President has one great sense of humor or has never been west of Chicago.

CHAPTER THIRTY TWO

Qualifications of Congressmen

The members that serve in the House of Representatives and the Senators should all be held to qualification standards to hold their positions. These standards should be for newcomers and the holdovers from prior elections. All the members should have a sixty day grace period to become qualified.

Requirements for all Members of Congress

What about a testing requirement?

The members of the Senate and the House of Representatives would have to pass a licensing procedure to make sure that they know what is in the Constitution of the United States. We have to become licensed to perform something as simple as driving an automobile, sell insurance, sell securities, sell real estate and many other professions. Why not make the members of Congress know something about the United States Constitution and the Amendments? A test could be made up of a battery of 500 questions and everyone would have to take an examination containing 100 questions and have a passing score of at least 80%. These questions could be made up by a group of law professors at our leading institutions of higher learning and be put into a question bank and the 100 would be randomly chosen by computer to make sure that the people taking the test would not know which questions that they would be getting. They would actually have to know the United States Constitution and the Amendments in order to pass the test. This requirement will be for any politician running for the office of the President, Vice President, Congress and all political appointees. The incumbent members of Congress will have 90 days to comply with these requirements.

What about requiring payment of all taxes?

All members of the Congress, the President, the Vice President, the Justice Departments and every czar or cabinet member that is appointed by the President will be required to show proof that they do not owe any State Income Taxes, Federal Income Taxes or local property taxes. This also includes any member of the staffs. No exceptions.

The following formation will confirm the need for enforcing the payment of all income taxes prior to appointment to an office in the federal government:

TAXES OWED BY CONGRESSIONAL EMPLOYEES ARE $9,300,000...

A news article on September 9, 2010 by Politics Daily reported that there were 638 congressional employees that owed $9.3 million in back taxes.

The paper used Internal Revenue Service data to determine that about 4% of the workforce on Capital Hill owed overdue federal income taxes. That $9.3 million was a small fraction of the over a $1 billion owed by federal employees across government.

It is unknown if any Senators or U. S. Representatives are among these taxpayers. The Post indicated the average unpaid tax bill in the Senate was $12,787, while the House average was $15,498.

IT GETS BETTER!! The Post found that 41 employees of the Executive Office of the President of the United States owed a total of $831,000 in overdue back federal taxes.

Representative Jason Chaffetza (R-Utah) said. "If you're on the federal payroll and you're not paying your taxes, you should be fired."

Let's Hope that they get legislation passed that will enforce the payment of all taxes or the employee is fired. That includes the Senators and Representatives of the House.

A current poll was taken asking if "Obama Good or Bad for Our Economy?" The poll was taken by Newsmax.com. The results of the poll on September 11, 2010 were as follows:

What is your opinion of Barack Obama?

75,002 or 75.49% voted **UNFAVORABLE.**

Do you believe Barack Obama is helping American business? 75,590 or 75.39% voted **NO.**

Do you believe Republicans are right in describing President Obama's policies as "socialist'? 75,848 or 76.79% **AGREE.**

Do you support President Obama's economic policies? 75,200 or 76.48% voted **NO.**

It appears that the majority of the American citizens are going to be looking for representatives that want to represent the citizens of the United States.

That is why it is so important that the representatives are screened to make sure that they have the qualities that are required to be one of the 535 individuals that are making the decisions for the remaining 308,000,000 Americans.

What about absolute proof of citizenship and education?

All members of the Congress, the President, the Vice President, the Justice Departments and every czar or cabinet member that is appointed by the President will be required to show absolute proof that they are American Citizens. This will be in the form of a certified copy of the birth certificate from the hospital where they were born. In addition, all the above mentioned officers will provide proof of their educational and military background. No exceptions.

These requirements should be investigated prior to allowing anyone to run for a public office. We need to know that the people that are running for offices in our government are qualified and proper to hold the office that they are running for. That should be both at the State and Federal level.

Every person that is running for public office must be required to provide accurate and complete financial disclosure statements.

What about law abiding representation?

There should be term limits placed on both the Congress and the House of Representatives. A balanced budget should be required every year. If the budget is not balanced then lower the wages of every Senator and Congressman by 20 percent. Most of them are very rich and it will not change their lifestyle. When a bill is passed that will effect the American citizen then it should apply to the members of Congress and the House of Representatives. The honor of being a Senator or Congressman should not be a lifetime career.

Eliminate all pork projects that are added to legislation for the benefit of a few instead of the entire country. If the add on to a bill is not qualified to pass on its own merit then it probable is not for the good of all the people of the United States.

The campaign rules need to be fixed. All politicians should be required to use the same amount of funds in their election campaign. The government provides matching funds which will even the playing field. The current system just promotes the buying of votes from the candidate that is able to secure the most funds. The exceptions could be anyone using their personal wealth to pay for their campaign. If a candidate is committed enough to spend their money to have the chance to further the development and betterment of the United States should be applauded. They are not living off the rest of the citizens. Think about it, would you spend your own money? That takes real dedication and they are not looking for a handout.

The government needs to start enforcing the laws against kickbacks of any time. That goes for the President, all the Senators, Representatives and all other appointed officials in the government. It also applies to the lobbyist and group caught trying to buy votes on any legislation.

There should be a cooling off period after any legislation is written so that every member that is required to vote has had an opportunity to read the entire bill. This will give every Senator or Representative an opportunity to ask questions about the bill before the vote is taken. We can not allow for any more of the legislation being passed like the healthcare bill that Nancy Pelosi recommended passing so that the members could find out what was in the bill. That will go down as one of the stupidest remarks ever uttered by the Chairman of the House of Representatives.

The government needs to quit forcing bills upon the citizens that are against the will of the American citizens. No more back office deals.

This chapter is an easy victory for Sarah Palin. We all know that the President has not provided proof of his citizenship or any records from his college days. It makes one wonder, doesn't it?

CHAPTER THIRTY THREE

American Citizenship

A quote from the Gettysburg Address: "Government of the people, by the people, for the people, shall not perish from the earth."

The country needs to take the actions required to return our nation to the one our founding fathers dreamed about when they wrote the Declaration of Independence and the Constitution. Your citizenship is your sacred possession.

Our founding fathers determined that to become a citizen, one must take the oath of allegiance. By doing so, an applicant swears to: support the Constitution and obey the laws of the United States; to renounce any foreign allegiance and/or foreign title; and bear arms for the Armed Forces of the United States or perform services for the government of the United States when required.

The requirements are very clear and when are the President and Department of Homeland Security going to understand them and enforce them. Deport every one of the illegals and their anchor babies. They would not qualify for citizenship and are here against the laws of our country.

The legal citizens of this great country are not accepting the challenge of electing representatives in Congress that are willing to stand up and pass the legislation that will return our nation to respectability.

America the Beautiful will return when our government becomes willing to be politically incorrect and start thinking about the American citizens and their rights. It is way past time for this to happen. The President and the Director of Homeland Security are not acting in the best interest of our country. It is difficult to understand why they choose not to protect our borders from the invasion by illegals from all different types of countries. It just happens that vast majority of the illegals are coming from Mexico.

Just think about what a beautiful place California could return to when the 10.8 million illegals are sent back to Mexico. Not to mention that they would be able to balance their budget within a year without all of the entitlements that the state is providing to these illegals. Wake up and make your state the pride of the Pacific.

There is a daily parade of illegals marching through the Sonoran Desert in Arizona and that is why we need to have our troops patrolling the border. It is a daily occurrence all along hundreds of locations on the border. We need to secure our border. How many of these illegals that are crossing are terrorists? No one knows.

The citizens of Arizona would like everyone who plans on boycotting them, to come on down and see the great contribution the Mexican Nationals and other illegal immigrants have blessed the once drab looking Sonoran Desert with. So why not take a vacation this summer and stroll on down immigrant Highway to see for yourself all the wonderful abstract works of garbage art that they have left for us to enjoy on their trail to freedom in America. When is the government going to stop this invasion?

The requirements to become a citizen of the United States are that all applicants must be at least 18 years old. An applicant must have been lawfully admitted to the United States for permanent residence. Lawfully means having been accorded the privilege of residing permanently in the United States as an immigrant in accordance with all of the immigration laws. Individuals who have been lawfully admitted as permanent residents will be asked to produce an I-551, Alien Registration Receipt Card, as proof of their status.

An applicant shall be eligible to file for citizenship when they have been lawfully admitted for permanent residence. They must have resided continuously as a lawful permanent resident for at least 5 years prior to filing. They may not leave the United States for a period totaling no more than one cumulative year.

An applicant must show that he or she has been a person of good moral character for the statutory period. An applicant is also permanently barred from naturalization if he or she has been convicted of an aggravated felony as defined in section 101(a)(43) of the Act on or after November 29, 1990. A person also cannot be found to be a person of good moral character if during the last five years he or she: has committed and been convicted of one or more crimes involving moral turpitude. Has committed and been convicted of 2 or more offenses for which the total sentence imposed was 5 years or more. Has committed and been convicted of any controlled substance law, except for a single offense of simple possession of 30 grams or less of marijuana. If an applicant for citizenship has been confined to a penal institution during the statutory period as a result of a conviction for an aggregate period of 180 days or more they will not be eligible. Has committed and been convicted of two or more gambling offenses or is or has earned his or her principle income from illegal gambling. Is currently or has been involved in prostitution or commercialized vice or has been involved in smuggling illegal aliens into the United States. Is or has been a habitual drunkard or is practicing or has practiced polygamy. Has willfully failed or refused to support dependents or has given false testimony, under oath, in order to receive a benefit under the Immigration and Nationality Act.

Well, that will just about take care of the illegal immigration problem. Now all we have to do is make sure that our government understands the rules and deports all of the illegals that are corrupting our country.

A few other facts that the illegals need to know are the rules about becoming a citizen. An applicant must show that he or she is attached to the principles of the Constitution of the United States. To become a citizen an applicant must be able to read, write, speak and understand words in ordinary usage of the English language.

Since this is a requirement to become a legal citizen why then is the government printing documents in Spanish to appease the Hispanic population? Obviously these people are not supposed to be legal citizens and therefore should not be allowed to vote. Why are there so many different signs all over that are in Spanish? Why then do we need to press 1 for English? Why do our schools have to have the teachers know how to speak Spanish?

"PRIDE IN AMERICA"

I'm proud to be an American

I'm proud of the "Pledge of Allegiance"

I'm proud of the "National Anthem"

I'm proud to display the "American Flag"

I'm proud to defend the "American Freedoms"

I'm proud to communicate in "English"

I'm proud of freedom of "Religion"

I'm proud to be an American

God Bless the United States of America

Thomas R. Meinders

CHAPTER THIRTY FOUR

Summary

What every elected representative of the federal government need to consider in the course of rebuilding America to what the majority of the Americans truly desire!!

Every American should be very proud to fly the American Flag. It would be a beautiful sight to see every home displaying the flag everyday. The American Flag is the only flag of the United States of America. We all need to understand and respect our flag. We should be careful and make sure that the flag we purchase and fly is "Made in the USA".

The United States of America needs to start enforcing the laws regarding immigration into the United States. The citizens of the United States are American and not Mexican Americans. If you do not want to be classified as an American then why did you come here?

Well, Senator Reid is up the underhanded policies that are the trend with the Obama administration. The Democrats are trying to pass legislation to repeal the "Don't Ask and Don't Tell" bill and attach Reid's "Dream Act" as an add on to the original bill. This and all future administrations need to understand that every bill that is presented by either the Congress or the House of Representatives needs to be for the benefit of all the citizens and be able to stand alone so that the passage will be on the merits of the individual bill. The policy of attaching legislation that everyone knows will not pass to a bill has to be stopped.

The repeal of the "Don't Ask and Don't Tell" bill is opposed by every commanding general in all four branches of the military. They want to have studies about how it is going to affect the military prior to trying to repealing the bill. What harm can it do to find out whether it is a good for the military or not? The Obama lemmings want to make sure the repeal is passed while it controls the Congress and House of Representatives. That way they can appease the Hispanics at the same time. The underhanded policies are what are making so much dissatisfaction among the voting public.

The administration is fully aware that the stand alone "Dream Act" would not have a snowballs chance in hell of passing on the merit of the bill. This is just more sleazy politics in an attempt to try and shore up more votes from the Hispanic community.

THE FIRE CHIEF SAID:

In South Los Angeles, a 4-plex was destroyed by a fire.

A Mexican family of six, all welfare recipients and gang members lived on the first floor; they died.

An Islamic group of seven, all welfare cheats, all illegally in the country from Kenya, lived on the second floor, and they too, all perished in the fire.

Six Los Angeles Hispanic Gang Bangers and ex-cons lived on the third floor and they too, died.

A lone, white couple lived on the top floor. The couple survived the fire.

Jesse Jackson, John Burris and Al Sharpton were furious. They flew into Los Angeles and met with the fire chief, on camera. They loudly demanded to know why the Blacks, Black Muslims and Hispanics all died in the fire and why only the white couple lived.

The fire chief said, "it's simple they were at work."

When you consider all of the information regarding the qualifications of Palin and Obama it becomes a clear choice that Sarah Palin would make a much better President of the United States.

There is debate about whether Sarah Palin could win in 2012. The other candidates include Mike Huckabee, Mitt Romney, Newt Gingrich, Tim Pawlenty and Ron Paul to mention a few. All of these candidates present the same rhetoric as President Obama. None of the other candidates for the office of President has the courage to tell the American people exactly what they are going to present to the American people or how they are going to achieve their plans. Sarah Palin needs to tell the world what she is going to do and how she is going to accomplish what she promises. Sarah Palin runs away from the competition with her charisma and ability to generate excitement among the voters.

LATE EDITIONS:

Dear Concerned American, your action is needed to stop legislation IMMEDIATELY!

You see, Harry Reid and Nancy Pelosi are scheming to pay back their union boss benefactors in a special "lame duck" session before newly elected pro-Right to Work Congressmen and Senators take office in January.

Any day now, you and I could reach the final United States Senate showdown on Big Labor's Police and Firefighter Monopoly Bargaining Bill (S. 3194).

In fact, recently an International Association of Fire Fighter's union operative told political magazine *The Hill,* "Majority Leader Reid very much wants to bring the bill up."

If passed, S. 3194 could force every police officer and firefighter in the country under union boss control, override state and local labor laws across the nation and lead to mammoth state and local tax hikes.

And your United States Senators could determine the fate of this union boss power grab.

That's why it's vital you contact your Senators today and demand a vote against S. 3194 at every opportunity.

<u>You see, your Senators are under enormous pressure from Big Labor to vote for the Police and Firefighter Monopoly Bargaining Bill</u>.

But you and other citizens who are opposed to forced unionism can thwart the union bosses' scheme.

That's why it's vital you send your Senators a free action fax IMMEDIATELY and urge opposition to this toxic union boss power grab.

You see, all you need to do is take a look at California and Illinois to see what the rest of the nation has in store should S. 3194 pass.

California is facing a budget deficit of over $19 billion thanks to out-of-control government union bosses and their outrageous demands.

Illinois is facing a $13 billion shortfall that is over half of the state if Illinois's budget.

Dropping down a level, the city of Vallejo, California, actually went bankrupt after nearly 75 percent of its budget was spent on satisfying the demands of the union agreement covering police and firefighters.

And the Mayor of Lancaster, Pennsylvania, recently stated that struggling cities are "handcuffed" by public sector monopoly bargaining.

So please contact your Senators IMMEDIATELY and demand a vote against the Police and Firefighter Monopoly Bargaining Bill.

Your Senators could be the key votes.

This late edition to the book should make Sarah Palin the overwhelming choice for the next President of the United States.

Forbes's Article on Obama

In case you haven't seen this --- it has not been widely covered.

After reading this article, I have a better understanding of what Obama is doing. What I do not understand is what the people who backed and are backing him have in mind for the USA.

This may be the only article you will see examining where, what and why Obama does what he does. No wonder the White House is up in arms about the article. They brought the Forbes White House Bureau Chief in to rake him over the coals. It's pretty revealing.

Obama's Problem with Business

Dinesh D'Souza, 09.18.10, 07:40 AM EDT

Forbes Asia Magazine dated September 27, 2010

Barack Obama is the most anti-business president in a generation, perhaps in American history. Thanks to him the era of big government is back. Obama runs up taxpayer debt not in the billions but in the trillions. He has expanded the U.S. government's control over home mortgages, investment banking, health care, autos and energy. The *Weekly Standard* summarizes Obama's approach as omnipotence at home, impotence abroad.

The President's bizarre actions mystify critics and supporters alike. Consider this headline from the Aug. 18, 2009 issue of the Wall Street Journal: "Obama Underwrites Offshore Drilling." Did you read that correctly? You did. The Administration supports offshore drilling, but drilling off the shores of Brazil. With Obama's backing, the U.S. Export-Import Bank offered $2 billion in loans and guarantees to Brazil's state-owned oil company, Petrobras, to finance exploration in the Santos Basin near Rio de Janeiro--not so the oil ends up in the U.S. He is funding Brazilian exploration so that the oil can stay in Brazil.

More strange behavior: Obama's June 15, 2010 speech in response to the Gulf oil spill focused not on cleanup strategies but rather on the fact that Americans "consume more than 20% of the world's oil but have less than 2% of the world's resources." What does this have to do with the oil spill? Would the calamity have been less of a problem if America consumed a mere 10% of the world's resources?

The oddities go on and on. Obama's Administration has declared that even banks that want to repay their bailout money may be refused permission to do so. Only after the Obama team cleared a bank through the Fed's "stress test" was it eligible to give taxpayers their money back. Even then, declared Treasury Secretary Tim Geithner, the Administration might force banks to keep the money.

The President continues to push for stimulus even though hundreds of billions of dollars in such funds seem to have done little. The unemployment rate when Obama took office in January 2009 was 4.6%; now it is 9.8%. Yet he wants to spend even more and is determined to foist the entire bill on Americans making $250,000 a year or more. The rich, Obama insists, aren't paying their "fair share." This by itself seems odd given that the top 1% of Americans pay 40% of all federal income taxes; the next 9% of income earners pay another 30%. So the top 10% pays 70% of the taxes; the bottom 40% pays close to nothing. This does seem unfair to the rich.

Obama's foreign policy is no less strange. He supports a $100 million mosque scheduled to be built near the site where terrorists in the name of Islam brought down the World Trade Center. Obama's rationale, that "our commitment to religious freedom must be unshakable," seems utterly irrelevant to the issue of why the proposed Cordoba House should be constructed at Ground Zero.

Recently the London *Times* reported that the Obama Administration supported the conditional release of Abdel Baset al-Megrahi, the Lockerbie bomber convicted in connection with the deaths of 270 people, mostly Americans. This was an eye-opener because when Scotland released Megrahi from prison and sent him home to Libya in August 2009, the Obama Administration publicly and appropriately complained. The *Times*, however, obtained a letter the Obama Administration sent to Scotland a week before the event in which it said that releasing Megrahi on "compassionate grounds" was acceptable as long as he was kept in Scotland and would be "far preferable" to sending him back to Libya. Scottish officials interpreted this to mean that U.S. objections to Megrahi's release were "half-hearted." They released him to his home country, where he lives today as a free man.

Theories abound to explain the President's goals and actions. Critics in the business community--including some Obama voters who now have buyer's remorse--tend to focus on two main themes. The first is that Obama is clueless about business. The second is that Obama is a socialist--not an out-and-out Marxist, but something of a European-style socialist, with a penchant for leveling and government redistribution.

These theories aren't wrong so much as they are inadequate. Even if they could account for Obama's domestic policy, they cannot explain his foreign policy. The real problem with Obama is worse--much worse. But we have been blinded to his real agenda because, across the political spectrum, we all seek to fit him into some version of American history. In the process, we ignore Obama's own history. Here is a man who spent his formative years--the first 17 years of his life--off the American mainland, in Hawaii, Indonesia and Pakistan, with multiple subsequent journeys to Africa.

A good way to discern what motivates Obama is to ask a simple question: What is his dream? Is it the American dream? Is it Martin Luther King's dream? Or something else! It is certainly not the American dream as conceived by the founders. They believed the nation was a "new order for the ages." A half-century later Alexis de Tocqueville wrote of America as creating "a distinct species of mankind." This is known as American

257

exceptionalism. But when asked at a 2009 press conference whether he believed in this ideal, Obama said no. America, he suggested, is no more unique or exceptional than Britain or Greece or any other country.

Perhaps Obama shares Martin Luther King's dream of a color-blind society. The President has benefited from that dream; he campaigned as a nonracial candidate, and many Americans voted for him because he represents the color-blind ideal. Even so, King's dream is not Obama's: The President never champions the idea of color-blindness or race-neutrality. The race issue simply isn't what drives Obama.

What then is Obama's dream? We don't have to speculate because the President tells us himself in his autobiography, *Dreams from My Father*. According to Obama, his dream is his father's dream. Notice that his title is not *Dreams of My Father* but rather *Dreams from My Father*. Obama isn't writing about his father's dreams; he is writing about the dreams he received from his father.

So who was Barack Obama Sr.? He was a Luo tribesman who grew up in Kenya and studied at Harvard. He was a polygamist who had, over the course of his lifetime, four wives and eight children. One of his sons, Mark Obama, has accused him of abuse and wife-beating. He was also a regular drunk driver who got into numerous accidents, killing a man in one and causing his own legs to be amputated due to injury in another. In 1982 he got drunk at a bar in Nairobi and drove into a tree, killing himself.

An odd choice, certainly, as an inspirational hero. But to his son, the elder Obama represented a great and noble cause, the cause of anti-colonialism. Obama Sr. grew up during Africa's struggle to be free of European rule, and he was one of the early generation of Africans chosen to study in America and then to shape his country's future.

I know a great deal about anti-colonialism, because I am a native of Mumbai, India. I am part of the first Indian generation to be born after my country's independence from the British. Anti-colonialism was the rallying cry of Third World politics for much of the second half of the 20th century.

Anti-colonialism is the doctrine that rich countries of the West got rich by invading, occupying and looting poor countries of Asia, Africa and South America. As one of Obama's acknowledged intellectual influences, Frantz Fanon, wrote in *The Wretched of the Earth*, "The well-being and progress of Europe have been built up with the sweat and the dead bodies of Negroes, Arabs, Indians and the yellow races."

Anti-colonialists hold that even when countries secure political independence they remain economically dependent on their former captors. This dependence is called neocolonialism, a term defined by the African statesman Kwame Nkrumah (1909--72) in his book *Neocolonialism: The Last Stage of Imperialism*. Nkrumah, Ghana's first president, writes that poor countries may be nominally free, but they continue to be manipulated from abroad by powerful corporate and plutocratic elites. These forces of neocolonialism oppress not only Third World people but also citizens in their own countries. Obviously the solution is to overthrow the oppressors. This was the anti-colonial ideology of Barack Obama Sr. and many in his generation, including many of my own relatives in India.

Obama Sr. was an economist, and in 1965 he published an important article in the *East Africa Journal* called "Problems Facing Our Socialism." Obama Sr. wasn't a doctrinaire socialist; rather, he saw state appropriation of wealth as a necessary means to achieve the anti-colonial objective of taking resources away from the foreign looters and restoring them to the people of Africa. For Obama Sr. this was an issue of national autonomy. "Is it the African who owns this country? If he does, then why should he not control the economic means of growth in this country?"

As he put it, "We need to eliminate power structures that have been built through excessive accumulation so that not only a few individuals shall control a vast magnitude of resources as is the case now." The senior Obama proposed that the state confiscate private land and raise taxes with no upper limit. In fact, he insisted that "theoretically there is nothing that can stop the government from taxing 100% of income so long as the people get benefits from the government commensurate with their income which is taxed."

Remarkably, President Obama, who knows his father's history very well, has never mentioned his father's article. Even more remarkably, there has been virtually no reporting on a document that seems directly relevant to what the junior Obama is doing in the White House.

While the senior Obama called for Africa to free itself from the neocolonial influence of Europe and specifically Britain, he knew when he came to America in 1959 that the global balance of power was shifting. Even then he recognized what has become a new tenet of anti-colonialist ideology: Today's neocolonial leader is not Europe but America. As the late Palestinian scholar Edward Said--who was one of Obama's teachers at Columbia University--wrote in *Culture and Imperialism,* "The United States has replaced the earlier great empires and is the dominant outside force."

From the anti-colonial perspective, American imperialism is on a rampage. For a while, U.S. power was checked by the Soviet Union, but since the end of the Cold War America has been the sole superpower. Moreover, 9/11 provided the occasion for America to invade and occupy two countries, Iraq and Afghanistan, and also to seek political and economic domination in the same way the French and the British empires once did. So in the anti-colonial view, America is now the rogue elephant that subjugates and tramples the people of the world.

It may seem incredible to suggest that the anti-colonial ideology of Barack Obama Sr. is espoused by his son, the President of the United States. That is what I am saying. From a very young age and through his formative years Obama learned to see America as a force for global domination and destruction. He came to view America's military as an instrument of neocolonial occupation. He adopted his father's position that capitalism and free markets are code words for economic plunder. Obama grew to perceive the rich as an oppressive class, a kind of neocolonial power within America. In his worldview, profits are a measure of how effectively you have ripped off the rest of society, and America's power in the world is a measure of how selfishly it consumes the globe's resources and how ruthlessly it bullies and dominates the rest of the planet.

For Obama, the solutions are simple. He must work to wring the neocolonialism out of America and the West. And here is where our anti-colonial understanding of Obama really takes off, because it provides a vital key to explaining not only his major policy actions but also the little details that no other theory can adequately account for.

Why support oil drilling off the coast of Brazil but not in America? Obama believes that the West uses a disproportionate share of the world's energy resources, so he wants neocolonial America to have less and the former colonized countries to have more. More broadly, his proposal for carbon taxes has little to do with whether the planet is getting warmer or colder; it is simply a way to penalize, and therefore reduce, America's carbon consumption. Both as a U.S. Senator and in his speech, as President, to the United Nations, Obama has proposed that the West massively subsidize energy production in the developing world.

Rejecting the socialist formula, Obama has shown no intention to nationalize the investment banks or the health sector. Rather, he seeks to decolonize these institutions, and this means bringing them under the government's leash. That's why Obama retains the right to refuse bailout paybacks--so that he can maintain his control. For Obama, health insurance companies on their own are oppressive racketeers, but once they submitted to federal oversight he was happy to do business with them. He even promised them expanded business as a result of his law forcing every American to buy health insurance.

If Obama shares his father's anti-colonial crusade, that would explain why he wants people who are already paying close to 50% of their income in overall taxes to pay even more. The anti-colonialist believes that since the rich have prospered at the expense of others, their wealth doesn't really belong to them; therefore whatever can be extracted from them is automatically just. Recall what Obama Sr. said in his 1965 paper: There is no tax rate too high, and even a 100% rate is justified under certain circumstances.

Obama supports the Ground Zero mosque because to him 9/11 is the event that unleashed the American bogey and pushed us into Iraq and Afghanistan. He views some of the Muslims who are fighting against America abroad as resisters of U.S. imperialism. Certainly that is the way the Lockerbie bomber Abdel Baset al-Megrahi portrayed himself at his trial. Obama's perception of him as an anti-colonial resister would explain

261

why he gave tacit approval for this murderer of hundreds of Americans to be released from captivity.

Clearly the anti-colonial ideology of Barack Obama Sr. goes a long way to explain the actions and policies of his son in the Oval Office. And we can be doubly sure about his father's influence because those who know Obama well testify to it. His "granny" Sarah Obama (not his real grandmother but one of his grandfather's other wives) told *Newsweek*, "I look at him and I see all the same things--he has taken everything from his father. The son is realizing everything the father wanted. The dreams of the father are still alive in the son."

In his own writings Obama stresses the centrality of his father not only to his beliefs and values but to his very identity. He calls his memoir "the record of a personal, interior journey--a boy's search for his father and through that search a workable meaning for his life as a black American." And again, "It was into my father's image, the black man, son of Africa, that I'd packed all the attributes I sought in myself." Even though his father was absent for virtually all his life, Obama writes, "My father's voice had nevertheless remained untainted, inspiring, rebuking, granting or withholding approval. You do not work hard enough, Barry. You must help in your people's struggle. Wake up, black man!"

The climax of Obama's narrative is when he goes to Kenya and weeps at his father's grave. It is riveting: "When my tears were finally spent," he writes, "I felt a calmness wash over me. I felt the circle finally close. I realized that who I was, what I cared about, was no longer just a matter of intellect or obligation, no longer a construct of words. I saw that my life in America--the black life, the white life, the sense of abandonment I'd felt as a boy, the frustration and hope I'd witnessed in Chicago--all of it was connected with this small piece of earth an ocean away, connected by more than the accident of a name or the color of my skin. The pain that I felt was my father's pain."

In an eerie conclusion, Obama writes that "I sat at my father's grave and spoke to him through Africa's red soil." In a sense, through the earth itself, he communes with his father and receives his father's spirit. Obama takes on his father's struggle, not by recovering his body but by embracing his cause. He decides that where Obama Sr. failed, he will succeed. Obama

Sr.'s hatred of the colonial system becomes Obama Jr.'s hatred; his botched attempt to set the world right defines his son's objective. Through a kind of sacramental rite at the family tomb, the father's struggle becomes the son's birthright.

Colonialism today is a dead issue. No one cares about it except Obama. He is the last anti-colonial. Emerging economies such as China, India, Chile and Indonesia have solved the problem of backwardness; they are exploiting their labor advantage and growing much faster than the U.S. If America is going to remain on top, it has to compete in an increasingly tough environment.

But instead of readying us for the challenge, our President is trapped in his father's time machine. Incredibly, the U.S. is being ruled according to the dreams of a Luo tribesman of the 1950s. This philandering, inebriated African socialist, who raged against the world for denying him the realization of his anti-colonial ambitions, is now setting the nation's agenda through the reincarnation of his dreams in his son. The son makes it happen, but he candidly admits he is only living out his father's dream. The invisible father provides the inspiration, and the son dutifully gets the job done. America today is governed by a ghost.

This article can be viewed along with the photos on the Internet at: www. forbes.com

When you consider all the information contained in this book it makes you wonder just how gullible the voters of the Democratic Party really are. I don't know about you but the Republican Party has my vote for the next President of the United States America needs a President that has the courage to stand up to the politicians and work for what the American people want. It is about time for the change for the better.

My additional thought was that if we conducted a poll about any topic on any subject there would never be 90% of the participants that agree with the presenter. Then how is it that 90% of the black community voted for Obama in 2008? That seems to be the worst form of racism that could possibly happen in America. How about forgetting the

color of the candidate's skin and vote on the programs that they are presenting that will benefit all of the Americans?

Make sure that you and every American that you know goes to the polls and votes in 2012. Vote for the candidate you feel will represent what you believe is best for the United Sates of America.

ABOUT THE AUTHOR

I was born in Grundy Center, Iowa on October 21, 1937 and raised in Cedar Falls, Iowa until I enlisted in the United States Air Force. I have served my country for 8 years, 1 month and 6 days and have two honorable discharges to show for it. I am currently raising my 9 year old son as a single parent and living on social security. It really makes me mad that the government can give the members of Congress a pay raise while freezing the citizens that are dependent upon social security. I have been in the stock brokerage business for about 20 years and an accountant for about 25 years. During the last 10 years I have attempted to help start-up companies to have a method of raising capital. As with all start-up companies some of them made it and the majority of them did not. I have been blessed with reasonable intelligence and have the ability to use common sense. I have also written the following books: "A Beautiful America" "America Can Recover" "Proud To Be American" and "My American Dream". For more information on my views and photos visit my websites:

www.thomasmeinders.com

www.americancitizenspac.com

www.my-american-dream.org

www.ingramcontent.com/pod-product-compliance
Lightning Source LLC
Chambersburg PA
CBHW030254290526
45785CB00001B/86